I0110000

ENGINEERED CONFLICT

STRUCTURAL VIOLENCE AND THE FUTURE OF BLACK LIFE IN CHICAGO

DAVID OMOTOSO STOVALL

Haymarket Books
Chicago, Illinois

© 2026 David Omotoso Stovall

Published in 2026 by
Haymarket Books
P.O. Box 180165
Chicago, IL 60618
www.haymarketbooks.org

ISBN: 979-8-88890-462-6

Distributed to the trade in the US through Consortium Book Sales
and Distribution (www.cbsd.com) and internationally through
Ingram Publisher Services International (www.ingramcontent.com).

This book was published with the generous support of Lannan
Foundation, Wallace Action Fund, and Marguerite Casey
Foundation.

Special discounts are available for bulk purchases by organizations
and institutions. Please email info@haymarketbooks.org for more
information.

Cover design by Eric Kerl.
Cover photos (*left to right*): an abandoned Chicago school (n.d.);
Cabrini-Green Homes, Chicago Housing Authority (2008); a
plainclothes police officer (photo: Bob Simpson, 2016); drummers
march with the Chicago Teachers Union at the Bud Billiken Parade
(photo: Bob Simpson, 2015)

Printed in Canada by union labor.

Library of Congress Cataloging-in-Publication data is available.
Library of Congress Control Number: 2025948027

10 9 8 7 6 5 4 3 2 1

PRAISE FOR

ENGINEERED CONFLICT

"In *Engineered Conflict*, Stovall reveals that the disproportionate violence in Chicago's Black communities is not random or pathological—it is designed through policy. From the CHA's Plan for Transformation to CPS's Renaissance 2010, he exposes how urban planning, disinvestment, and the politics of disposability have systematically destabilized Black neighborhoods. This is the definitive scholarly work on the structural roots of Chicago's violence in the early twenty-first century."

—**Lance Williams**, professor and author of *King David and Boss Daley: The Black Disciples, Mayor Daley, and Chicago on the Edge*

"A book we've sorely needed. Drawing together historical and political analysis, experience from his deep embeddedness in Chicago's neighborhoods, and theoretical acumen, Stovall illuminates many forces of structural violence that our communities intuitively understand as interrelated. *Engineered Conflict* offers new language for seeing the tangled ties that bind school privatization, organized abandonment, and the carceral state. With his trademark energy and clarity, Stovall leads us toward an abolitionist vision, guided by tales of the sites where that vision has come to life."

—**Eve L. Ewing**, author of *Original Sins, Ghosts in the Schoolyard*, and *1919*

"You can feel the love on every page of *Engineered Conflict*, David Omotoso Stovall's remarkable new book. His love for humanity, and specifically for Black people, is palpable—he embraces the creativity and durability, the courage and stamina, the human spirit and soul. His love for Chicago—his home, his community, his safe space, and his battlefield—is also recognizable. But this is no shallow hookup or fairy-tale romance; this is an intimacy based on lived experience, driven by compassion and attachment, and edged with sadness and outrage. Stovall keeps a keen eye on the many ingenious ways Black people have survived and thrived under unspeakable assault as he explores the systems designed and manufactured by the powerful to make selective humanization seem natural, mass incarceration necessary, injustice expected, and white supremacy inevitable. Stovall brings his whole self to this work, leaving nothing on the shelf; here is a community organizer, an activist, an eminent scholar, an engaged (and enraged) intellectual. This is an urgent book, an illuminating and necessary beacon for these world-shaking times, and David Stovall is the perfect messenger."

—**Bill Ayers**, author of *Demand the Impossible! A Radical Manifesto*

"Both battleground and blueprint, David Stovall maps the calculated violence of the intersections of school closings, public housing demolitions, and police terror to reveal not isolated crises but a coordinated assault on Black life. With an unmatched attention to rigorous detail coupled with aching love, Stovall mourns what's been stolen while honoring the ongoing tradition of fierce resistance, Black fugitivity. Timely, urgent, and unflinching, the book pulses with truth and testimony: of loss, of lineage, of uprising."

—**Erica R. Meiners**, coauthor of *Abolition. Feminism. Now.* and coeditor of *How to End Family Policing: From Outrage to Action*

"*Engineered Conflict* is essential reading for anyone working to understand the impact of urban neoliberalism on Black communities and the strategies for resisting it."

—**Alex S. Vitale**, author of *The End of Policing*

To Geoffrey Dwight Banks
(1975–2024)
We will continue to build and grow your gardens

CONTENTS

ACKNOWLEDGMENTS

Writing this book was not a solitary project. The following acknowledgments recognize the people and places that were instrumental in bringing this book into reality.

Ada and Ronald Stovall (mom and dad), Irene Juaniza (Asawa and my partner—your undying love and support is what gets me through). Daniel Solórzano and the Research Apprenticeship Course through the Center for Critical Race Studies in Education at the University of California, Los Angeles (UCLA). Emily Pierce (for magnificent assistance throughout the book project). Amanda Lewis, Ivan Arenas, and Deana Lewis of the Institute for Research on Race and Public Policy (IRRPP) at the University of Illinois Chicago (UIC). Mark Canuel and Linda Varva of the Institute for the Humanities (UIC). Allison Sutton and Sumayya Ahmed of the Black Metropolis Research Consortium (University of Chicago). Na'ilah 'Nasir of the Spencer Foundation. Sonya Douglass, founder of the Black Education Research Center (BERC), Teachers College, Columbia University. Ezekiel Dixon-Roman of the Edmund W. Gordon Institute for Advanced Study, Teachers College, Columbia University. Sarah Rothschild (Quest Center of the Chicago Teachers Union). Nommo writing crew: Ann Aviles, Erica Davila, and Richard Benson II. Daily Writing Rebels crew: A. Naomi Paik, Nadine Naber, Katherine S. Cho (especially for deepening the concept of engineered conflict), Nicole Nguyen, and Vivienne Tan. National writing crew: Aja Reynolds, Farima Pour-Khorshid, Patrick Camangian, David Philoxène, Edward Currameng, Tracy Lachica Buenavista, and Dimpal Jain. History crew: Ivon Padilla-Rodriguez, Clare Kim, and Hayley Negrin. IRRPP Write-on-Site crew: Susila Gurusami, Ash Stephens, and Danielle Beaujon. New writing crew: Darius Bright, Asif Wilson, Tara Betts, Reggie Royston, and Lilly Padia. Readers: Eve Ewing, A. Naomi Paik, Rhoda Freelon, Lance Williams, Rachel Weber, and Lisa Lee. Damon Williams of the #LetUsBreathe Collective, Martine Caverl of Ujimaa Medics, and Richard Wallace of Equity and Transformation (EAT). Hellen Schiller (Chicago City Council), Olaminji O'Connor (Communiversity), Ethan Michaeli (Resident's Journal), Dimitri Nesbitt, and Andrea Craft (for the amazing maps).

Chicago coffeeshops: Sip and Savor (43rd Street location); Afro Joe's Coffee and Tea; Fairgrounds Coffee (University of Chicago, Fulton Market, Wells Street, and Oak Park locations); Bridgeport Coffee (31st Street location); Jackalope Coffee and Tea House; Collectivo Coffee (Milwaukee Ave. and Damen Ave. locations); Pilot Project Brewing Company; The Brewed Coffee House; Sipping Turtle Café; Magnifico Coffee Roasters; Volumes Bookcafe; A Cup of Joe Coffee House (Pilsen location); Gracias Maria; Two Shades Café; Sleep Walk Chocolateria and Café; Bittersweet (Pilsen location); Froth Chicago; Ground Up Coffee and Bites; Star Lounge Coffee Bar; Surge Coffee Bar and Billiards (Montrose location); Dayglow Coffee; Buzz Coffee (closed, sorry to see you go); Chiya Chai Café (Logan Square location); Intelligentsia Coffee (Milwaukee Ave. and Bryn Mawr locations, both closed); Standing Passengers; The Bourgeois Pig; Coffee, Hip-Hop and Mental Health; Pedestrian Coffee (Belmont Ave. location); Osmium Coffee Bar; XMarket; Sweet Moon Café; The Perfect Cup; First Sip Café; Nabala Café; Passion House Coffee Roasters (OG spot on Kedzie)' The Long Room; Jennivee's Bakery and Café; Elie Tea Bar;

The Coffee Studio; The Understudy Coffee and Books; Kribi Coffee (Madison Street location, Forest Park); Qamaria Yemeni Coffee Co. (Chicago Ridge); Queen B Café; and Addis Café (Oak Park).

Coffee shops outside of the Chicagoland area: Coffeebar (Reno, Nevada); Hand Craft Coffee Company (Reno, Nevada); Star Village Coffee (Reno, Nevada); Hub Coffee Roasters (Reno, Nevada); Dig It! Coffee Co. (Las Vegas, Nevada); O Coffee (New York City); Groundwork Coffee (Venice, California); 10 Speed Coffee (Los Angeles, Sawtelle Boulevard and Santa Monica Boulevard locations); Cafe Ruisseau (Santa Monica, California); Hilltop Coffee and Kitchen (Inglewood, California); Hawai'i Coffee Company (Honolulu, Hawai'i); The Coffee Fox (Savannah, Georgia); The Sentient Bean (Savannah, Georgia); Superbloom (Savannah, Georgia); Origin Coffee Bar (Savannah, Georgia).

Day One crew: Darius Bright, Dwayne Preston, Thomas Johnson, Charles Clemons, Jason "J-Grilla" Green, Rahsaan Moore, Gladstone "Stone" Sanders, Reginald Breshears, Creighton Barr, Phloe Pontaoe, Matt "Bucho" Hodges, Cryssida Green, Shuntita Moore, Natacha Smith, Dinorah "Dino" Lozano, Robert O'Leary, Carla O'Leary, and Kenyatta "Kay-Kay" Bright.

BLUEPRINT OF ABANDONMENT

MAPPING ENGINEERED CONFLICT, MAPPING RESISTANCE

David A. Philoxène

Structural violence operates along a continuum, blurring the boundaries between institutional oppression, interpersonal brutality, and self-destructive behaviors, all of which are fueled by systems of inequality and exclusion.
—Philippe Bourgois and Nancy Scheper-Hughes,
Continuum of Violence

Cities are not neutral landscapes; they are structured to make some people feel welcome while rendering others disposable. This reality is perhaps most visible in the logic of hostile architecture, a term that describes the intentional design of urban spaces to discourage rest, congregation, or the presence of marginalized populations. Benches are fitted with dividers to prevent unhoused people from lying down, spikes are embedded in storefront ledges to deter loitering, and public spaces are increasingly saturated with surveillance technologies that regulate movement and presence.[1] These interventions are justified under the rhetoric of "urban improvement" and "public safety," yet their function has never been about creating more accessible or inclusive environments. Rather, they work to manage, exclude, and erase—ensuring that urban space prioritizes commerce and capital over broader human needs.

But hostile architecture does not stop at the built environment; it is part of a broader system of spatial governance that extends beyond physical structures into the policies that dismantle schools, demolish housing, and militarize neighborhoods under the guise of urban renewal. It transforms the quotidian into a battleground, turning public institutions into sites of containment rather than care.[2] The real question is not simply how these spaces function, but for whom they were designed. This is the central provocation at the heart of David Omotoso Stovall's *Engineered Conflict: Structural Violence and the Future of Black Life in Chicago*, a book that refuses to take urban policy at face value and instead helps us understand the deeply racialized logics that shape the built environment, public institutions, and everyday life.

The Engineered Costs of Conflict

In his award-winning album *To Pimp a Butterfly*, Kendrick Lamar asks, "How much does a dollar cost?"[3] The question appears deceptively simple. At first glance it appears economic—about charity, about an individual's choice to give or refuse. Should he spare a dollar for an unhoused man? Should he feel responsible? What is the cost of giving, and what is the cost of refusing? As the song unfolds, it becomes clear that the dilemma is deeply structural, political, moral, and even existential. Across Lamar's internal monologue he realizes that his refusal was never just about money—rather, it was a test of his own humanity, including our collective complicity in systems that create deprivation and exclusion.

If Lamar's song forces the listener to reconsider the cost of a single dollar, Stovall's work forces us to reckon with the cost of entire communities being gutted by policy decisions framed as neutral, inevitable, or even necessary. Just as Lamar initially sees the song's unhoused man as the problem, rather than questioning the system that produced his suffering, so too do dominant narratives frame school closures, housing demolitions, interpersonal conflicts, and police violence as disconnected crises rather than deliberate mechanisms of racialized control. The challenge *Engineered Conflict* presents is clear: We must ask not only who pays but also who constructs the terms of that payment and why. Like Lamar's realization, Stovall's work forces us to see beyond individualized narratives of hardship and into broader logics of racial capitalism that govern whose lives are sustained and whose are rendered disposable.

Poor Black communities, across generations, have long borne the costs of engineered containment. The price is extracted through schools that punish rather than educate, through housing policies that segregate rather than shelter, through economies that exploit rather than sustain. These costs are not incidental. They are engineered.

Yet within this system, individuals are forced to make impossible choices, ones that often appear personal but are, in reality, structurally imposed. The refusal of a dollar is framed as an ethical dilemma, but what of the broader refusal of a nation to value Black life? What of the calculated governance decisions that dismantle public infrastructure, displace entire communities, and intensify surveillance and control? The moral weight so often placed on the choices of the marginalized is rarely applied to the institutions that engineer their disposability.

The Spatial Strategies of Racial Containment

In *City of Quartz*, Mike Davis describes the rise of fortress urbanism, where cities are designed as spaces of exclusion, built to enforce segregation through architecture, policing, and policy.[4] Stovall extends this critique, showing how the architecture of racial containment—through the destruction of public institutions, neighborhood displacement, and carceral expansion—is deliberately designed to control Black life. These mechanisms do not just create inequality—they make it inescapable. Schools disappear, forcing Black students into unfamiliar and adversarial neighborhoods. Public housing is razed, leaving families stranded and in-between. Police fill the void, patrolling the very instability that the state has manufactured.

Stephen Haymes reminds us that urban policies have long been a form of racialized containment, structuring both access to resources and the boundaries of exclusion.[5] His work on pedagogy and Black urban struggle situates the destruction of Black public institutions as part of a larger strategy of racial capitalism, where land use and educational policy function as tools of governance rather than service. This same pattern appears in Chicago's dismantling of public schools and mass displacement of residents, echoing what Rashad Shabazz describes in *Spatializing Blackness*—that the architecture of segregation does not merely confine Black people to particular spaces but also produces carceral geographies, where the built environment itself enforces surveillance, restriction, and control.[6] As such, the policies examined in

Engineered Conflict are not just about displacement, though they are in part, but also about the very creation of conditions in which Black life itself is regulated, hyper-policed, and assailed.

I recognize these same dynamics from my own work in Oakland, California, where young people are often forced to navigate racialized geographies of safety and risk with survival strategies that reveal their acute spatial awareness.[7] Violence, as they understand it, is not merely confined to individual acts or discrete moments—it is instead diffusive, stretched across the landscape, saturating the everyday. Stovall captures this reality with precision. Here, his work reminds us that policies are not abstractions; they are lived realities that shape how people move, survive, and dream within their environments.

Mapping a Black Geography

Stovall's analysis is deeply rooted in the intellectual tradition of critical Black geographic thought, a field that insists on the centrality of race, space, and power in understanding diasporic realities, including the Black urbanscape. At its core, this expansive tradition reveals how Black life and spatiality are simultaneously produced, policed, and resisted within the logics and system of racial capitalism. It recognizes that space is not neutral or apolitical; rather, it is shaped by histories of enslavement, colonial dispossession, and racialized economic exclusion.

Echoing Fanon's admonishment that "violence is a tool of dehumanization," we remember that violence is not only physical, but also a structuring force that defines the very parameters of existence for the colonized.[8] Violence, in this sense, is inscribed onto the landscape, determining who has access to security, to mobility, to rest, to resources, and ultimately, to life itself. In the case of *Engineered Conflict*, this Fanonian framework helps us understand how urban planning, school closures, and policing are interlocking mechanisms of spatial control, designed to restrict Black life to specific geographies of containment. These are not simply bureaucratic decisions; they are, as Fanon warns us, acts of epistemic and material warfare.

Yet this tradition of Black geographic thought also signals ruptures and refusals. McKittrick, for instance, reminds us that Black geographies are spaces of transgression as well as containment.[9] While Black life is forced to navigate and negotiate geographies that are shaped by anti-Blackness—where state policy and urban infrastructure are not merely indifferent to Black survival but actively structured to curtail it—McKittrick insists that Black geographies are also sites of insurgent spatial practices, of subversion, of alternative world making. This dialectic—containment and refusal, repression and resistance—is precisely what Stovall foregrounds. He reveals how state violence is mapped onto the city itself, determining not only where Black communities are pushed but also how they are forced to adapt, strategize, and resist.

Here, Black life is not purely reactive or victimized. Stovall insists on showing us spaces of possibility—where residents create new forms of sociality, where resistance takes shape in everyday acts, where survival itself becomes a radical refusal of disposability. These acts of counter-design—from mutual aid to alternative educational spaces—disrupt the logic of hostile urbanism, insisting that Black life is not a problem to be managed but a future to be nurtured. This is what makes *Engineered Conflict* not just a critique, but a tool for rethinking the very relationship between Blackness and urban space. And as a political (and geographic) project, abolition, as Stovall reminds us, is not just about tearing down oppressive systems; it is equally about building the spaces we need and deserve. His work highlights community-based resistance, from the #LetUsBreathe Collective to Ujimaa Medics, as acts of abolitionist world building. These movements show us that resistance is not just about surviving the world as it is but about creating the world that should be. For educators, policymakers, and organizers, this book serves as both a challenge and a guide.

A Call to Action:
Refusing Disposability, Reimagining Space

Stovall forces us to confront the full weight of cost—not just in terms of economic displacement but in the psychic, communal, and generational tolls extracted from Black communities. What is the cost of engineered conflict? Who absorbs that debt, and who profits from the balance? More importantly, this book also reminds us that resistance—rooted in Black ingenuity and collective care— remains a powerful force against disposability. It pushes us beyond sanitized narratives of urban development and urban life to confront the deeper stakes of anti-Black logics and spatial control. Stovall's work insists that engineered conflicts demand equally deliberate resistance—and as a tool for scholar-activists, it serves as a compass for what engaged scholarship can and must be.

As you engage with this book, I invite you to examine the spaces you inhabit, the policies that shape them, and the lives they include— or exclude. *Engineered Conflict* is more than an account of Chicago; it is a challenge to rethink how we design, govern, and imagine urban life. For those willing to take up this charge, it will unsettle, inspire, and, most critically, push us toward strategy. If this book reveals how the world has been arranged, it also demands that we refuse its terms.

It is my profound honor to introduce this work.

ABBREVIATIONS

BIG	Blacks in Green
BD	Black Disciples
BGDN	Black Gangster Disciple Nation
BNC	Bar None Crazy
CHA	Chicago Housing Authority
CORE	Caucus of Rank and File Educators
CPD	Chicago Police Department
CPS	Chicago Public Schools
CRP	Critical Race Praxis
CRSA	Critical Race Spatial Analysis
CRT	Critical Race Theory
CTU	Chicago Teachers Union
CVL	Conservative Vice Lords
DOJ	United States Department of Justice
EAT	Equity and Transformation
GD	Gangster Disciples
HUD	Department of Housing and Urban Development
IVL	Insane Vice Lords
NPIC	Non-Profit Industrial Complex
OCBAC	Obama Community Benefits Agreement Coalition
OPC	Obama Presidential Center
POAH	Preservation of Affordable Housing
PWA	Public Works Administration

Ren 2010	Renaissance 2010 (Chicago Public Schools)
SSI	Small Schools Initiative
STL/EBT	Saint Lawrence/E-Block Territory
STOP	Southside Together Organizing for Power
TIF	Tax Increment Financing
TVL	Traveling Vice Lords
TWO	The Woodlawn Organization
U of C	University of Chicago
UCCS	University of Chicago Charter Schools
UCWHS	U of C Woodlawn High School
VL	Vice Lords
WECAN	Woodlawn East Community and Neighbors
WESP	Woodlawn Experimental Schools Project
WPA	Works Progress Administration
WPIC	Woodlawn Preservation and Investment Corporation

ENGINEERING CONFLICT IN THE "NEW" CHICAGO

The more complex a capitalist empire gets, the more unclear who the spontaneous target is and the less people want to hit something of the empire, just each other.
—Tongo Eisen-Martin, "Like Normal-Speed Bullets Changing a Normal Life"

Where Tongo Eisen-Martin's commentary on his birthplace of San Francisco is parallel to the lives of many Black Chicagoans, his reflections compel us to consider the conditions that make conflict almost inevitable. My hometown of Chicago, Illinois, has been framed recently as an epicenter of "violent crime" (particularly in the form of gun violence), where the victims and the people responsible for harm are primarily Black. But the story is more complex than this narrative of

1

pathological Black criminals roaming the streets. If structural violence
is understood as "the multiple ways in which social, economic, and
political systems, including income inequality, racism, homophobia,
and other social exclusion, expose particular populations to risks and
vulnerabilities leading to increased morbidity and mortality," then
Chicago (and everyplace like it) has a structural violence problem.[1] If
structural abandonment is, as taken from critical geographer Ruth Wilson Gilmore, the "intentional disinvestment in communities leading to
the gradual disappearance of safe housing, reliable jobs, clean water,
healthy food, and a social safety net which, in turn, create opportunities for privatized social services, redevelopment, and increased police
presence and criminalization as a way to fill the cracks of a compro-
mised social infrastructure," then Chicago is an epicenter of planned
abandonment.[2] Eisen-Martin's perspective challenges us to understand violence beyond the acts that result in immediate bodily harm
or death, and to begin to consider the structural conditions behind
them. I read Eisen-Martin's statement as a provocation, challenging us
to understand how individuals respond to structural violence.

As a meditation on structural violence and Black resistance, this
book contemplates the following questions: First, *Under what conditions can a system make people hit each other?* Second, *As these people
continue to hit each other, what conditions make it difficult for them to
strike back at this system?* Finally and most importantly for those who
have decided to resist, this book is also asking: *What are Black Chicagoans doing to address the situation while building new realities for themselves and the people they care about?*

*Engineered Conflict: Structural Violence and the Future of Black
Life in Chicago* is an amalgamation of conversations, observations,
and research over a twenty-five-year period. One of the more jarring
observations comes in the form of picture I took at a local gas station near my house. The picture is from the corner of 66th and Stony

Island, where a residential building was demolished to make way for a new commercial development. I didn't at first notice the gaping hole made by the wrecking ball as I stopped to get gas at the station next to the demolition, and once I turned around, I was shocked at the devastation. The stark visual of an incomplete demolition is directly reflective of engineered conflict; it is the moment when residents understand that something is coming to replace a building, and that it will not be for them. Heightening the realization for me in this case was the fact that the brother of a good friend used to own the building being destroyed. I couldn't help but imagine how much he had sold the building for, and how many people had been displaced from the residence. When I showed the picture to a friend, she alerted me to the idea that, for populations deemed disposable, the "frayed white picket fence is an allegory for the squandered American dream." She went on to explain that the vacuum represents how white supremacy takes from our communities "until we are left on empty."[3] *Engineered Conflict: Structural Violence and the Future of Black Life* contemplates disposability (being left on empty) and what communities are willing to do to resist it.

I have been talking about the concept of engineered conflict in community and formal educational spaces over the last two decades, but my attempts to articulate my observations and research in a book have always presented a number of challenges. When I first started talking to people about the concept of engineered conflict, Middle East/North Africa scholar Atef Said asked me, "Conflict engineered by whom and for what purpose?" As a Chicagoan, my initial response was, "Engineered by the City of Chicago, for the purpose of instilling in its Black population an understanding that few will be accepted, and that those who do not comply are disposable." While not a joyous response on the surface, I consider my response to be *fugitive*, meaning that I understand that the rules and regulations of the state do not work for those who have been deemed disposable. Because these rules and regulations do not work for certain groups of Black people in Chicago, a fugitive response deviates from the narrative that violence is solely caused by a few "bad actors." To the contrary, if we consider the idea that violence (particularly shootings and gun homicides) is often heightened by a planned abandonment, then we can understand how a city can intensify violence in certain communities. As tensions grow in a moment with severely limited access to education, affordable housing, living-wage employment, and health care, Black people are often villainized for a situation that they did not create. In a city that moves to isolate and contain many of its low-income and no-income Black residents, *Engineered Conflict: Structural Violence and the Future of Black Life in Chicago* considers how violence operates structurally, opposing the narrative that violence is solely a problem of individuals. Because violence is a structural problem, it is also intensified by white supremacy (racism) and capitalism.

How to Make a Killer

For the remainder of this account, the term *engineered conflict* will refer to a collective set of policies and practices created, maintained, and expanded by local, state, or federal entities to ensure the disposability of poor and working-class Black people, with specific regard to housing, education, and law enforcement. The collective grouping of these three entities heightens the possibility of clashes between individuals or across groups, often with fatal results. *Engineered Conflict: Structural Violence and the Future of Black Life in Chicago* calls into question the conditions that heighten the probability of violence. In this book, engineered conflict lies at the nexus of school closings, the destruction public housing, and police violence, all of which solidify the disposability of Black bodies in Chicago in the name of "progress." It is the place where violence between individuals and structural violence from state-sanctioned entities converge, deepening the precarity of certain Black residents of the city. In challenging the usual despair that comes with considering engineered conflict, the remainder of the book argues that understanding how conflict is engineered is central to developing resistance to the prolonged, permanent, and structural punishment imposed on the bodies of Black people.

A specific personal example is connected to an informal conversation I had with two members of the Chicago Police Department (CPD). One was a basketball teammate of mine in high school who revealed to me that he used to work in a gang tactical unit. When I told him about the project I was working on, he instantly suggested that I speak to one of his former commanding officers in the unit. Despite my initial apprehension, I agreed. When we were finally able to talk on a three-way call, the retired officer revealed to me that he had talked to my friend about my interests and stated that he totally agreed with me. In fact, he said, it might be a little more intense than I realized. Even though I was initially confused at his statement, I

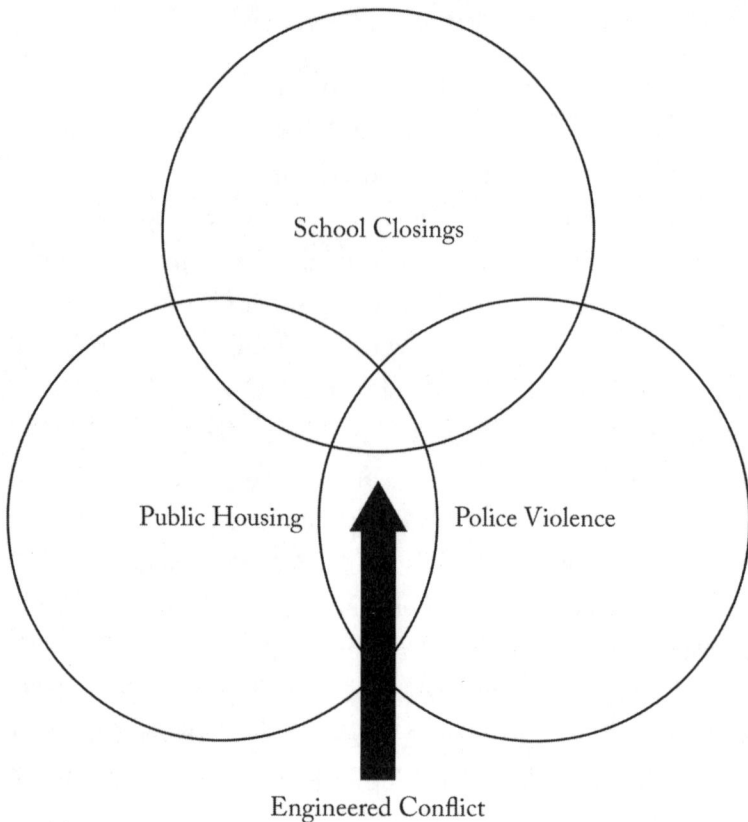

continued to listen. I use italics to highlight our conversation as it so clearly articulates how engineered conflict works in Chicago:

> *I want to tell you how to make a killer. First you don't have a place for them to live. Second, you don't have a place for them to work. Third, you don't have a place for them to go to school. Fourth, and most important, you hire me to contain them, with the hope that they will eliminate each other in the places designated for their containment. We know as a police department that no child is born with a natural propensity for crime. What we do know, however, is that conditions can make crime more of a possibility.*[4]

His own reflections on what he told me were even more chilling. He finished his statement by saying, *In fact, that's not how you make a killer; it's how you make a monster.*

Beyond the intensity of his commentary, the most important component of our conversation was his understanding that the dehumanization of people, often by way of stereotype or innuendo (*killer* or *monster*), can become a reality by conditions that are largely *manufactured.* Black youth do not have a "natural" propensity for violence. Instead, the conditions that people find themselves in (lack of quality education, affordable housing, police violence, etc.) deeply impact whether or not they will be involved in a violent act.

When considering structural violence, the most critical element to consider in Chicago is that horizontal violence (violent acts between individuals or members of a group) is often deeply influenced by vertical violence (violence that comes from a state institution). For these reasons, the book does not use homicides as the focal point by which to criminalize and/or fetishize Black death. Indigenous scholar Eve Tuck warns against "damage-based" research that centers "deficit narratives," reinforcing images of inherent deviance.[5] The point is never to dilute the impact of the loss of human life; any death is serious and should be taken as such. I ask us rather to consider how that loss, the result of acts of individualized violence, is deeply impacted by the policies and actions of the state. Rarely are systems or institutions (in this case a city) charged with being the instigators of conflict. In response to the documented spike in homicides in Chicago during 2016 (762 recorded in the calendar year), a national narrative described the city as overrun with criminals intent on victimizing its residents.[6] The purported solutions include "tough-on-crime" legislation that includes law enforcement targeting "high-crime" areas or tougher punishments for violent infractions. This narrative failed to take into account the mitigating factors that increase the chances of violent conflict. As mainstream media highlights the story of the grieving family or the violent offender, missing is any differentiation between vertical and horizontal violence.

More specifically missing from this conversation is a discussion of the impacts of segregation. Chicago is one of the most segregated cities in the country. If you are isolated within a certain grouping of people for extended periods of time, interactions with new groups could aggravate tensions. This will be an important theme throughout this book as we consider the thousands of Black residents who have been displaced and forced to relocate to communities they are unfamiliar with. Commonly discussed in media outlets and by law enforcement solely as a "gang problem," the ideas of hyper-segregation, structural abandonment, and marginalization are more complicated. In fact, in some instances, gang activity in the traditional sense of large conglomerates has significantly diminished over the years. Yet, as discussed in detail in chapter 3, Chicago's City Council and CPD continue to engage in strategies intended to eradicate gangs, which backfired immediately. These policies do little to halt crime, but they do evidently result in increasing rates of incarceration for Black residents of Chicago communities already struggling through chronic disinvestment and destabilization.

A Story of Red X's and Pay Phones

As someone who was born and raised in the city, I have always understood Chicago's symbols to represent explicit lines of demarcation or direct foreshadowing. I place the tag "direct" on foreshadowing because of a unique relationship certain symbols have with particular neighborhoods. For example, if you lived in certain neighborhoods in Chicago in the early to mid-1990s, the red X was a familiar and perplexing symbol. It physically marked buildings designated for demolition, and at the same time alerted residents of the displacement and gentrification to come.

Pay phones, too, have a particular relationship to the demarcation of space in Chicago. Where pay phones are currently understood as obsolete technology, at one time they were a significant mode of telecommunication in many poor and working-class Black communities throughout the city. Before the rise in cellular technology, one of the improvements to telecommunication was wireless communication by pagers. Instead of waiting for a call from a landline, pagers provided relative immediacy for both sender and recipient. If you received an electronic page and you were not near a landline, the pay phone was the device used to reply to the alert. Because pay phones were used by people who took part in the informal economy (sometimes in the sale and distribution of outlawed drugs), members of city government, along with CPD, developed experimental strategies to reduce communication via pay phone, in what they thought would be a key component in the War on Drugs.

One strategy was to turn pay phones off after 10:00 p.m. in specific low-income, working-class Black neighborhoods. Another was to limit pay phones to outgoing calls, a policy instituted in certain South and West Side neighborhoods in 1990 to curb suspected drug dealing.[7] A year later, Chicago's City Council ran a pilot program in the 8th and 37th wards that would end phone service in the early evening.[8] Internally known as the "Hang Up on Bad Guys" program, the initiative prohibited anything except outbound calls via credit card, collect call, or through the operator from 6:00 a.m. to 6:00 p.m. City Council and CPD's idea was that if suspected drug dealers' communication could be eliminated at the point of the sale, it would make their enterprise more difficult to maintain. Though there was no data supporting this strategy's success, it became an important optic to demonstrate the city's commitment to curbing the drug trade. As discussed in detail in chapter 3, there is a common theme in law enforcement that large-scale actions aimed at reducing crime rarely produced the desired results. In many instances, the strategies actually intensified conflict in certain communities throughout the South and West Sides of the city. The red X and pay phone serve as dual images for sites of engineered conflict through the process of containment and/or removal.

These strategies were primarily enacted in Black communities. Though drug sales occurred in other parts of the city, the focus was on Black communities, where the majority of drug sales were perceived to occur. The State Street Corridor, for example, was given special attention by law enforcement, as discussed in chapter 2. This was where the Robert Taylor Homes were, the largest public housing complex in the world at one time, between its construction in 1965 and the first demolitions in 1995. Originally developed as temporary housing for Black residents who could not find housing on the South and West Sides of the city, the corridor was the primary provider of housing for large families with children who did not have large incomes. Further adding to the population density of the corridor were Stateway Gardens, Dearborn Homes, Harold Ickes Homes, and Hilliard Homes. All of these developments except for the Dearborn Homes and Hilliard Homes have since been razed, and large swaths of the area remain vacant, making the former magnitude of the corridor difficult to conceptualize. At one point in time over 25,000 people lived on this continuous, four-plus-mile stretch of street. More incredible is the fact that at one time the entire neighborhood was served by only one high school (Jean Baptiste Point DuSable High School), despite the fact that two other high schools were in proximity to the State Street Corridor (Paul Laurence Dunbar Vocational High School and Wendell Phillips High School).

Upon the destruction of over 80 percent of the corridor, Black families were first dispersed throughout the South and West Sides of the city, then to Western and Southern rim–adjacent suburbs, slowly moving to outer-rim suburbs, then to central Illinois, Southern Wisconsin, Iowa, and Minnesota.[9] Given the mass exodus of Black families from the city or displacement to other parts of the city, there is specific meaning for poor and working-class Black people who have remained in the city. Their experiences with displacement, depopulation and organized abandonment are real and apparent from the shuttering of schools, lack of affordable housing, and violent experiences with law enforcement. For these reasons, I subscribe to Michael J. Dumas's assertion that:

> Any incisive analyses of racial(ized) discourse and policy pro-
> cesses . . . must grapple with cultural disregard for and disgust
> with blackness . . . . Deeply and inextricably embedded within
> racialized policy discourses is not merely a general and gener-
> alizable concern about disproportionality or inequality, but
> also, fundamentally and quite specifically, a concern with the
> bodies of Black people, the signification of (their) blackness,
> and the threat posed by the Black [person].[10]

Complicating the process of "improvement" as long-term state-sanctioned violence, the efforts by city government to isolate certain Black communities for either gentrification or extreme isolation and containment is a historical strategy. In Chicago, the concern of the city with certain Black bodies (read poor, unemployed, housing insecure, food insecure, underemployed, etc.) is to remove them as part of a long-term improvement strategy. It is a process that is germane to engineered conflict, as schools are closed, public housing is demolished, and surveillance/containment strategies by law enforcement are increased in areas with large concentrations of poor, working-class Black people.

The "De-Blackening" of Chicago

I agree with education scholar and activist Eve Ewing's assertion that Chicago is in a process of "de-Blackening" itself. I borrow this term from a conversation that she and I had about certain neighborhoods experiencing significant drops in Black populations. "De-Blackening" is a process that captures the realities of race, space, and place. At the same time, the specificity of "de-Blackening" to Black people is not to discount Chicago's rich and contested history of Black, Indigenous, Latinx, and Asian solidarity in organizing for equitable education, housing, and employment. The attempt here is not to participate in an "oppression Olympics," arguing which group is the "most oppressed." To do this would be to pit one group against another in a fight for the scraps of resources brushed from the table of white supremacy. Instead, I offer a specific perspective, particularly in relationship to the nexus of public housing and school closings that almost exclusively targets working-class/low-income Black residents in specific neighborhoods. Eighty-eight percent of the schools closed between 2001 and 2013 were schools that almost exclusively served Black families.[11] There is a similar relationship with public housing, whose residents were almost 95 percent Black at the time of the Chicago Housing Authority's (CHA) Plan for Transformation in 1999.[12] These material realities present a unique relationship between the city and a particular set of Black residents that is explicitly rooted in isolation and containment. As for law enforcement, Latinx populations are also deeply impacted by police violence and policies of containment, but there is a unique relationship for Black populations due to the collection of Black street organizations (i.e., gangs) in Chicago. The particular significance to Black residents in Chicago comes in the form of strategies that were used to target street organizations, resulting in the splintering of Black organizations and the creation of a new set of dynamics in Black neighborhoods experiencing marginalization in the form of isolation and disinvestment.

Census data reveals that Chicago has lost over three hundred fifty thousand Black residents since 1980, with almost two hundred fifty thousand departures occurring since 2000.[13] This dynamic has deeply impacted schools and housing, as many schools on the South and West Sides of the city have depopulated. Because depopulation is not a simple phenomenon of people leaving the city for new opportunities, we must also consider factors that push residents out of the city. In light of disinvestment, the removal of resources from certain neighborhoods, it becomes difficult to remain, a process similar to school pushout, when the policies of a school make it more difficult for a young person to remain a student there. Just as students are "pushed out" of schools due to zero-tolerance policies and other mechanisms of criminalization, the material realities of historical and contemporary policies make it difficult for poor and working-class Black residents to remain in the city.

The trinity of engineered conflict (school closings, destruction of public housing, and police violence) pairs itself with population loss at the same time as Chicago positions itself as a twenty-first-century hub for business, tourism, and other forms of development. Although these dynamics do not occur in a vacuum, they push us to ponder a hefty contradiction regarding Chicago's racialized neoliberal advancement at the expense of certain populations of Black people.

Black people in Chicago remain connected to the stories of Black people in other parts of the country and planet, where our disposability has been normalized under the flawed tropes of "development" (i.e., gentrification) and "free-market strategies" (i.e., school privatization, privatization of public goods, etc.). As Black bodies are racialized in Chicago, they are also positioned in opposition to whiteness and the ruling classes in New York City, Los Angeles, San Francisco, Oakland, Houston, Miami, Seattle, Atlanta, Detroit, Milwaukee, London, Madrid, Rio de Janeiro, Toronto, Montreal, Rome, and Paris. In all of these locales, Black people are refusing the spoils of the neoliberal state and developing formations to "live in and despite" the war raged against Black bodies.[14] Education scholar DeMarcus Jenkins reminds us that the aforementioned set of policies are reflective of a spatial imaginary of anti-Blackness, where Black people are deemed "undesirable and therefore extractable from spaces and places that have been envisioned for their exclusion."[15] Housing, or the lack thereof, has deeply contributed to Chicago's twenty-plus-year purge of Black people, setting the stage for conflict for those that remain.[16] Many of the spaces where Black bodies have been forcibly vacated have been marked by developers as "desirable," "up-and-coming," and "walkable." These terms may appear innocuous to most, but for others they serve as dog-whistle signifiers for permanent removal. In some instances, these demarcations are subtle. Where they are unnoticeable to some, to others they are a clear sign of things to come.

Chicago's "Revenge" on Its Poor and Working-Class Black Residents

Returning to Eisen-Martin's comments in the opening epigraph, some would consider engineered conflict to be Chicago's attempt at revanchism, or "vengeance after a loss or defeat." After the masses of Black people that came to the city in the Great Migration of the early and mid-twentieth century, the city soon expressed its disdain for certain segments of its Black population through abandonment and containment, particularly in education, housing, and law enforcement. In the current moment, as the city expands and deepens its commitment to neoliberal development (particularly the privatization of public entities like parking meters, tollways, and airports) the "losses" are interpreted by the state as delays in the ability to capitalize on its capacity to rid the city of its "undesirable" elements (in this case, poor/working-class Black people).

Layers of obstruction and failure at the government/administrative level make way for the city's recent and historical maneuvers in education, housing, and law enforcement. All three operate as material and ideological sites for containment and marginalization of large groupings of Black residents on the South and West Sides of the city. Where the city has never expressed "defeat" in the sense of direct loss as the result of a land-based war, it has deemed certain Black people to be the enemy and utilized a myriad of policies and practices to declare them disposable. The twentieth-century political and material "wars" of local, state, and federal governments (i.e., the war on poverty, war on drugs, the counterintelligence program of the FBI's COINTELPRO, etc.) have continued into the twenty-first century as continued wars on poor and working-class Black people. Despite the severity of the circumstances, Black people in Chicago have engaged in a perpetual struggle to claim their humanity since our arrival to the city en masse in the early twentieth century. In recognition of the collective will to resist, *Engineered Conflict: Structural Violence and the Future of Black Life in Chicago* engages the logics of displacement, disinvestment, and disposability in relation to the resistance of poor and working-class Black people in the city.

A "New" Gentrified Chicago

Since the 1970s, the city of Chicago, like other urban centers across the globe, has engaged in numerous efforts to reshape its reputation as a city riddled with violence and urban blight. Reframing the city as the "new" Chicago, local government, real estate developers, and large businesses interests have coalesced strategies through entities like the Civic Committee of the Commercial Club of Chicago to further shift Chicago to "a knowledge-based, computer-driven information technology and service sector."[17] Given the shift to an hourglass economy, with a very wealthy group in power and a significant number of people relegated to the low-wage service-sector economy at the bottom (with very few people in the middle), the removal of manufacturing and industry has shifted education, housing, employment, health care, and food distribution in cities across the world. As Chicago created or repurposed new segments of its public schools for the well-to-do (currently known as selective enrollment schools), it has also engaged in a collection of gentrification maneuvers intended to boost its business, tourism, and housing profile regionally, nationally, and internationally. In these instances, gentrification lays bare the function of structural violence. The layers of the process aren't always as simple as a process of one group of wealthier (usually whiter) people moving in and another group of poorer, people of color being moved out.

One of the instruments to ignite the process of gentrification was Chicago's commitment to "revitalize" historically blighted areas. Beginning in the 1990s, the City of Chicago's Department of Planning would post signage throughout the city that had "Neighborhoods Alive" at the top and the number "21" in the middle. The "21" was a nod to the Chicago 21 Plan developed in 1971 under the administration of Richard J. Daley, the first of the Daley family to rule the city for over twenty years. The Chicago 21 Plan was a development strategy to re-develop twenty-one wards in the city, with the purpose of curbing and reversing White flight.[18] More than fifty years later, the city is littered with new public works signs with the City of Chicago flag on the edges and the words "Building a New Chicago" or "Chicago Works" at the center. Given the boom in development in the central business district, some North Side neighborhoods, and particular sections of the Near West Side and South Side (most of them adjacent or in proximity to the central business district), the question remains: *A new Chicago for whom?*

The question is answered in part when we begin to interrogate structural approaches to distributing public funds. Beginning in the late 1980s, the city utilized a funding mechanism for blighted areas known as tax increment financing (TIFs). Where the original purpose was to jump-start economic development in areas that were historically disinvested, the move has instead resulted in billions of public dollars being diverted from public use to private projects that have been pitched to the city by legions of developers. As a financial instrument, TIFs freeze the rates of property taxes, which were supposed to go to a geographic area's community infrastructure (e.g., schools, roads, infrastructure, small business grants, etc.). Any increased taxes inside of the earmarked district are collected by the city and distributed to any project of the alderperson's liking.[19] Where the initial TIFs were used to infuse dollars into blighted areas, by the late 1990s the vast majority of dollars were distributed to entities that served the mayor's interests. Structurally this has worked well for the central business district, with the La Salle Street TIF district being the largest and most valuable in the city.[20] Yet, in a glaring contradiction, there are no parts of the LaSalle Street TIF district that suffer from blight, and few neighborhoods have been able to utilize TIF dollars to support crumbling infrastructure or provide health services in the form of mental health clinics. Residents have instead witnessed the development of the primary tourist attraction in the downtown area, Millennium Park, along with private development in the South and West Loop communities. During this time a portion of the West Loop (the meatpacking district of Fulton Market) has become one of the most expensive places to live in Chicago. Predating this moment and ever since, wealth disparity in the city has risen to insurmountable levels as the public commons has been all but eroded. Parking meters and toll roads that once served as revenue streams for the city are now held by private entities, while charter schools operate as private entities that run a public good. Meanwhile, areas on the spatial and economic margins of the city have been ignored. Eve Ewing is correct that "this form of violence creates systems with which death and despair are quiet but inevitable, and the weapons at hand are history, policy and racism."[21]

Engineered Conflict Is Powered
by Gentrification to Disorient Us

Chicago is comprised of seventy-seven neighborhoods, fifty political wards, and twenty-five police districts. Many refer to Chicago as a tale of two cities, one abundantly wealthy, the other isolated and disinvested. This can serve as a broad descriptor for those unfamiliar with the city, but to any long-term resident of Chicago the city stands as a collection of seventy-seven universes, with fifty nonsensical gerrymandered city council political districts, contained by twenty-five militarized police zones. All of these are spatial iterations that hold formal and informal borders. In a hyper-segregated city, the names of some neighborhoods are well known to their residents, while others are mistaken for other communities. Sometimes asking someone where they live is an exercise in misdirection. People will offer the name of the neighborhood because it was the name that their realtor told them or because it is the name commonly offered by long-time residents. The gentrified or gentrifying neighborhoods of Pilsen, Wicker Park, Bucktown, West Town, Roscoe Village, Lakeview, Logan Square, Albany Park, Rogers Park, South Loop, West Loop, Streeterville, West Haven, Lincoln Park, Andersonville, East Garfield Park, Kenwood, Oakland, Grand Boulevard, Douglass, Bronzeville, Woodlawn (particularly East Woodlawn), Hyde Park, and Humboldt Park share some version of the process of uneven development. Spatially, these communities are all located in proximity to the central business district or another valued amenity (rail transit, lakefront property, public parks, full-service grocery stores, etc.).

Depending on the situation, gentrification and engineered conflict can appear uneven, layered, and sporadic. Some points can feel like lull periods, where little is happening in terms of displacement. Soon after it can feel like there is a constant barrage of people being forced to move while their schools are being closed. Soon after again, new buildings are erected as older ones are gutted and redeveloped. As capital is rearranged in Chicago from a manufacturing to a service-sector economy built for the few, the realities of race, place, law enforcement, and school are central. For those in Chicago experiencing the rapid rate of gentrification, there is often a feeling of disorientation. I often tell people who have left the city that if they returned to their former neighborhood, they may not know where they were. Single-family homes have been replaced by huge cookie-cutter monstrosities designed by one of a few architectural firms. Developers broker with these firms, creating a distribution of buildings that are almost identical across neighborhoods. Independent, mom-and-pop stores are razed for new big-box retail outlets, tech hubs, coffee shops, shared workspaces, retro-fitted fitness centers, and boutique hotels. Places formerly known as neighborhood staples are replaced by trendy restaurants and specialty shops that cater to the new gentry. For a person experiencing this in real time, it can feel like the world you knew is crumbling around you. New neighbors come with new rules while the population of the local school receives a significant gentry of white students who are "new" to the neighborhood. Soon after, the same school may establish a "friends of" organization that provides extra funding. This appears cordial at first, until the children of long-term residents of the community can no longer attend due to a "specialty" tag that has been placed on the school along with new academic qualifications. From a housing perspective, many long-term residents are forced to leave their neighborhoods due to rising rents, unreachable home prices, and exponentially rising taxes. In the words of scholar-activist David Philoxène on his home of Oakland, California, gentrification often has me "writing on memory and loss while experiencing my own."[22]

As in other large cities, gentrification in Chicago is place-driven, dependent on the nuances of the local political economy. A commonly shared joke among people of color experiencing gentrification is that you know it's happening when white people feel comfortable enough to jog in the neighborhood, walk their dog, or sunbathe in the local public park. The trendy independent or commercial cafés, hipster bars, and retail boutiques come later. In other iterations of gentrification, the white artists come first, due to cheap rents for loft space that can double as exhibition and living quarters. Once they've populated the area, they are joined by more affluent white families seeking to "lay roots" in the neighborhood and repopulate the neighborhood public school. Sometimes these families may find the city too challenging to navigate and move on to wealthy white suburbs where they feel "more comfortable."[23] As a native Chicagoan, I read being "more comfortable" as code for the idea that living in proximity to certain groupings of people of color (read poor, working-class Black people) is still cause for alarm.

When people actively resist forces that persistently work to isolate and contain them, they are often caught between pride and discontent. When I stake my claim as a born-and-raised Chicagoan at academic or community gatherings, I do so with the knowledge that many physical spaces lodged in my memory no longer exist. I know that even before the COVID pandemic, many of these places were forced to close as a result of neoliberalism's myriad of rationales. David Harvey's notion that gentrification occurs through "accumulation by dispossession" stands as a literal depiction of life in Chicago.[24] As community spaces are deemed blighted or valuable, the combination of city planners and private developers move in, dispossessing people of communities that they've come to know as home. Chicago must contend with the fact that actual lives are in the balance of its development aspirations, but it cannot so long as

it continues to place cost-benefit analysis before the human component of displacement. In the spirit of this reality, I am moved by the
work of education scholar Patrick Camangian's work on colonization, in which he explains:

> It is not in the interests of the oppressed to consider the
> redeeming values of their oppression. Considering the "good"
> that has come from colonial rule is a violently liberal pontif-
> ication. Any supposed good that comes from the erasures of
> indigenous peoples in the Americas, the enslavement of Afri-
> cans and the feudal exploitation of many others is an apology
> for genocide, dispossession and exploitation.[25]

The same applies to Chicago, substituting the term *gentrification*
for his use of *colonial rule*. Gentrification in Chicago, like engineered
conflict, is loaded, complex, and layered, but there is one principle
that stands firm: *There is no such thing as "good" gentrification.* Parallel
to colonization, when a community is gentrified the disposable are
racialized and sorted along the lines of class, gender, age, (dis)ability,
and sexual orientation in colonization, and are soon discarded. Physically, some Chicago neighborhoods are valued due to their proximity
to rail transportation, major thoroughfares, quality-of-life amenities,
the lake and the central business district, effectively known as "the
Loop." Others are prioritized solely for their distance from Black and
Latinx residents. The remaining Black communities like Englewood,
Austin, Garfield Park, West Garfield Park, North Lawndale, Roseland,
and Auburn Gresham, have large swaths of residents that rarely venture outside of their specific neighborhoods. These are the communities that serve as the epicenters of engineered conflict. It is in these
places that the majority of schools have been closed, public housing
has been demolished, and the bulk of homicides occur.

The tiers of uneven community change in Chicago have reached the level of absurdity. Urban planning scholar Janet Smith (1962–2022) would remind me that in some Chicago neighborhoods, "the gentrifiers are gentrifying the gentrifiers."[26] Landlords, homeowners, and business owners that were part of earlier iterations of gentrification are being replaced by venture-capital conglomerates as new skyscrapers line the neighborhoods adjacent to the central business district. Some are completely residential, while others are a combination of retail and residential dwellings. Due to exorbitant rents or housing prices, these dwellings are largely inaccessible to Black Chicagoans who reside in the outer rings of the South and West Sides of the city. While a few poor Black people (or other people of color) will be allowed to work in these areas, most are relegated to low-wage service-sector employment. Beyond their service to the wealthy, once they leave their site of work, if they live in a neighborhood targeted by speculative development, gentrification can make them strangers in the spaces that many have called home for generations.

As the city executes its plan to build a "new" Chicago, long-time residents can only leave or resist. Adding to the complexity of life in Chicago are communities where community resistance is still present, where the conflict is visible and apparent, and *Engineered Conflict: Structural Violence and the Future of Black Life in Chicago* focuses its efforts on these sites of contestation. Some neighborhoods targeted for gentrification still stand as contested spaces, as community residents are in an active struggle against displacement. Taking this into account, *Engineered Conflict* is concerned with communities that are physically and spatially marginalized, as some operate as sites of resistance, where community residents organize with each other to collectively address the poor conditions they face. As an interrogation of state-sanctioned structural violence, the book ponders the question posed by Samudzi and Anderson: "Why not directly challenge the authority of oppressive political institutions when our social placement primes us to do so?"[27]

To "Engineer" Conflict

I am not using the concept of engineering to wax poetic on the historical imprint of the Burnham Plan of the early twentieth century, or the legacy of the Chicago School of architecture. Instead, my inquiry of engineering begins with *the elimination of human error*. I was introduced to this concept in engineering by higher-education scholar Katherine S. Cho in a conversation at the Research Apprenticeship Course (RAC) at UCLA in 2018. As a field of study and implementation, she explained to me, engineering is broadly concerned with form, function, and the elimination of human error. Engineers are consulted to find out if the load-bearing wall in a house can serve as the primary support mechanism for its roof. Along with other scientists, engineers can make sure airplanes are aerodynamically correct and can determine if automotive companies can improve fuel economy and safety. Alternatively, engineers can be used to perfect the war machine of local, state, and national governments. From drone attacks to border walls, engineering straddles the line between practical utility and destruction.

One key concept in understanding engineered conflict and state-sanctioned violence in Chicago is *intention*. Most notably used in the field of cognitive engineering, *intention* is the "highest level specification of a desired action."[28] As Donald Norman writes,

> The intention may result from conscious decision making or from subconscious processing. The important point is that it is a high-level specification that starts a chain of processing that normally results in the accomplishment of that intention. An error in the intention is called a *mistake*. An error in carrying out the intention is called a *slip*.[29]

If Chicago's primary interests are to strengthen its connection to capital as a provider of amenities, services, corporate destinations, and

tourism to the people it deems valuable, then the city is bound to engineer a set of conditions to make those things available for those people. If poor Black people are not considered members of this group,
they will be thought of like engineering "mistakes" and "slips." The loss
of viable employment, affordable housing, and access to healthy food
options and health care has rendered many Black residents of the city to
the deep margins, both spatially and materially. Taking these dynamics
into account, the purpose of this book is to examine the dynamic that
continues to deepen the margins of poor/working-class Black people
in the city. Although individuals are blamed for Chicago's violence, a
deeper, layered analysis would reveal that the conditions where violence occurs in the city can be engineered. Because poor Black people interrupt the city's goals to construct itself as hub for tourism
and international investment, *Engineered Conflict: Structural Violence
and the Future of Black Life in Chicago* considers the places where this
grouping of Black people live, go to school, experience police violence,
and resist attempts by the state to dispose of them.

The point here is not to incite conspiracy theory. Instead, it is to
understand the contestations of Black life in Chicago under a set of
rules and conditions that have kept significant portions of the population at the margins. The immediate narrative of news outlets contends
that interpersonal horizontal violence (primarily homicides by gun violence) is the driving factor in displacing Black people. However, history,
policy, and geography provide an alternative understanding of the ways
that poor/working-class Black people are marginalized. It also allows
us to develop a deeper understanding of Eisen-Martin's assertion that it
becomes easier for people to hit each other if they can't see how structural violence and planned abandonment keeps them isolated.

Where it is known that stressors (particularly long-term stressors like
housing insecurity, lack of quality education, and continued police violence) can heighten conflict, the absence of any discussion of engineered

conflict allows mainstream media outlets and public opinion to reduce violence to a singular act or event. Because homicides are tried in the criminal legal system as singular events, they miss an understanding of violence as state-sanctioned and structural. Engineered conflict is a kind of gradual violence, described by environmental justice scholar Rob Nixon as "slow-paced but open-ended, eluding the tidy closure . . . imposed by the visual orthodoxies of victory and defeat."[30] As poor and working-class Black residents of the city are displaced, they are also blamed for their demise. Where the violence of homicides and physical harm is often jolting and quick, engineered conflict slowly grows and develops into an entity that allows the powerful to take over the spaces filled with people who have been deemed disposable.

Complicating Home

I have a profoundly complex relationship with Chicago. On the one hand, it is home—the place of my birth and formative development, and the primary site of the justice-centered work I do with students, teachers, families, community members, and other comrades. On the other hand, it is also the place where I have been exposed to deep levels of trauma and violence, whether it be personal or structural. As a collection of reflections, research, and concerns I raise as a lifelong Chicagoan, my experiences provide space to couple optimism with unflinching critique.

I am aware that my view of Chicago is deeply informed by how I occupy my specific identities as a cisgender, straight Black male from the South Side of the city employed as a university professor. At the same time, these identities serve as reminders of the fact that the city at any given point in time could deem me either acceptable or disposable. Because I call Chicago home, I owe it an unapologetic discussion that excavates its layers of fracture, containment, marginalization, and isolation. Some may read my musings on Chicago as overly harsh and unfair. In response, I offer that because white supremacy is overly harsh and unfair, its function by way of engineered conflict can only be discussed on the same terms, simultaneously highlighting the importance of community resistance to disposability.

Scholar and fellow Chicagoan Eve Ewing identifies the moment when community members come to grips with the permanent closure of their neighborhood school as "institutional mourning," which she describes as the "social and emotional experience undergone by individuals and communities facing the loss of a shared institution they are affiliated with." Ewing's meditation on school closings reflects the tragedy of losing an institution that operates as a central hub for community interests. While others wonder why people would mourn a place that they consider dysfunctional, Ewing is correct that the fight to save such places represents a fight against people "losing their very world."[31] Her terminology resonates with me as a Chicagoan in that these losses of pieces of home can appear to be insurmountable. As sudden as school closings appear, they are also layered and reflective of the type of "slow violence" that occurs in a city that is constantly shifting.[32]

Where there can be pride in a community institution like a school, it is also positioned against the reality that large swaths of Black Chicagoans struggle to live here. Thousands of Black Chicagoans have been burdened by exorbitant parking tickets and red-light camera violations.[33] In some areas, especially in or in proximity to a gentrifying neighborhood, rent or property taxes have increased exponentially.[34] Until 2018, if you tried to make a collect call from the Cook County Jail, your call could be as much as fifteen dollars an hour.[35] Depending on your situation, the city punishes you for trying to live in it.

At the same time, there is also the contradiction that the city was erected on wrongfully appropriated land rooted in an uneven set of arrangements with Indigenous nations. Where these contradictions are not commonly discussed amongst Chicagoans, I also live in recognition that the places we call "home" remain deeply contested. I take into account contestation and resistance simultaneously in a way similar to bell hooks's conception of *homeplace*:

> Historically, African-American people believed that the construction of a homeplace, however fragile and tenuous (the slave hut, the wooden shack), had a radical political dimension. Despite the brutal reality of racial apartheid, of domination, one's homeplace was the one site where one could freely confront the issue of humanization where one could resist.[36]

For over half a century Chicago has served as my homeplace—an often fragile and conflicting site of explicit marginalization, isolation, resistance, and self-determination. From these realities I understand the struggle for homeplace in Chicago as a commitment by Black people to humanize ourselves in the face of intense repression. Some may read the following pages and still feel I've gotten the story wrong. At the same time, I lean on the words of Carlo Rotella, that "the places in which we live, especially the places in which we grow up, lastingly mark and shape us: neighborhoods live in us."[37]

Engineered Conflict as an Expression of Racialized Neoliberal Capitalism

Returning to Eisen-Martin's opening epigraph: If you live in a city structurally attempting to render you disposable, it can be difficult to see those experiencing the same suffering as potential comrades in struggle. It is even more difficult when enemies are manufactured by way of continued displacement, hyper-segregation, and dispossession. People are quicker to consider each other as the opposition (or "opps") than they are to identify the true enemy of white supremacy and late-stage racialized capitalism. When you are preoccupied with lack of quality education, housing insecurity, few work options outside of low-wage service-sector employment, police violence, lack of health care, and food insecurity, you no longer see the purpose of striking the real enemy, and it becomes easier to hit each other instead.

As in Eisen-Martin's San Francisco, the untenable costs of daily sustenance in Chicago leaves those who historically have the least with even less. When people are pressed under these conditions, tensions can run high, yet when a violent act occurs blame is placed solely on the individual who has engaged in it.[38] Instead of considering people who are in conflict with one another as "bad actors," we should grapple with the idea that much of this conflict is engineered through structural processes, with the goals of either containment or outright removal. In other words, the conditions of many poor and working-class Black people in Chicago are part of an organized abandonment, with the hope that this group will continue to hit (and kill) each other in perpetuity.

The story of engineered conflict appears uneven at first, because there are so many layers to it. To unpack the layers, it is important to understand *conjuncture*. Stuart Hall offers the idea that a conjuncture is the historical moment when "different social, political, ideological and economic contradictions that are at work in society come together to give it a specific and distinctive shape."[39] I agree with Hall and Massey that conjuncture "forces you to look at many different aspects, in order to see what the balance of social forces is and how you might intervene or have a better idea of how to intervene effectively."[40] The layers of school closings, the destruction of public housing, and police violence under racialized neoliberal capitalism must be understood both individually and collectively, as a conjuncture. To some, the layers I am describing amount to no more than the "natural" progression of cities, as Chicago tries to remain relevant in a shifting globalized economy. For others, the moment is clear—engineered conflict in Chicago is the brutal, violent, and inhumane result of organized abandonment while the city explicitly determines who is valuable and who is disposable.

I also understand that the term "racialized neoliberal capitalism" deserves some discussion. Neoliberalism, as David Harvey defines it, is "a theory of political economic practices that proposes that human well-being can best be advanced by liberating individual entrepreneurial freedoms and skills within an institutional framework characterized by strong private property rights, free markets and free trade"; engineered conflict is deeply influenced by neoliberalism's free-market rationales for determining the needs of a population.[41] Neoliberalism is reflected in the city's shift from manufacturing to a privatized, service-sector economy backed by financialization (goods and services to be traded and speculated on by way of financial institutions). If we couple this with racial capitalism, the idea that "racial exploitation and capital accumulation are mutually enforcing," we can understand engineered conflict as an expression of racialized neoliberal capitalism.[42]

The overlapping layers of school closings, the destruction of public housing, and law enforcement reveal a complex set of entanglements that are often excluded from mainstream media discussions on homicide. Because conjuncture requires description of "a kind of complex field of power and consent and looking at its different levels of expression," the "political, ideological, cultural and economic" moment in Chicago is key in understanding engineered conflict.[43] When the majority of poor, working-class Black people in Chicago face housing instability, lack of affordable health care, lack of quality education, and unsustainable low-wage service-sector work, neoliberalism rhetoric says that it is because they did not make the right "choices"; their disposability is thus normal, right, and good. For example, when a charter school pitches their services to a historically underserved community, what they are saying to parents and family members is "You've had forty years of something that's been unacceptable, so choose us—what we're offering can't be worse." In so doing, the families on the margins that do not choose the charter school option are reduced to people who have made "poor choices" and are deserving of their lots in society. We know, however, that the schools and housing in the areas with the largest masses of people in this predicament are not there due to "bad choices."

The contract-buying system in the West Side neighborhood of North Lawndale provides a prima facie example. Documented extensively in the work of Beryl Satter and Ta-Nehisi Coates, the contract-buying system overcharged Black residents for housing, creating a situation where many families were unable to keep up with repairs.[44] This was not a system where Black people made bad choices; they made the only choices they had, as they were locked out of traditional mortgage systems by local and federal government. Coupled with disinvestment from the city beginning in the mid-1960s as well as extraction and organized abandonment by way of the state, blight in North Lawndale was bound to result, for which Black residents were blamed, not taking into account the external conditions. As Black people were deemed unworthy of investment from the state, private business owners (in this case real estate brokers and mortgage lenders) were allowed to run roughshod over residents with little to no oversight or regulation.[45] Because there can be no discussion of Black life in Chicago without acknowledging the complex and shifting realities of race, class, gender, age, (dis) ability, and sexual orientation, it is in these layered realities that we are able to understand the necessity of Black people's refusal to accept things the way they are.

With this in mind, the purpose of this book is not to have its readers sit in despair. While racialized neoliberalism places all blame on the individual for not taking advantage of opportunities provided to them, and insists that the public sector should be privatized and left to the will of the free market, there are others who actively refuse these notions.[46]

As a contribution to the larger conversation on Black self-determination, the hope is that a discussion of engineered conflict might sharpen our analysis of the situation, allowing for an intelligent, forward-thinking collective resistance. Critical geographer Rasul Mowatt states it explicitly in relationship to self-determination:

> The state must regulate via policy to establish a rule of law, whether it abides to those laws itself or not. The state must regulate via force to dictate and control behavior . . . . Without this abandonment and regulation, we, the citizenry would come up with our own version of a society instead of the fabricated Society that is given. Self-determination threatens consignment.[47]

Such refusals mandate the creation of spaces that operate to meet one's needs, regardless of what the state says you should do. The clearer we are about the function of engineered conflict, the better prepared we will be to defeat it. Discussed in detail in chapter 5, several community organizations in Chicago are engaging the current moment with deep intention, taking into account the forces that work to marginalize them.

Critical Race Spatial Analysis and Engineered Conflict

Over the last thirty years I've worked in numerous capacities with young people and families on issues of education, housing, and the school-prison nexus. As a community-engaged scholar and practitioner, I have tried as an individual and within collectives to confront the realities of white supremacy as an organizing principle of life in the United States and around the world. From my time as a graduate student in the late 1990s I have utilized Critical Race Theory (CRT) and Critical Race

Praxis (CRP) to engage and grapple with the complexities and layers of white supremacy in the form of state-sanctioned violence and structural racism. I have dedicated this section of the introduction to discussing the central frames of CRT, CRP, and Critical Race Spatial Analysis (CRSA) to give readers a sense of the way I am using the concepts to frame engineered conflict in the book.

Critical Race Theory is a construct emerging from legal scholarship, first intended to identify the legal system in the US as one that is rooted in race, class, and gender oppression. From its genesis as legal theory in the 1980s, scholars in education, humanities, and the social sciences have taken it on to understand white supremacy as foundational to life in the western hemisphere and other parts of the globe. My own scholarship has been in a subfield of CRT known as Critical Race Praxis. The original intent of CRP was to push proponents of CRT to begin to think about what the theory means on the ground, with people who are actively resisting racism and other forms of oppression. Championed by legal scholar Eric Yamamoto, CRP's primary purpose is to encourage scholars to spend "less time with abstract theorizing" and more time in communities experiencing injustice.[48] Central to the construct is what he refers to as *race praxis*, which includes four components: the conceptual (how we understand an issue and the work that needs to be done to address it), the performative (the actual work to be done), the material (the resources needed to perform the work), and the reflexive (our reflections on our work for the purposes of improving future efforts).

Another subset of CRT, Critical Race Spatial Analysis, is of particular importance to this book. As an "explanatory framework and methodological approach that accounts for the role of race, racism, and white supremacy in examining geographic and social spaces," it also allows the ability to challenge "white supremacy within these spaces as part of a larger goal of identifying and challenging all forms of subordination."[49] As a critical race theorist, my sentiments converge with Velez and Solorzano in the attempt to "reimagine 'spatial' research and teaching tools that work for racial justice, and expanding the reach and use of these tools to eliminate subordination in and beyond the academy."[50] *Engineered Conflict: Structural Violence and the Future of Black Life in Chicago* is a Critical Race Spatial Analysis project, given its commitment to understand the spatial and racial ramifications of Black disposability in Chicago.

Throughout the text I will use the terms *white supremacy* and *racism* synonymously. Differing from popular notions of the former term to exclusively describe white nationalist terror, I understand white supremacy as the perception of the views and values of Western-European-descended, able-bodied, cisgender, heterosexual, Christian males as normal, right and good—with any other racial or ethnic group rationalized as strange and subsequently targeted for marginalization or elimination. Philosopher Charles Mills (1951–2021) offers that this "racial contract" goes unspoken but understood in every aspect of life in the US. His use of the concept of a social contract suggests that white supremacy operates contractually as an agreement between those deemed to be white and those who have been determined to be the object of domination.[51]

Articulating the realities of white supremacy requires intentional and direct language. Given the ubiquitous and totalizing nature of racism, I use italics throughout the book to emphasize contradictions, intensity, and thoughts, to resemble the inflections of human expression. As the state has determined certain segments of Black communities to be disposable in Chicago, my meditations on this phenomenon attempt to reflect the spirit of resistance held by community members seeking to confront attempts to render them nonexistent.

I borrow from critical educator and scholar Michael Dumas on how to address Blackness and work by Black people. I take his lead in my attempt to speak to the complexity of Black life in a city steeped in racist policies and practice:

> In my work, I have decided to capitalize Black when referencing Black people, organizations, and cultural products. Here, Black is understood as a self-determined name of a racialized social group that shares a specific set of histories, cultural processes, and imagined and performed kinships. Black is a synonym (however imperfect) of African American and replaces previous terms like Negro and Colored, which were also eventually capitalized, after years of struggle against media that resisted recognition of Black people as an actual political group within civil society . . . . I choose to use uppercase to signify that what is being imagined here is the material Black body.[52]

I intentionally embrace his departure from traditional rules of grammar to emphasize the political project of resistance and self-determination in Black communities. Additionally, unless referenced in a primary source, I refrain from the terminology of *crime* and replace it with *harm, conflict,* or *violence.* Because crime is socially constructed, the term is often used to pathologize events that cause harm in Black communities.[53]

There are also a number of terms that will reappear throughout the manuscript. Where they are often read as overlapping, I use each term intentionally to articulate the nuances of engineered conflict as a process. *Hyper-segregation* refers to historical, social, and spatial realities inflicted by state-sanctioned policies to keep members of certain racial/ethnic groups in certain geographic areas. *Dispossession* speaks to the process of removing cultural practices and material resources used by communities to claim their humanity. *Marginalization* is the process by which individuals and groups are removed from the process of decision-making that impacts their lives. I use *isolation* to reference the physical, social, and ideological project of permanently locating individuals and/or groups far away from resources that would allow them to improve their conditions. Aligned with *marginalization* and *isolation, containment* operates as a physical description of the impact of law enforcement on the communities it hits hardest, as the movement of people there is highly regulated and surveilled in a specific geographic location. *Disinvestment* is the process by which resources are systemically removed from communities, creating challenges in maintaining infrastructure. *Displacement* is another physical description of the process whereby groupings of people are removed from one physical place to another, where it is often more difficult to access basic necessities due to unfamiliarity and lack of access. *Disposability* is the all-encompassing aspect of rationalizing individuals or groups as unworthy of humanity. In this instance, they are left without resources and the means by which to take care of themselves in ways that are fruitful and relevant. These terms are critical in understanding the depth and specificity of the results of organized abandonment.[54]

Overview of Chapters

Chapter 1, "Schools as Sites of Displacement and Dispossession: School Closings in the Gentrified City," places school closings inside the construct of "slow violence," where residents of a neighborhood experience a gradual erasure, reminiscent of a crumbling building that slowly erodes until it is reduced to rubble. Students from Austin High School in the West Side, for example, were displaced to a distant school in an unfamiliar neighborhood. Because school closings are commonly thought of only as the shuttering of a physical building, the chapter expounds on the idea that there are numerous forms of school closure in Chicago. Without being explicitly closed, schools can be merged, moved into newly closed buildings, or made into "turn-around schools," where an entire school staff is summarily fired and replaced by a new staff. All of these situations represent a type of closure, and when coupled with hyper-segregation they can lead to residents of a neighborhood becoming perpetually contained in spaces that are void of life-sustaining entities (not just quality education, but also living-wage employment, access to health care, etc.).

Chapter 2, "Plans That Did Not Transform: The Chicago Housing Authority's Commitment to Engineered Conflict," interrogates the Chicago Housing Authority's (CHA) Plan for Transformation. Touted as a solution to the problem of disrepair in CHA housing, the plan in its entirety never came to fruition. What happened instead was extreme displacement and the destruction of over 80 percent of Chicago's public housing. When former public-housing residents were displaced, many of the schools that served residents were closed due to rapid population loss. When the displaced residents arrived to new communities, conflict ensued rapidly.

Chapter 3, "This Is Not a Gang Problem—It's a White Supremacy Problem with Policy and Spatial Implications," begins with strategies by the Chicago Police Department (CPD) in the late 1990s specifically aimed at curbing gang activity and illicit drug sales. It also speaks to the theory posited by CPD that they were "outgunned" by warring gang factions. Instead of a theory of hyper-violent youth, the chapter looks at the fracturing of gangs (referenced as *street organizations*) as a generative part of engineered conflict. Through the process of displacement and the failure of incarceration strategies originally used on members of organized crime outfits (commonly known as the Mafia), the strategies did little to curb violence. Instead, as engineered conflict, the policy and tactical maneuvers by CPD and other law enforcement agencies actually increased violence in certain communities, as tensions became inevitable.

Chapter 4, "When It All Comes Together—Race, Place, Schools, and Policing in Woodlawn," provides an example of what engineered conflict looks like in one Chicago neighborhood. Visual representations of engineered conflict, as a combination of school closings, razed public housing, and homicides, are paired with a historical analysis of uneven development. As a neighborhood that has recently been "valued" by the city, Woodlawn has rapidly transitioned from a space of despair to a destination for developer's desires. The community provides a critical example of what engineered conflict looks like in real time, as housing, education, and policing strategies have drastically shifted in the neighborhood.

Chapter 5, "Black Fugitive Futures," looks at three grassroots community organizations (the Let Us Breathe Collective; Equity and Transformation [EAT]; and Ujimaa Medics) and the forms of resistance they utilize to combat marginalization and isolation. As the Black body has been made strange ("queered") in the gaze of white supremacy, these organizations also recognize the centrality of women and young people in movement building.[55] Each organization's work is framed as an example of resistance to engineered conflict. By providing the introductory steps of what it will take to ensure the future of Black life in Chicago, their analysis and organizing strategies center necessity and intent.

CHAPTER 1

SCHOOLS AS SITES OF DISPLACEMENT AND DISPOSSESSION

SCHOOL CLOSINGS IN THE GENTRIFIED CITY

The Centrality of School Closings in Engineered Conflict

Over the last few years, I have made it practice in classes, workshops, and public speaking events to ask a basic question on how to understand the concept of engineered conflict in relation to school closings: *What is the best way to start a fight that you don't take part in?* The answers range from "instigating" to "starting a rumor" to "lying." After people offer their suggestions, I offer the image of two rival schools. If the people I'm talking with are seated in rows, I will have the audience imagine the room being divided in two, with each side representing a different high school. I continue by asking the group what would happen if one side of the room's high school was closed and everyone there was sent to the rival high school (in this case, the people on the other side of the room). In many instances, the very first answer they give me is "fights." My following question to the group is: *What if you did that forty-nine times in one summer?*

I like to begin with this example because it allows people who are unfamiliar with the situation in Chicago to imagine the conditions that certain groups of young people and their families endure. At the same time, it also pushes me to consider another question: *If it is known that conflict is likely to ensue in these situations, why would a city make a policy of creating them? And why would it do so in schools that primarily serve working-class/low-income/no-income sectors of its Black population?*[1]

An Austin Story and a Black Chicago Story: Contextualizing White Flight, Isolation, and Precipitous Disinvestment in the City

One of the earliest examples of the city producing fights between individuals and groups in schools took place in the West Side neighborhood of Austin. Like many neighborhoods that isolate Black populations in Chicago, Austin offers a deeper understanding of engineered conflict's connection to neoliberal education, housing, and law enforcement policies. Many Chicagoans may locate the beginning of Austin's decline in the late 1990s, but history reveals an earlier genesis. Like many discussions on race and space, we can locate the City of Chicago's disinvestment in Austin in the late 1960s.[2] During this time period, the lifting of restrictive covenants* had allowed Black residents to move from the

---

* Once restrictive covenants were declared unconstitutional in the Supreme Court case *Hansberry v. Lee* (311 U.S. 32) in 1948, residents were legally able

Black Belt on the South Side into West Side communities like Austin and North Lawndale.[3] As Black residents began to arrive in Austin in the early 1960s, swaths of its white population left rapidly, providing one of the primary examples of white flight in Chicago. When Richard J. Daley, the first longtime power-wielding mayor of the city noticed the departure of Austin's white residents, he urged the superintendent of Chicago Public Schools (CPS), Benjamin Willis, to do something about it. Because schools are a primary anchor keeping residents in a community, the mayor figured if he wanted to appease white residents, one of the ways would have to be through the schools.

One of Willis's solutions was to grant white families a "permissive transfer," by which they could relocate to the school of their choice, further distancing themselves from Black students while remaining in the city. At the same time, Willis refused to support overcrowded schools in Black communities and began to place mobile units (popularly known as "Willis Wagons") in the playgrounds of schools with majority Black populations. These units were rarely repaired and were often dangerous due to lack of heat and shoddy plumbing. As Austin remained densely populated with Black residents, the majority of high-school-aged youth in the community attended a single high school, Austin High School.

Unfortunately, deindustrialization soon deeply impacted community residents. By the mid-1980s, as unemployment rose to crisis levels, people began to turn to underground economies (primarily in the form of drug sales) for sustenance. This created a unique relationship with the nearby affluent suburb of Oak Park, whose residents would come to

---

to purchase homes outside of what was historically known as the Black Belt on the city's South Side. From 1900 to 1954, over 80 percent of all Black people in the city lived in an eight-square-mile area. Once the ban was lifted, two West Side communities, Austin and North Lawndale, were spaces that Black people relocated to, along with newer migrating Black families from southern states. In both neighborhoods, Black people experienced the slow violence of disinvestment and isolation.

Austin to purchase narcotics. The Eisenhower Expressway (also known as I-290) received the nickname "the heroin highway" due to the number of white suburbanites traveling to Austin to purchase illegal drugs. Along with this came an intensified police presence in the community, that soon led to increased levels of arrests and other interactions with law enforcement.[4] Like many who exist under the gage of late-stage capitalism, some residents decided to "vote with their feet" and ended up leaving Austin. Black families that had the resources to leave Austin began to settle in communities in other parts of the city or left Chicago.[5] In light of the lack of resources at the grade school and high school levels, educational options in the neighborhood were considered scant, to the point where families that remained in Austin began to choose other high schools in the area if they were able to. (Discussed later in the chapter, this is one of the strategies utilized by charter schools to lure parents.)

In the context of Austin and its lone high school, urban planners Lugalia-Hollon and Cooper's observations are deeply insightful:

> Restless youth are the first to be kicked out of schools. The most traumatized are the most likely to be jailed. And those most in need of work are the least eligible for employment. Policymakers have not just avoided addressing the problems of unemployment, struggling schools, addiction, and mental illness in African-American communities; they have actively punished people suffering from these conditions.[6]

The issue here is not whether city government recognizes this. Instead, the city often moves to the rationale of containing violence to the extent that the concerns don't seep out to the areas the city has deemed valuable. Because government remains content with its ability to keep the "problems" confined to a particular geographic area, Lugalia-Hollon and Cooper are accurate in stating that policymakers have been willing to wage a "war on neighborhoods" where the city and developers pay to ensure absence and loss rather than economic revitalization . . . though this spread of punitive logics and policies, the war on neighborhoods has reshaped households, residents, businesses and local organizations. It has further hollowed out the valleys while the surrounding mountain continues to thrive.[7]

Discussed in more detail later in this chapter, when Austin community members first got word of the proposed closure of Austin High School by way of phase-out in 2004, they expressed concern at the fact that the largest geographic community area in the city would no longer have a neighborhood high school. As I paid attention to these rumblings, my first concern was: What would happen to the students who lived in Austin's attendance boundary?

Unfortunately, CPS did not have a good answer. There was no comprehensive plan for schools that received students arriving from closed schools.[8] As Austin High School moved toward closure, displaced students from the West Side neighborhood were not sent to a neighboring high school, but to Roberto Clemente (Clemente), eight miles away.[9] The decision was strange, considering the city's hyper-segregation. When students were sent to Clemente, they had to cross numerous spaces of unfamiliarity, popularly thought of solely as "gang territories," running the risk of being in harm's way. The gang narrative is only a partial truth, as regional segregation in itself can create deep tensions within a city. When those same students arrived at Clemente, tensions were high and conflicts resulted. While some of these were connected to street organizations, others were due simply to students' unfamiliarity with each other.

As students continued to fight during the school year, the school enacted repressive discipline strategies. One of the policies enacted by school leadership at Clemente was particularly prison-like: School security guards were placed at fifty-foot intervals around the perimeter of the lunchroom, with the rule that the guards could never be out of each other's sight. These are almost verbatim the rules of a prison mess hall. Leadership in the building comfortably forgot that if you create carceral conditions in a school, students will pick up on it very quickly. If young people feel as if they've been imprisoned in the place where learning is supposed to happen, any respect or care for that place and the people in it will leave immediately. To the chagrin of CPS, this strategy did not curb fighting amongst students. Frustrations ran so high that Clemente's principal abruptly resigned with a year and a half left on her contract, via phone call while on vacation in Brazil. She did not alert her administration, teachers, students, or their families of her departure.[10]

The closure of Austin High School served as a linchpin moment for me in beginning to theorize what engineered conflict looks like in public schools. In Clemente, many of the early conflicts were interracial, as Black and Latinx students who had traditionally attended neighborhood schools in a hyper-segregated city found themselves in prolonged contact with each other for the first time. It is incorrect to blame young people solely for the fights. Instead, the conflict was engineered, the result of the closing of Austin High School, which was itself the culmination of policies and practices that have declared certain sectors of Black life disposable.*

School Closure in Black Chicago

Although the closure of Austin High School resulted in tensions between Black and Latinx students, other school closures in majority Black communities led to intraracial conflict. In considering this

---

* Austin was "reopened" in 2006 as three small schools. Two of the small schools have since closed, while the other has a student population of under two hundred.

shift, as schools closed in majority Black communities, the connection to neoliberal racialized capitalism becomes clearer. Pauline Lipman's scholarship is instructive here.

> The struggle over education in Chicago is about more than schools. It is about race and capital, state violence, claims to urban space and political power . . . . Resistance to education policy is an expression of the rejection of neoliberal policies to remake the city for capital accumulation and to simply abandon, contain or drive out those whose lives do not matter and are, in fact, disposable in a context of corporate hegemony, elite consumption and whiteness.[11]

In Chicago, the neoliberal relationship between schools and poor/working-class Black communities on the South and West Sides of the city, like Chicago's long history of segregation, is explicit both visually and spatially. Within CPS, the differences between schools are stark and evident. Any passerby could look at the conditions of the neighborhood and quickly understand the conditions of its schools. Neoliberal logic would blame the conditions of the school on a community that "doesn't care" about the building, but another perspective would identify the history of disinvestment and marginalization that produced them. The largest single set of school closings in the history of the United States raised alarms in 2013, but Chicago's history of mass school closings goes back to the early 2000s. Where cities like Detroit, New Orleans, Philadelphia, Houston, and Pittsburgh have faced the devastation of school closings, the unique dynamics of school closings in Chicago reveal an intimate relationship between the destruction of public housing and the practices of law enforcement. Given that there have been almost 150 school closures in Chicago since 2000, a closer look allows us to complicate closure as both process of and rationale for abandonment.

Policy Contradictions, Mayoral Control, and the Generative Closing Power of Ren 2010

Except for the closings in the spring of 2013, much of the actual violence of closings happens slowly. In many instances it isn't always evident that closings are part of a process that meets the policy goals of a city, especially in Chicago, where schools operate under mayoral control. One of these goals is regarding capital accumulation, with schools used as a lever to keep wealth in the city (despite its depopulation of Black residents). Because it is well known that the primary determinant for a family purchasing a home is the school it is in proximity to, the City of Chicago continues a process of funneling resources to a set of selective enrollment schools primarily maintained for white affluent residents and upper-middle-class families of color.* Since the 1995 educational policy shift to mayoral control, the mayor's office was granted sole authority over district schools, with the power to serve as arbiter in *any* school-related decision of their choosing. The mayor also had the responsibility of appointing the school board, which is generally responsible for final approval of school-related issues (e.g., financial matters, curricular shifts, contract procurement, approval of new schools, etc.), and maintains the ability to overturn any decision made by the board. Facilitated under the twenty-two-year mayoral tenure of Richard M. Daley (son of Richard J. Daley, who was also mayor of the city for twenty years), this system has become a blueprint for numerous cities in the US desiring

---

* The City of Chicago has a set of selective enrollment schools that are difficult to gain entry to. For admission, students need a particular test score on a standardized test to qualify to take the admissions test to qualify for the selective enrollment lottery. Admission to the top school of your choice is not guaranteed, and gaining access to the lottery is a challenging process for those who do not possess the capital to navigate a complex system. Where the population of CPS as a district is almost 90 percent Black and brown, and white students make up less than 10 percent of the district's population, selective enrollment schools are almost 50 percent white.

to centralize control of their school systems.[12] Mayoral control* ended after the November 2024 election, but the two mayors following the second Daley administration (Rahm Emanuel and Lori Lightfoot) used it extensively, and only to cater to the desires of the wealthy.[13]

Mayoral control should be considered one of the introductory measures for school closings and engineered conflict for several reasons. School closings in Chicago are birthed out of a policy initiative developed in the early 2000s. Operating from the "Left Behind" report created by the Civic Committee of the Commercial Club of Chicago (the conglomerate representing multinational corporate business interests in the city), CPS proposed to target up to seventy "chronically underperforming" schools to be closed or "repurposed," and to open one hundred new charter, contract, or performance schools in their place by 2010.[14] The mandate, dubbed Renaissance 2010 (Ren 2010), was introduced to the press in July of 2004 at a meeting at the Commercial Club.

Most of the targeted schools were in Black communities that had experienced numerous forms of disinvestment. The first pilot of Ren 2010 was scheduled to take place in the mid-South region of the city, a collection of four neighborhoods (Kenwood, Oakland, Grand Boulevard, and Douglass) that were experiencing different levels of disinvestment or gentrification.[15] Here the city saw a "test market" for a strategy rollout it thought would get little resistance. Fortunately, because community members knew about the strategy, they were able to resist and slow the policy from overtaking existing neighborhood schools.[16]

The classification of schools in Ren 2010 is critical, as each of the three distinctions the policy mandated for new schools (charter, contract, or performance) has a particular relationship to the closing or

---

* The City of Chicago is set to end mayoral control with the establishment of a fully elected school board. In 2024, eleven of the seats were appointed by the mayor and ten were elected. Two years later, in 2026, elections will be held for the eleven currently appointed seats, leading to a fully elected board by fall of 2027.

reconfiguration of existing schools. In brief: Charters are institutions approved by the state; contract schools are designated for individuals or groups that have secured individual contracts with the city to create schools; and performance schools are schools originally configured to receive a set of resources allowing them to specialize in a particular content area.[17] Because the majority of charter schools are not unionized, the proliferation of charters had a union-busting function, as fewer teachers would have access to membership in the Chicago Teachers Union (CTU). Contract schools were a close cousin to charters in terms of funding formulas, but are in direct partnership with the city, rather than the state. Despite their classification as public schools, both charters and contracts are not required to provide union protection. These new policy changes were spun to community residents as providing "choice" and "options" in the "education marketplace."[18] But because they were instituted around the same time as the city's decision to raze public housing and expand law enforcement in the same areas, they only served to produce engineered conflict.

Complicating School Closure
Attendance Boundaries, Neighborhood
Public Schools, and Privatization

When most of us hear that a school is closed, our thoughts move to a situation where people no longer have access to the building, the physical structure is locked, the structure lies vacant until demolition, or some type of "repurposing" takes place. In Chicago, repurposing includes the conversion of the school to luxury living spaces that are no longer affordable to long-term residents of the gentrifying neighborhood. Yet demolition and repurposing are only two forms of closure. In Chicago, engineered conflict challenges us to contemplate multiple forms of closure, particularly in relation to housing and law enforcement strategies. This chapter considers five forms of closure, each with its own unique relationship to the process of engineered conflict. Working against the idea that school closings in Chicago are the inevitable result of the "unfortunate" conflu- ence of economic and population events, I accept here Lipman's challenge to understand the role that race, capital, state-sanctioned violence, polit- ical power, and the right to the city play in the process of school closures.

Although neighborhood attendance boundaries have become less significant in Chicago after the enactment of policies promoting school "choice," they are still important in understanding decreasing CPS enroll- ments beyond Black population loss in the city. Beginning with a city policy enacted in 1863, Black and white students were forced to attend separate schools.[19] Black students historically were not allowed to attend schools outside of the areas they were regulated to live in,[20] and restric- tive covenants made selling homes to Black families outside of a particu- lar area illegal.[21] This dynamic has not changed significantly in Chicago, where over 70 percent of Black students continue to attend segregated schools.[22] Given the intimate connection between housing and education in any municipality, schools in Chicago followed an identical path. Hyper- segregation, compounded by white flight from the city in the 1960s and '70s, shifted schools and neighborhoods that were historically white to school buildings and communities that were almost 100 percent Black.

When neighborhood attendance boundaries were in effect, stu- dents who lived in a specific neighborhood were usually "assigned" to the school they lived closest to. The boundaries were designated by dis- tricts, with the attendance areas for K–8 schools being geographically smaller than those drawn for high schools.* Students were traditionally

---

* Neighborhood attendance boundaries are determined by CPS's Office of Planning and Data Management. Career Academies at the high school level do not have attendance boundaries. Some Science Technology Engineering and Mathematics (STEM) Academies and schools with Fine Arts designations also do not have attendance boundaries. See the district's map of boundaries at https:// schoolinfo.cps.edu/schoollocator/index.html.

only allowed to attend a school outside of an attendance boundary if they
were accepted to a magnet school (now referred to as a "selective enrollment" school) or attended a school with what is known as "citywide"
enrollment, primarily reserved for what used to be known as "vocational"
schools (currently known as Career and Technical Education [CTE]
schools). Yet even these were segregated, with Black students attending
citywide schools located in predominantly Black communities, which
very few people even knew had citywide attendance boundaries, leaving
parents and students confused about the citywide specific differences
between neighborhood schools and schools with a citywide attendance
designation. I myself didn't know until much later in life that schools
like Chicago Vocational Career Academy (formerly Chicago Vocational
School [CVS]), Paul Laurence Dunbar, and Neal F. Simeon High School
were all schools with a citywide attendance boundary. James H. Bowen
High School was listed as my neighborhood high school, but I lived closer
to CVS. Because my friends went to both Bowen and CVS, I thought
my community just had two neighborhood high schools. The citywide
boundary was a layer that few Chicagoans outside of CPS paid attention
to. Because these schools provided pathways to vocational careers, they
were sought after by community residents, but because of historical de
facto and de jure segregation, these schools remained filled with primarily Black students from the surrounding neighborhoods.*

At the grade school (K–8) level there were other distinctions before
the advent of Ren 2010. While the majority of K–8 schools had neighborhood attendance boundaries distinction, other classifications emerged.
The first notable one was magnet schools, which came by way of a
1980 consent decree declaring that the city was insufferably segregated,

---

* *De facto* segregation referring to the process of keeping certain communities isolated, regardless of laws that may declare segregation to be illegal. *De jure* segregation referring to the legal process that disallows certain people to live in particular
neighborhoods, meaning it is actually legal to segregate populations.

permanently locking students of color out of educational opportunities.[23] The federal court decision allowed students from across the city to take a test for admission to a school with enough resources to attract students from all parts of the city, often the crown jewels of their districts.[24] They were not, however, accessible to most Black people in the city, especially if they did not meet the admissions qualifications. By the late 1990s, there were many more distinctions for K–8 schools, including charter schools, Regional Gifted Centers, Science Technology Engineering and Mathematics (STEM) Academies, and fine arts academies. At the high school level, the system of neighborhood public schools is so disheveled that more than 75 percent of high school students attend a high school other than their neighborhood high school.[25]

The neighborhood attendance boundary, while at first appearing as just another confusing layer in the classification labyrinth of CPS, is of specific importance when considering engineered conflict and the ways schools are depopulated, especially considering that the city is losing its Black population at an increasing rate. Like gentrification, school depopulation in some instances appears to be a gradual process. In other instances, it can feel rapid and abrupt.

Five Configurations of School Closure

The first set of school closings in Chicago went through a traditional trajectory, with the shuttering or demolition of their buildings. As time progressed, school closings became more complex, as CPS began to use a number of mechanisms that constitute closure in various configurations. In their account of all these mechanisms, Rachel Weber, Stephanie Farmer, and Mary Donoghue provide an important framing of the intimate connection between school closings and the process of engineered conflict.[26] Their inquiries illustrate the pivotal role of schooling, particularly the process of how CPS "rendered school facilities serving a majority

African-American student body as more disposable, precarious and inse-cure."[27] The practices of CPS before, during, and after Ren 2010 describe a progression with devastating effects, often resulting in displacement and upheaval. Where the results are clear, the process of getting to actual clo-sure is nuanced, providing a more complex story in policy and practice.

Integral to this discussion is the concept of underutilization. In an attempt to "rightsize" school buildings in the district by bringing enrol-ment capacity in line with the physical space of the school, deeming school buildings underutilized was determined to be the closure mech-anism that would save significant amounts of money. Each school was given a utilization rate placed in comparison to its building's design capacity (sometimes referred to as its "maximum capacity"), deter-mined by the number of homerooms (classrooms) in a building times thirty. Any building with enrollment under 20 percent of its maximum capacity was considered underutilized.[28] CPS would then "rightsize" such buildings by bringing enrollment capacity in line with the physical space of the school. The neoliberal language of *rightsizing* is important, as it is the same word economic speculators and corporate entities use when they argue for moves that make the most financial sense. The use of neoliberal rhetoric may appear insignificant, but it becomes import-ant when we understand that it does not allow for alternative solutions. If members of the public who are unfamiliar with the rhetoric of school closings hear that a building is "underutilized," they will assume that the problem is best solved by closure or some form of consolidation. In reality, when we begin to enter the conversation about why buildings were actually "underutilized," we see that many of these schools were using classrooms to accommodate diverse learners with pronounced disabilities, as well as for community space.[29]

The four types of closure named in the Weber et al. report (consoli-dation, closing/closure, phase-out, reconstitution/turnaround) are cen-tral in understanding the complexity of school closure as a practice that coincides with the loss of public housing and the proliferation of law enforcement policies. This account also considers a fifth, underrecognized designation, namely consolidation/closure by charter. Below are brief explanations of each process.

1. ***Consolidation***: Two or more schools are combined into a single school. Students from the closed school are reassigned to the consolidated school facility.

2. ***Closing/Closure***: A school is shuttered and students are reassigned to one or more neighborhood receiving school.

3. ***Phase-Out***: Enrollment in certain grades gradually ceases each school year until a school closes or is consolidated with another school.

4. ***Reconstitution/Turnaround***: The principal, staff, and teachers of a school are dismissed and a new set of professionals is hired to reorganize the school and curriculum. The school is reopened as the open-enrollment attendance-boundary public school, serving the same children.[30]

5. ***Consolidation/Closure by Charter***: A charter school is erected near a neighborhood public school and begins to accept and retain students that would originally attend the neighborhood public school that it's close to.

Each type of closure is explained in detail below, with its specific connection to engineered conflict.

Closing/Closure: Immediate Depopulation

Closing/closure is the most straightforward category for school closings. The first direct closures hit hardest in neighborhoods where public housing had been demolished in the early 2000s.* As this escalated throughout

---

* This is directly connected to the Chicago Housing Authority's "Plan for Transformation," where all high-rise public housing was demolished and low-rise developments

the city in historically Black neighborhoods, students from communities with significant levels of public housing experienced high mobility rates as they were shifted from school to school. Before the 2013 closures, the space where this was most prominent was the State Street Corridor. Highlighted in the map at the end of this section and discussed in detail in the following chapter, the State Street Corridor at one time housed the most populous set of public housing units in the world. Upon first glance, it would appear as if the school buildings in this neighborhood were closed and/or demolished sequentially, from north to south. In reality the buildings were demolished absent of a particular order, except that they coincided with decreasing populations of the schools, which resulted from the closure of public housing buildings in the corridor. Because many schools shared the same neighborhood boundaries, some schools closed within months of each other. From 2001 to 2006, seven buildings and six schools (Attucks, Williams, Terrell, Colman, Raymond, Hartigan, and Douglass) were closed and/or reoccupied in the area.[31] Five of these schools were on the same street. This is significant to engineered conflict in Chicago as direct closure is often the result of displacement of public housing residents. As they were forced to move to different communities, a series of conflicts occurred in their new neighborhoods.

Consolidation: Confusing in Place and Name

Consolidation was probably the second most abrupt processes of closure, particularly for students, teachers, and families after the spring 2013 closures. As school districts communicated the terms and conditions of closure between the months of April and July of 2013, the scramble for families was chaotic, especially those with children with special needs or who required bussing. When two schools were consolidated, the

---

were built throughout the city. Since the mid-1970s, public housing has been almost exclusively Black.

lower-performing school would be closed, with its students sent to the higher-performing school (often called the receiving school). For students that were sent to the receiving school, the displacement could be shocking. Taking into account that most community tensions are often rooted in unfamiliarity, many consolidated schools experienced a significant number of fights in the first years of consolidation.[32] Two examples of particular significance are the consolidation of two sets of schools, one on the North Side and the other on the South Side of the city. Both are of particular importance to engineered conflict as Black students were displaced without the type of thoughtful planning necessary to ease tensions between students entering new and unfamiliar environments.

Austin O. Sexton Elementary School (Sexton) on the South Side neighborhood of Woodlawn was a school experiencing disinvestment in a number of forms, particularly in the lack of resources for students with special needs or who required academic supports. Woodlawn was placed on probation, while John Fiske Elementary School (Fiske), less than three blocks away, was deemed to be higher performing. Fiske remained open; Sexton was closed and consolidated. The closure of Sexton may seem straightforward, but the physical conditions of the two schools' buildings complicated the matter. CPS declared Fiske to be a building in disrepair, Sexton's larger and in better condition. Given this dynamic, CPS decided that the best maneuver would be to physically close Fiske and move all of the students to the Sexton building. The students in the Sexton building would remain in their original building, with the newly added Fiske students. However, because Sexton was "closed" due to underperformance and underutilization, the name of the Sexton building was changed to Fiske, and administration and staff from Sexton were fired. Fired teachers and staff could reapply for their positions, but only a few did. Sexton administration (the principal, assistant principal, and office clerks) had to look for employment elsewhere. The Fiske administration and staff took over the Sexton building, creating an unusual situation for Sexton students required to start over with a group of unknown teachers from three blocks away. If this reads as confusing, imagine what it means for the families who find themselves in these situations.[33]

In the early years of the merger, the staff from Fiske saw significant numbers of fights between students. Students from Sexton felt as if they were not wanted, and began to express their frustrations against Fiske students. This continued for the first two years of the merger, as engineered conflict played out in the hallways of the newly named Fiske school and the holdover students from Sexton were expected to grin and bear it.[34]

On the North Side neighborhood of Uptown, students at the Mary E. Courtenay Elementary Language Arts Center were merged with Joseph Stockton Elementary. Similar to Fiske and Sexton, the schools were in close proximity to each other. Additionally, like the Fiske and Sexton merger, the higher-performing school building (Courtenay) was physically closed as students, staff, and administration were sent to the "closing" school (Stockton). "Closing" is placed in quotes because the Stockton students were not displaced physically, but the name of the building was changed to Courtenay, along with the Stockton staff and administration being fired.[35] Fights ensued as Courtenay students merged with Stockton and spatial rivalries became prevalent.[36] Courtenay's students feared merging with Stockton, many of whose Black students came from low-income or housing-insecure families navigating poverty at a higher level than the majority of Courtenay students.

Missing from the conversation around fights at merged schools is the sense of loss experienced when your home school is closed and you're allowed to stay in the building with students from the new school who are viewed as "smarter" or better than you, based on an arbitrary measure (high-stakes testing). As your teachers are fired, new teachers come in who have no relationship with you. Frustrations are bound to heighten in an environment where one set of students is valued while another is "tolerated." These conditions would frustrate even any adult. This is significant to the concept of engineered conflict, as violence is often the outcome of frustrations that go unaddressed. Ironically, ten years after the merger, due to the city's consistent depopulation of Black residents and Uptown's rising housing costs, families have decided not to choose Courtenay. The 2024–25 school year attendance data reports that the building houses 221 students in a school that can seat almost one thousand.[37]

Reconstitution/Turnaround: Different Name, Same Results

Reconstitution is also a drastic form of closure, where the entire staff and administration of a school would be fired and replaced. In 1996, 109 CPS schools were placed on "probation" and threatened with drastic measures if they did not improve performance. Of the thirty-eight high schools that were placed on probation, seven (DuSable, Englewood, Harper, King, Orr, Phillips, and Robeson), all of them over 90 percent Black at the time of the action, were reconstituted.[38] The following description demonstrates the intense nature of reconstitution for the seven high schools:

> All teacher and staff positions were vacated, but former staff were allowed to apply to be retained in their previous position. Across the seven schools, about 30 percent of teachers were not retained; at individual schools the number not retained ranged from 20 percent to 60 percent. Some of those not reappointed to their old jobs found new jobs in other schools (a few in other reconstituted schools). About one-third of these teachers were not able to find new permanent jobs.[39]

Over twenty years later, Harper, Englewood, and Robeson have closed. King went through a phase-out process and is now a selective enrollment high school. Discussed in detail in a later section of the chapter, DuSable, Phillips, and Orr are severely depopulated and perpetually face the threat of closure.

In the early moments of reconstitution, the bulk of the blame for inadequate performance was placed on teachers and administrators, as they had the most proximity to students who were not meeting the standards. Framed as a job performance issue, if teachers and administrators could not improve test scores and other performance indicators, they would be fired under the policy of reconstitution. In 2004, when Ren 2010 was introduced as a reform mechanism in CPS, the process of "reconstitution" was renamed to "turnaround." The process remained the same, with similar results. Schools that were chronically underperforming were not prioritized in the turnaround strategy and often found themselves in similar situations when coupled with neighborhood depopulation.

Missing from CPS's analysis is the fact that many schools placed on probation had not received the resources necessary to address educational concerns. This is important in understanding engineered conflict as schools that serve Black students navigating deep precarity (i.e. poverty, housing insecurity, lack of access to living-wage employment, lack of access to health care, police brutality/surveillance, etc.) are primarily judged by performance indicators on high-stakes tests. In some instances, when schools don't meet the testing standards set by the district or state, academic support programming focused on learning is replaced with stringent and deeply carceral strategies aimed at instilling student discipline. Longitudinally, it creates a situation where students who've historically had the least amount of resources to support learning can find themselves in schools with even less. Replacing content with test preparation and punitive discipline is not a viable solution for schools that have the highest need. In some instances, the inability to provide learning support, combined with fear of conflict in school buildings (like Clemente in the early 2000s), leads to the adding of security staff, including an increased presence of members of the Chicago Police Department.[40]

Phase Out: Reconsidering Austin High School

When I first heard of the closing of Austin High School and the relocation of its students to William H. Wells (Wells) and Roberto Clemente (Clemente) High Schools over five miles away, my first thought was, "What person in central office thought this was a good idea?" Soon after, my thinking went to, "Of course, a person who does not know Chicago or care about students of color in Chicago." Beyond my initial disgust at the closing, I soon came to know that Austin's story as a neighborhood high school was rife with disinvestment, like other low-income/ no-income Black communities in Chicago facing issues with regard to housing, law enforcement, and interpersonal and structural violence. I was especially baffled by the decision because there are two schools that are much closer than Clemente and Wells: Charles Allen Prosser High School (Prosser) and Edwin G. Foreman College and Career Academy (Foreman) are both just over four miles away from Austin High School. The reason given was that Foreman and Prosser did not have available seats for the displaced Austin students, but gentrification made space for them in Wells and Clemente, regardless of the absurdity of travel distance between schools and ongoing neighborhood tensions.

Austin High School's story is significant and highlights how engineered conflict is produced specifically through policy and process.[*] In both sets of closings (those before and after 2013), the city's rationale takes us into a longer story of structured disposability. Where

---

[*] Because the community and the high school share the same name, I make the distinction between the high school and the neighborhood in this chapter.

neoliberalism attributes the fault of neighborhood and school decline solely to community members, the story of Austin High School reveals a different story. When neoliberalism manifests itself in Chicago's policy decisions to contain and isolate poor Black low-income/ no-income families, school closings become a central component. I knew the Austin community and its high school from previous work, but I was not aware of the numerous changes that took place at the high school during the late 1990s and early 2000s. When I heard that the school would stop accepting freshmen and students in the Austin High School attendance boundary in the spring of 2004, I had the inclination to think that this was connected to a larger plan.

Watching Austin students being sent to predominantly Latinx Wells and Clemente, I couldn't help but think of the potential for conflict. As many Black students live in hyper-segregated communities and may not be in contact with people from neighborhoods in different parts of the city, there was the greater chance that conflict could occur along the lines of race, class, and neighborhood of origin. I am careful not to refer to this solely as conflicts between "gangs," as it does not speak holistically to the realities of years-long neighborhood conflict facilitated by hyper-segregation. Where some youth may have affiliations with street organizations, there are also tensions between communities and rival schools that will also lead to conflict. Similar to its destruction of public housing, the city's decisions to engage in the massive structural shifts to close schools housing abjectly refuses to consider neighborhood relations deeply shaped by legacies of hyper-segregation.

The shortest distance between Austin High School and Clemente is almost 8 miles. Wells is almost equidistant at 7.4 miles away. To outsiders, this may seem like a relatively short distance between schools if someone has access to public transportation, but to Chicagoans in a hyper-segregated city, traveling 8 miles is akin to traveling between galaxies. Where popular media outlets discussed it as crossing "gang lines," this is more of a distortion than the reality. If you take into consideration the fact that traditional large gang structures have been splintered, conflicts can arise just along the lines of neighborhood residence. In a city where tensions are already high, given lack of access to viable employment, health care, quality education, and housing, they can be heightened when residents from different neighborhoods meet. Students throughout the city understand this tension and often do not venture to other communities, especially if they rely on public transportation for travel.

Clemente and Wells were considered viable spaces because they had the largest number of available seats. The reason for that, however, was gentrification in the neighborhoods of Humboldt Park (where Clemente is located) and West Town (where Wells is located). Clemente and Wells began their individual descents into depopulation as both communities were losing their population of high-school-aged youth. Because housing prices were unattainable for many families in both neighborhoods, they were often forced to move to other parts of the city or to the suburbs. When considering engineered conflict, the complexities of school depopulation should be coupled with gentrification, disinvestment, lack of living-wage employment, and the establishment of charter schools in proximity to remaining neighborhood schools. This set of relationships creates an instance where some residents become perpetually contained in spaces that provide limited access to life-sustaining institutions (quality education, living-wage employment, access to health care, etc.).

Under the rationale of not having viable educational options in the neighborhood, CPS shuffled the lives of displaced Austin students, shipping them off instead of dedicating resources to the neighborhood high school. Ironically, Austin attempted to engage in an experiment in changing the direction of the school's academic trajectory, but the damage had been done when the school moved toward closure when it stopped accepting freshmen.[41]

Consolidation/Closure by Charter:
Almost Unnoticeable on the Surface

Taking a more subtle form than the deterioration witnessed in phase out, depopulation/closure by charter school is the most difficult type of closure to recognize. When charters were sanctioned to operate in Illinois in 1996, there were numerous distinctions that primed them to replace neighborhood public schools. Charter schools were originally thought of as places for innovation in teaching and supportive of teachers' unions (actually where the concept originated) and community control, but they quickly morphed into a mechanism of racialized neoliberal capitalism.[42] This transition is visible in Illinois, where many of the first applications for charter schools were originally led by community organizations who wanted to pursue educational strategies aimed at reaching the youth they were working with. But this moment was short-lived, and charters quickly became a corporate industry, securing branding agreements through educational management organizations (EMOs) that garnered profits by way of contracts with school districts. Once charters were identified as a "growth market," the structure shifted, where EMOs would "shop" their models to communities through several dubious practices.[43] Currently charters do not have neighborhood attendance boundaries and operate on a lottery system for admissions.* Even though most students attend charters in or close to their respective neighborhoods, there is significant variance in charters along the lines of curriculum, discipline, and accessibility.

As a market entity, the pitch that charters put to communities would position them as a new "experiment" that would improve educational outcomes for students who decided to attend. Events that would usually

---

* Where most students are able to get into the charter of their choice through the lottery system, there are densely populated charter schools that rely heavily on the lottery process, as they consistently receive more applications than they have seats for admission.

operate as community orientation meetings (sometimes referenced as an "open houses") would include raffles of expensive electronics and household appliances. Families who had historically been starved of resources were enticed by this practice to apply for admissions, but many soon realized it was merely a ploy to get students in the door. Essentially, the sales pitch from EMOs to families was, "You've had forty years of madness, misappropriation, and exclusion—We don't know exactly what it is that we're doing, but there's no way it can be worse than what you already have!" Ironically, to this day, there is no discernable evidence that charters as a whole outperform traditional neighborhood public schools.[44]

Public school districts like CPS appreciate charters because they lower the cost burden of the district. EMOs would be responsible for a portion of the operating costs, and the district only responsible for covering the remainder of the expenditures. Because charter schools are public schools run by private entities, they mirror the management structure of public housing in Chicago, where the remaining buildings, while still operating as a public entity, are managed by private corporations. For charters, this public-private partnership resulted in staunch opposition to union organizing and strict discipline policies that included monetary fines for being out of uniform and other demerits.[45]

In reference to engineered conflict, the advent of charter schools reveals another depopulation mechanism that is deeply connected to the neighborhood attendance boundary. The push for charter schools in Chicago, begun by Arne Duncan, increased the number of privately run public charter schools from zero in the mid-1990s to 133 in 2014, serving approximately 57,000 students in Chicago. The rapid growth of the charter-school movement has only accelerated the decline of neighborhood high school enrollments. As a result, "'some 10,000 high school students and 6,000 elementary school students of CPS students, [sic] travel as far as six miles to get to school each day, crossing boundaries of race, class, and opportunity."[46] In the current moment, the hard and fast rule of the compulsory neighborhood attendance boundary has weakened considerably. Where charter schools have shifted the reality of neighborhood attendance boundaries, they are also important in understanding school closure as a process that is not completely centered in population loss in the city. In contrast with the other forms of closure, closure by charter could be described as a "slow burn" instead of a hostile takeover. Even though it is a deliberate process, the effects are not as immediate as direct closure, consolidation, or reconstitution/turnaround. In many instances, there are charters who set up their new school in a formerly closed building that is in close proximity to a neighborhood public school. In the most extreme instances, the charter can set up shop less than a block from the neighborhood public school. Of the neighborhood public schools that were closed between 2000 and 2013, the average distance to a charter school was .61 miles away, while the schools that stayed open were on average 1.017 miles away from a similar charter school.[47] This spatial reality should not be taken as coincidence; instead, it should be understood as a component of charter proliferation that cannibalized the populations of neighborhood schools on the South and West Sides of the city.

Running the Gambit of School Destruction: The Conundrum of Orr HS

Orr Academy High School (Orr) serves as an important vehicle by which to understand engineered conflict, particularly as it is one of the few CPS schools that have experienced all of the first four forms of closure (consolidation, closing/closure, phase-out, reconstitution/turnaround). In all of its iterations, the school stands as one of the earliest and most egregious cases of failed corporate school reform in the city. Named in honor of late nineteenth- and early twentieth-century labor leader Rezin Orr, the school was originally an elementary school when it opened in 1918.

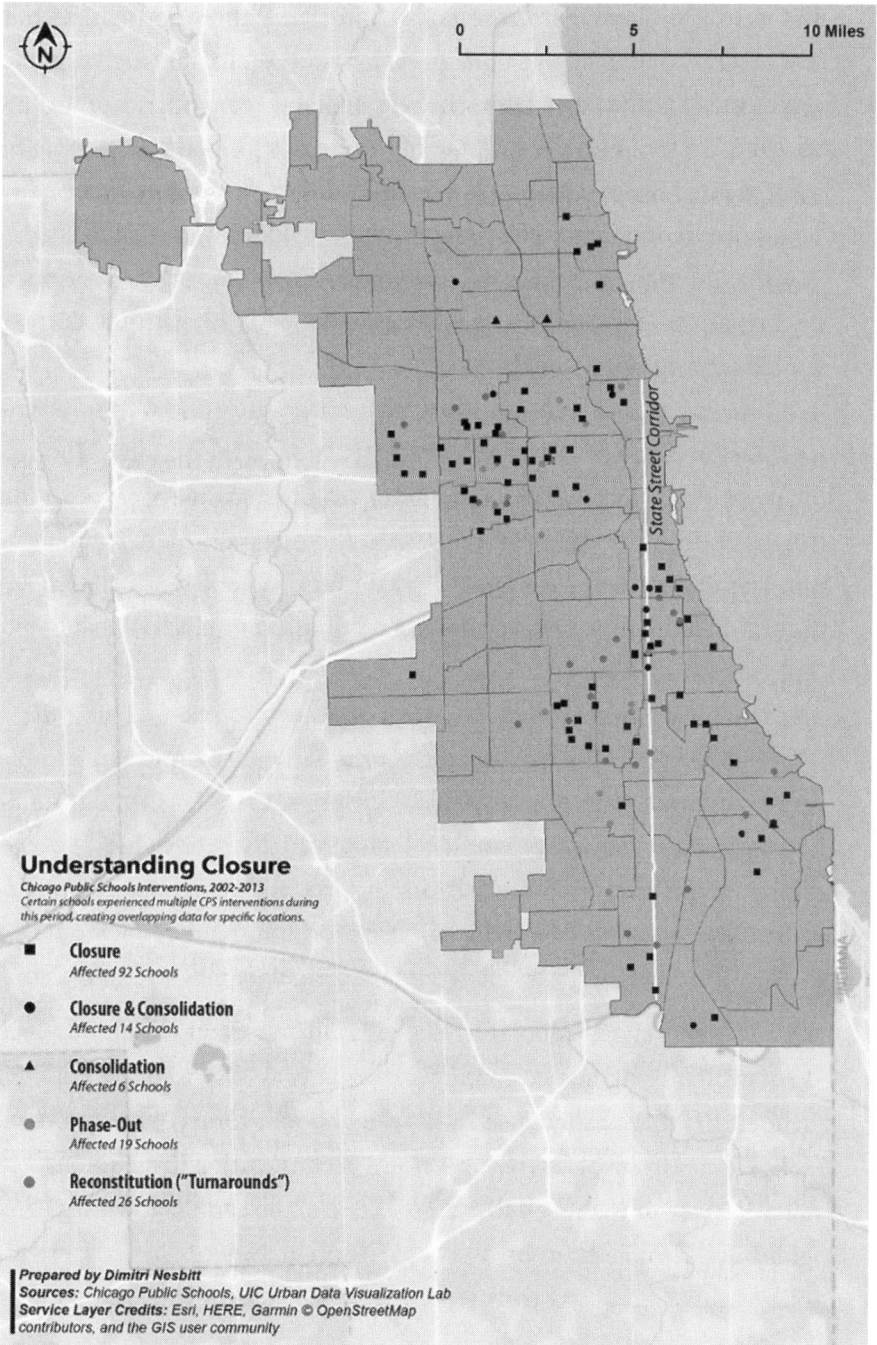

0   5   10 Miles

State Street Corridor

Understanding Closure

Chicago Public Schools Interventions, 2002-2013
Certain schools experienced multiple CPS interventions during
this period, creating overlapping data for specific locations.

■   **Closure**
     Affected 92 Schools

●   **Closure & Consolidation**
     Affected 14 Schools

▲   **Consolidation**
     Affected 6 Schools

●   **Phase-Out**
     Affected 19 Schools

●   **Reconstitution ("Turnarounds")**
     Affected 26 Schools

Prepared by Dimitri Nesbitt
Sources: Chicago Public Schools, UIC Urban Data Visualization Lab
Service Layer Credits: Esri, HERE, Garmin © OpenStreetMap
contributors, and the GIS user community

In the 1920s it became a branch of Austin High School. By the 1940s it had shifted back to a vocational program for seventh- and eighth-grade boys. After a fire that destroyed the school, it was temporarily, from 1958 to 1962, housed in the Our Lady of the Angels program. Beginning in 1962 it operated as a branch of Marshall High School. When it became an official stand-alone CPS school in 1966, an addition was placed in the Marshall building to relieve overcrowding. When enrollment continued to increase, a new site for Orr was approved in 1970, with the current building being completed in 1973.

Integral to Orr's relationship with corporate school reform and engineered conflict is the physical construction of the building. Though many people may associate the school-within-a-school concept to the small-schools movement of the 1990s, there was also a movement in the late 1960s and early '70s to create high schools with specializations.[48] Structurally, Orr was designed around four clusters that could hold five hundred students each. Each of the four sections of the building had its own large lecture area, seminar rooms, labs, and dining areas. During the late 1970s and throughout the early '80s some high schools were constructed to house spatial "clusters" of students in the building for certain specialties. Students could usually choose between the building/mechanical trades, performing arts, and/or media. The physical architecture of the building lent itself to a multiple school model, as each cluster was identical, allowing for curricular and structural autonomy, depending on how leadership chose to utilize the space.*

As the population of the West Humboldt Park community began to decline, Orr began to experience particular forms of disinvestment. When academic performance waned due to the removal of resources in the form of teaching staff and academic programming, Orr was

---

* The four physical clusters of Orr could be used to house individual grade levels (sophomores, juniors, etc.) or curricular focuses (building trades, performing arts, media, etc.).

targeted for reconstitution. The original plan to offer curricular specializations for students quickly became a mechanism that pitted the
schools in the building against each other.

From its first reconstitution in 1997, to a phase-out plan in 2000, to
its break-up into four small schools in 2002 (Applied Art Science and
Technology Academy, EXCEL Academy, Mose Vines High School, and
Phoenix Military Academy), and back to its consolidation and takeover
by the Academy of Urban School Leadership (AUSL) in 2008, the Orr
building is a standing testament to failed experimentation conducted on
Black bodies, despite consistent demands for quality education.[49] Currently the school is severely underpopulated. Mose Vines and Applied
Art Science and Technology Academy have closed, while Phoenix
Military Academy moved out of the Orr complex and now has its own
building. Since AUSL has lost its contract with the district, Orr has been
returned to CPS. It currently shares the building with KIPP One Academy, a charter school run by the national charter-management organization Knowledge Is Power Program (KIPP). Despite the turmoil of the
last twenty-five years, the school won three consecutive state basketball
titles in 2017, 2018, and 2019. Its current positioning as a basketball
powerhouse is most likely one of the factors that keeps the school open.

Death of the Neighborhood High School

Where the bulk of media attention has been placed on the 2013 closings
of K–8 schools, school closings at the high school level (usually in the
form of phase-outs) are of particular importance, particularly at the level
of the traditional neighborhood high school. There have been phase-outs
and a few charter takeovers of closed school buildings, leaving a set of
predominantly Black high schools with populations that have withered to
alarming numbers. The chart below provides a sense of the lasting effects
of the aforementioned forms of closure on neighborhood public schools.

LISTING OF DEPOPULATED NEIGHBORHOOD HIGH

Name of School	Percent Black
Manley Career Academy HS	92.5
John Marshall Metropolitan HS	97.9
Richard T. Crane Medical Preparatory HS	85.5
Austin College and Career Academy HS	94.7
Emil G. Hirsch Metropolitan HS	93.9
Chicago Vocational Career Academy HS	95.6
Hyde Park Academy HS	98.7
James H. Bowen HS	76.5
Christian Fenger Academy HS	96.3
Wendell Phillips Academy HS	91.7
Paul Laurence Dunbar Career Academy HS	95.9
Jean Baptiste Point DuSable HS Building (closed in 2023)	95.7
George H. Corliss HS	94.8
Percy L. Julian HS	96.2
Collins STEAM HS	95.2
Al Raby HS	88.6
Frederick Douglass Academy HS	96.2
Orr Academy HS	74.2

Sources: https://www.cps.edu/schools/find-a-school/ and Quest Center of the

SCHOOLS NEAR OR OVER 75 PERCENT BLACK

Co-location Y/N (school that shares the building)	Students enrolled in 2024–25	Building Capacity (in number of students)
N	147	1,296
N	211	1,296
N	280	1,365
N	140	1,776
N	96	960
N	591	2,184
N	733	1,800
Y (Baker College Prep Charter HS)	266	1,824
N	217	1,224
N	407	1,608
N	315	1,752
Y (Daniel Hale Williams Prep School of Medicine and Bronzeville Scholastic Academy HS)	141	2,136
Y (Butler Charter HS)	375	1,440
N	403	1,344
Y (North Lawndale College Prep Charter HS)	194	1,200
N	104	816
N	26	800
N	326	2,000

Chicago Teachers Union

Note that only three of these high schools (Bowen, Corliss, and Collins) share buildings with charter schools (co-locations). Even if we add the population of the co-locating charter school in the building, only Collins and Corliss have a student population that is more than 50 percent of the building's capacity. In both instances, the charter school is almost double the size of the neighborhood high school (Butler Charter HS has 652 students to Corliss's 291, North Lawndale College Prep Charter has 432 students to Collins's 223), contributing to an internal depopulation of the neighborhood high school. Of the stand-alone schools that are not sharing a building with a charter school, none are over 40 percent of the building's capacity. When we take into account neighborhood high schools with traditional attendance or citywide boundaries on the South and West Sides of the city, there are only two non–selective enrollment schools with a majority Black population (Kenwood Academy and Neal F. Simeon Career Academy High School) that are at or near full capacity.* The situation becomes even more stark when we consider that Kenwood and Simeon are both on the South Side, meaning that

---

* The discussion of Kenwood Academy requires nuance. While listed as a neighborhood high school with traditional attendance boundaries, their academic center (which is their seventh- and eighth-grade program) does not have attendance boundaries and is a selective enrollment academy. Through the selective enrollment process, students have to test in for admission. Students at the academic center are given priority among applicants to attend Kenwood for high school. This contributes to the fact that the school's demographics are actually more closely aligned with the selective enrollment high schools in Chicago, given that the high school's population of "low income" students (58.4 percent) is considerably lower than the district average (72.7 percent). The percentage of students who would be considered diverse learners (5.6 percent) is also considerably lower than the district average (15.3 percent). Despite its designation as a neighborhood high school, the academic center creates a situation where there are considerably more Black students from middle- and upper-income Black families.

there are no majority Black non–selective enrollment neighborhood public high schools on the West Side of the city that are at or near full capacity.

The high school population data, while a subset of the larger advent of school closings, are important to the concept of engineered conflict with specific respect to disposability. Because CPS as a district uses a per-student allotment for funding, it is impossible to have the things needed for the day-to-day functions of a high school.* Things like athletic programs, guidance/career counselors, school psychologists and nurses are out of the question, because the funding equation will not allow for the expenditures. If these buildings are operating anywhere between 10 and 45 percent capacity, it is extremely difficult for them to operate as robust centers of learning.

Although the list of schools targeted for closure in 2013 was reduced from 128 to 49, and high schools were kept off the list, many were already in the process of phasing out. Two specific examples are King College Prep and Jones College Prep. King, as a former neighborhood high school that was originally built as a performing-arts high school, had suffered from years of disinvestment. Jones, once a school for what was then known as the "secretarial arts," was a city-wide enrollment school that also experienced disinvestment, but was also located in the downtown area that still operates as an epicenter for uneven development/gentrification. Both schools were phase-outs, where the buildings laid dormant before they were "redeveloped" with new amenities. In the most extreme instance, Jones's redevelopment included a seven-story addition that almost tripled the size of the original school building. Tellingly, the new Jones

---

* The per-student allotment formula is a funding mechanism that distributes resource dollars to a building based on the number of students attending the school. The smaller the school's population is, the less access they have to resources.

structure required the demolition of a shelter for the unhoused, to remove the "unsightly" presence of people experiencing housing insecurity. As spaces for the "new Chicago," schools serve as a key component in the aesthetic and material reimagining of the city.

The Depopulation Machine: GoCPS

If we take the high school–population data from the earlier section as a barometer, it appears as if CPS has settled on depopulation as the norm for schools serving working-class, low-income/no-income Black students on the South and West sides of the city. Adding to the problem is a cleverly worded process and website (cps.edd/gocps) that appears to explain educational options for families in the district, but also creates a mechanism that almost guarantees the depopulation of certain schools. If a family wants to register a young person for any CPS school, they must use the GoCPS site.[*] The site appears self-explanatory, with deadlines for applications and other options. Families can subscribe to the site to get reminders and updates for registration deadlines and other important dates on the CPS calendar. Once inside the site, a family can type in the name of a school and get an overview that includes data on its racial composition, test scores, and other information (reports, programs, downloads, etc.). On the surface, the site appears to provide an accessible and viable interface for families to make informed decisions on schools throughout the city.

The problem arises in the next step. To choose a school, families are required to list their top ten choices on the GoCPS site. In

---

[*] For selective enrollment high schools, in addition to GoCPS, students must have a certain test score average as a seventh grader to qualify to take an entrance exam. Admission to K–8 selective enrollment schools also require an admissions test. The GoCPS application can be found at https://www.cps.edu/gocps.

the spirit of the rhetoric of "choice," families are not bound to choose neighborhood schools or schools inside their neighborhood attendance boundary. Schools that are chosen the most by families have the greatest chance to have high population numbers. Given the city's depopulation issue, most families get their first or second choice with non–selective enrollment schools. Where this initially sounds equitable and justice-leaning, it is important to consider families who do not have the means to travel to other schools. If we consider childcare and transportation concerns, some community members do not have the means to travel long distances and are best served by their neighborhood school. If there are not enough families that choose these neighborhood schools, it is almost certain that they will experience significant reductions in their student population.* Because GoCPS is universally required for all families registering students in CPS, the depopulation mechanism is engrained into one of the primary functions of the district.

If a family or individual makes a bad choice, then blame is placed on them for making the decision, without an understanding of the conditions that impact it. GoCPS, as a mechanism of the neoliberal state, creates the illusion that families are provided resources allowing for an informed decision. For some families the opposite is true. In the broader scope of engineered conflict, we see yet another example of whose bodies are cherished and whose can be thrown away.

---

* The translation option isn't immediately visible on the GoCPS site, so families who have a primary language other than English could have some initial difficulty with navigation. Additionally, the site could also be more difficult to navigate via phone, as it would require an internet interface. Though access to internet is thought of as commonly accessible, it is not for all families, particularly those without access to free Wi-Fi signals.

Safe Passage(?)

Another indication of of who is valued and who is disposable came in 2009, when the City of Chicago, under the leadership of Mayor Richard M. Daley, implemented the Safe Passage program. Yellow signs that read "Safe Passage" were placed on streets frequented by young people on their way to and from school. Like the red "X" signage on buildings soon to be demolished described in the introduction, Safe Passage routes serve as indicators for communities that are either in transition for development or have been marked for disposability. Following the tragic and virally distributed beating death of Fenger High School honor student Derrion Albert in 2009, the city came to grips with the fact that a tragic mistake had been made with the closing of one school and the subsequent consolidation with another school in a different neighborhood.[50] Community members had warned of the potential troubles that would be produced by the consolidation of George Washington Carver High School (Carver) and Christian Fenger Academy (Fenger), but by the time the city offered a solution it was too late. In this instance, the city's negligence is at issue, given the fact that there were numerous warnings about school consolidation on the South and West Sides of the city. The city only moved when the graphic nature of Derrion Albert's beating went viral and placed all eyes on Chicago.

Safe Passage is a program with a specific relationship with the police strategy of containment. Following CPS's inability to consider community concerns about the school closings that took place between 2000 and 2009, the city began a series of actions on the first day of school in September of 2013 (the school year following the forty-nine closings). South and West Side receiving schools (ones that would take in students from closed schools) had a visible and overt police presence. Squad cars lined the streets along Safe Passage routes. In some instances, fire engines parked on paths marked for Safe Passage, with armed police officers standing on top. Some schools had mounted police officers to oversee students' entrance and exit from school. Once again, the city's show of potential force was supposed to prevent any potential conflicts between new students and neighborhood residents, as thousands of students traveled to forty-nine new schools across lines of hyper-segregation and decades-old neighborhood tensions. But given the marked corridors and spaces where people could be physically contained against their will, it is difficult to imagine students feeling safe under these conditions.

Despite the city's attempt to present itself as aware of potential conflicts at the beginning of the 2013–14 school year, the heavy police presence waned by the second week of school. Where some violence was curbed on Safe Passage routes, there was not a wholesale reduction.[51] The constant in the research and reporting on Safe Passage is that it only works in areas where Safe Passage community workers have relationships with young people in the neighborhood.[52] A holistic view of the program would have us consider violence that occurs on Safe Passage routes before and after the designated hours. The security details on Safe Passage paths currently begin an hour before the start of school and ends two hours after classes end.

Spatial relationships in school closings are also connected to the military industrial complex. The person assigned to supervise Safe Passage after the 2013 closures was Tom Tyrrell, a former Marine colonel whose responsibility in the Marine Corps was hostage negotiation and hostage transport through war zones.[53] If Black students on the South and West Sides are reduced to de facto hostages then the police presence becomes less confounding. If the war theater is the city of Chicago, then there is little to differentiate between enemy combatants and Black residents who live in Safe Passage zones. Similar to the actions of the military, CPS and the Chicago Police Department have engaged in triage, where casualties are sorted to prioritize the treatment of the wounded, whether that be an individual person or a school that has experienced harm due to lack of thought and consideration in the process of closure. Those schools that can remain open are "treated" to the extent that they can remain open. Those that can't represent the casualties of war. Discussed in the next chapter, a similar fate was assigned to residents of public housing as the city lay down the terms and conditions of engineered conflict.

CHAPTER 2

PLANS THAT
DID NOT TRANSFORM

THE CHICAGO
HOUSING AUTHORITY'S
COMMITMENT TO
ENGINEERED CONFLICT

*Project: an individual or collaborative enterprise that is
carefully planned to achieve a particular aim.*[1]

Jay-Z's line about public housing in the song "Do You Wanna Ride?"—
"Why do you think they call it a project? Because it's a project"—while
distressing, is clear. His lyrics have always stood as some of the clearest
explanations of public housing as an "experiment." When viewing post-

war plans for public housing, the titles given to the building complexes in Chicago before they were named after actual people allude to a process that appears both tentative and speculative. Official titles like "Public Housing Administration Aided Project No. Illinois 2-19," first given to the Henry Horner Homes in Chicago, sound like they're speaking of some sort of ill-intended open experiment.[2] Even though it may not be discussed explicitly, the term *project* in public housing evokes negative connotations of a temporary dwelling where residents are regulated to live under the worst possible conditions. Because the images of neglect and disrepair are ingrained in our minds, we continue to think of public housing as dwellings of last resort. Where this train of thought may be more commonplace in today's thinking, it is not reflective of earlier iterations of public housing in the first half of the twentieth century. Coupled with the fallacy that all of the problems associated with public housing were the fault of its Black residents, this false notion should be placed in context, revealing a set of structural and historical concerns that rapidly reduced many of the housing complexes to sites of permanent disrepair.

I remember having a conversation with a good friend in the late 1990s about the future of public housing, soon after the Ida B. Wells Extension was demolished in 1997. My friend told me, "You know the Ida B.'s are coming down." My first response was, "What?" I was surprised: the Ida B. Wells Homes were different from the high-rise extension apartments to the east, which had been in disrepair for years. In theory, the low-rise Ida B. Wells Homes were better constructed and easier to maintain than the high-rises. Even though they had experienced neglect over the years, I thought CHA would move to refurbish them, for the sole reason that it would cost less to do so.

This was all taking place in the historic Bronzeville neighborhood, which is spread across the four neighborhoods of Kenwood, Oakland, Grand Boulevard, and Douglass, all of which comprise the mid-South region of the city. The connection to engineered conflict is stark, in that this was also the area where CPS announced its Renaissance 2010 plan that would close or repurpose twenty of the twenty-two schools that serviced the region. My friend and I soon came to find out that what was happening to the Ida B. Wells Homes was part of CHA's Plan for Transformation, which would become the largest public housing–redevelopment plan in the history of the United States.

It is important to note that public housing in Chicago was not always the housing choice of last resort. Where the Plan for Transformation was a poorly executed attempt to address years of neglect, a critical perspective of CHA history and policy challenges us to ask a few simple and straightforward questions. First. *How did things get this way?* Second, *If everyone knew the conditions were unlivable, why was the plan to rectify the situation so haphazard and incomplete?* For many Chicagoans and people who pay attention to housing issues locally, nationally, and globally, the answer to both questions is, *Because the Black people who are bearing the brunt of these conditions have been discarded and declared disposable.* Even if we consider the anemic maneuvers made by the Chicago Housing Authority (CHA) to improve conditions in public housing from the 1970s to the late 1990s, it is immediately noticeable that the well-being of Black residents was not primarily in mind. Because these residents are held in the least regard, it makes "logical" sense to the neoliberal state to put them in situations like the one suggested by Eisen-Martin in the introduction where they continue to hit each other. If conflict ensues, more strategies will be enacted to contain or remove them.

As happens with schools, questions about public housing are only raised when people are deep in crisis. Attention only comes to education and housing for poor/working-class Black residents in the most extreme instances, ignoring the longitudinal decline in resources needed for improvement. Education and housing, both essential life-sustaining entities, share an intimate relationship with each other in Chicago, and both are critical in understanding the structural components of engineered conflict. When both are shuttered and/or demolished, people are displaced to communities that are unfamiliar to them and the probability of violence increases. In Chicago, both public housing and public education systems can be extremely difficult to navigate, leaving families without the resources to fend for themselves. Critical anthropologist Catherine Fennell poses two important questions that make it easier to understand engineered conflict in relation to public housing:

> How do obsolete infrastructures such as decaying projects, shuttered factories and vacant homes linger in the sensibilities, solidarities and bodies of those who have spent lifetimes moving around them? How do these lingering sensibilities and solidarities now press into flesh, thought, feeling and action novel arguments concerning what might be owed to citizens who weathered the worst of such abandonment?[3]

The history of CHA is central to engineered conflict. With it we can understand how housing policies devolved from benevolence to outright animus for its Black residents. Emerging as a small agency focused on providing housing for people who were either housing insecure at the close of the Depression or working in the war effort during World War II, by the late 1970s CHA had evolved into an unmanageable entity revealing a confusing labyrinth of local, state, and federal housing policy. Once significant numbers of Black people had moved into high-rise CHA properties, the city's strategy of containment became one of disposability. If a project is an "enterprise that is carefully planned to achieve a particular aim," the mid-twentieth- and early twenty-first-century government "project" of public housing for Black people in Chicago stands as a deliberate exercise in abandonment.

The remainder of this chapter is my attempt to articulate the nuanced, layered, and intricate connection of public housing to engineered conflict. To make sense of the relationship, the chapter begins with CHA's early years and subsequent shift from serving majority white to primarily Black and poor residents, revealing the racialized nature of public housing. I then offer a challenge to the idea that housing was "better" in the early years of CHA, to show how it was already laying the groundwork for engineered conflict. From a discussion of the temporarily expedient and structurally dysfunctional high-rise CHA buildings, the Plan for Transformation is then brought into focus as the city's attempt to conceal its strategy of planned abandonment.

The Brief (but Contested) Moment of Sustainable Public Housing

In contrast to contemporary views on public housing, it is important to note that at one time, local, state, and federal governments collectively maintained a sustainable formula for public housing residents, who at the time were primarily white. Before it was reduced to an afterthought, public housing was far from being the choice of last resort in Chicago. Instead, it was viewed as a forward-thinking approach to address housing shortages and an overabundance of slum dwellings, especially for veterans and industry workers during and directly after World War II.[4] In the first twenty years of CHA (1937–1957), residents in the low-rise buildings were provided with social workers, fully resourced community centers, health clinics, new schools, and, for most buildings, playgrounds and open, manicured greenspace.[5] Building complexes often sponsored sports teams and social clubs, and hosted parades and other events centered in community pride.[6] The buildings were managed efficiently, allowing residents to develop personal relationships with each other and with the organizations that provided them support. From an onlooker's perspective, CHA housing developments had all the makings of sustainable communities.

Although this phase was brief and already filled with problematic policy decisions (particularly with regard to residential segregation), it allows us to begin to contemplate what state-sponsored, sustainable public housing could look like. In essence, local, state, and federal housing agencies actually *knew* what it took to provide viable housing for low-income residents but refused to do it in later iterations of CHA, when the residents became majority Black and poor. They made a concerted effort to create sustainable public housing when developments were only sprinkled with Black residents who would eventually use CHA as temporary residence. White residents were valued by the city, thought to be integral to its future development, whereas early Black residents in CHA were only tolerated, and only to the extent that they would be contained in certain geographic areas.

Contrary to popular belief, there was a moment in Chicago where public housing was considered structurally innovative and potentially paradigm-shifting. Buildings were built to "human scale," six stories high or lower. The land-to-building ratio always favored land, with ample space between buildings. Coupled with innovations in central heating with individual central heating plants for each development, the earliest low-rise iterations of public housing had the front-facing view as viable places for families to live.[7] At least at the surface level, and although still deeply fraught along the lines of race and class via residential segregation, the early days of public housing in Chicago were reflective of a commitment to the well-being of its residents.

In addition to support services, CHA had several contractual relationships that allowed them to keep rents low, while maintaining a surplus to address repairs. At the all-white Trumbull Park Homes, a contract with Wisconsin Steel Works and United States Housing Authority (USHA) incentivized CHA to keep rents low, to make sure there would be no surplus of funds, which would have to go back to USHA. This allowed CHA to offer rents as low as $20.55 for a three-bedroom apartment, including utilities. With these costs, CHA purchased utilities in bulk, making its cost per unit even lower. At these prices, only one-third of 1 percent of CHA rent was unpaid in 1941. Additionally, subsidies at the local and state level created a situation where CHA paid no real estate taxes on its properties. As a reciprocal model, CHA also paid 5 percent of its rental fees for schools and other services for residents in the early years, providing a sustainable model for renters.[8] Despite the current view of public housing as the least viable option, then, we must recognize that in some instances, government has demonstrated some responsibility, albeit primarily to white residents in the city.

The transition in Chicago from federal public housing to locally supported efforts is key in understanding containment by way of hyper-segregation. Built between 1935 and 1938 by the Housing Division of the Public Works Administration (PWA), soon to become consolidated into the Works Progress Administration (WPA), the first three federal housing developments in the city were the Trumbull Park Homes, Julia Lathrop Homes, and the Jane Addams Homes.[9] As a local-federal partnership between the City of Chicago and the PWA, the first set of public housing units were built by PWA funds, but were managed by the CHA, who were under contract with USHA. The local-federal relationship has significant bearing on CHA's mismanagement in the late twentieth century. The WPA sought to address slum clearance, lack of affordable housing for veterans, and lack of shelter for people working in the manufacturing industry before and during World War II. As these dwellings were originally designed to address the overabundance of slum dwellings and lack of housing throughout the city, CHA's first occupants were white residents in majority white neighborhoods.

Even in the early days of public housing in Chicago, the idea of containment, both spatially and racially, of Black people was a central fixture. Before we accept the claim that public housing was some sort of panacea for Black people, we ought to look behind the veil of newly built buildings and services being provided for residents. In name, federal public housing was not to support discrimination of any kind, but a combination of federal policy and de facto moves by the city meant Black families remained isolated. Take for example the Jane Addams Homes on the Near West Side. A small grouping of Black families were allowed to live in the Addams homes because they lived in the slum area where the new development would be built. When they moved in, however, they were contained to a certain section of the development, limiting their contact with other residents of the Addams Homes.[10] On the Northwest Side of the city, the Lathrop homes were built on a vacant lot in a primarily industrial area on the Chicago River, and the Trumbull Park Homes were built in proximity to the Wisconsin Steel Works on the South Side, in a predominantly white neighborhood to house the families of workers employed by the steel mill.[11]

The Ida B. Wells Homes are a unique case in the history of segregation in Chicago's public housing, in that they were exclusively built for Black residents on the South Side of the city. Originally scheduled to open at the same time as the Addams, Lathrop, and Trumbull Homes, the Wells Homes had the slowest rate of construction, even though the land was purchased around the same time as it was for the other developments, in 1934. When the construction of public-housing buildings was transferred to local entities in 1937, CHA, which was incorporated that year, could claim the Wells Homes as its first development.[12] This was also the same year that the United States Housing Act was passed. Because there was a provision that the racial make-up of a community could not be changed by a new development, the Wells Homes maintained its exclusively Black clientele from its construction to its demolition in the early 2000s.

Apartments in the Wells Homes were a significant improvement from mismanaged, privately owned slumlord buildings throughout the South Side. In addition to a fully functional health clinic, the Wells development was also the first CHA development to have a city park (property of the Chicago Park District) on its site. There were significant problems, however. When some of the dense slum housing was demolished to build the homes, residents were further overcrowded. In the first years of the development the number of applicants (18,000) far exceeded the number of available units (1,600).[13] Still, the management of Ida B. Wells made sure that families on the higher side of the income bracket were not given priority. On the contrary, early CHA management openly expressed concern for residents' well-being and were able to provide the necessary supports for families, regardless of income.[14]

My connection to this reality comes by way of my grandmother, Edna Stovall, who arrived in Chicago by way of Mariana, Arkansas, in 1938. She was able to secure a home in the Ida B. Wells Homes in 1941. At the time, due to restrictive covenants, my grandmother and other Black people could not own a home or rent an apartment outside of an arbitrary border. Through this process of "redlining," over 80 percent of the Black population was contained in an area of less than nine square miles, primarily on the South Side of the city. My father would tell me stories of how the Ida B. Wells Homes provided a technological advancement in the form of central heating. From the late nineteenth century to the mid-twentieth century, many of the homes in Chicago's Bronzeville community were kitchenette apartments, often heated by a coal stove in the middle of the apartment. In many instances, multiple families had to share kitchenettes. In addition to central heating, the Ida B. Wells Homes were primarily low-rise homes (mostly two-story buildings, with no building higher than six stories high) constructed with brick, allowing for more substantive protection from inclement weather. Because kitchenette buildings were often drafty with leaky plumbing, faulty electricity, shoddy construction, and lack of upkeep, the Ida B. Wells Homes represented a definitive upgrade from slumlord-run apartments.

By the end of WWII, five years into the existence of the Wells Homes, CHA had become big business. The agency had a staff of 449 people, including 295 maintenance staff and 154 administrative and clerical personnel.[15] CHA had over eleven thousand units split between permanent dwellings, temporary veterans' homes, and one rent-to-own property, also specifically for Black residents (the West Chesterfield Homes).[16] The buildings were regarded as efficient and well maintained. There were some mixed-race residences like the Cabrini Row Houses, originally built for workers in the war industry, but otherwise CHA housing was still deeply segregated. Developments in majority white communities like the Bridgeport Homes and Lawndale Gardens served as housing for people working in heavy industry throughout the city, while Black residents were also able to live in newly built complexes, like Wentworth Gardens, that were also managed by tenants with a degree of success. As restrictive covenants were lifted in the city in 1948, Black families could also live in the Frank O. Lowden Homes on Ninety-Fifth Street. CHA moved forward with developments on empty plots of land, like LeClaire Courts on the Southwest Side, for residents whose family members were working in postwar industries. As CHA entered its development boom through partnerships with the city and the federal government, claims of success could be made regarding the social experiment of public housing. However, the issue remained, *for whom and for how long?*

Not Halcyon Days—Only Different and Contested Ones

There is always the need to revisit the idea of CHA once being a "paradise." One of the most contested statements made in everyday, intergenerational conversations is, "Things were better in my day." I take to heart a warning my father offered to me jokingly, that once you hear a sentence that begins with "back in my day," the person is about to tell a lie. This was not to deny people's experiences, but to take them in context. A more accurate description would be to state that "things may have appeared to be better on the surface, but white supremacy did not leave us." To be precise, it would be more accurate to state that "things were different." Because neither is all good or all tragic, we know that nuance and deep contestation is eternally present in the lives of Black people. Embracing this reality allows us to understand a layered discussion that includes particularities and contrasts.

A discussion of the early days of CHA demands these distinctions. Political scientist Michelle Boyd reminds us that when people wax poetic about a historical period, they often bypass a discussion of the struggles that many families faced. Her reference to the practice as "Jim Crow Nostalgia" or "a yearning for and a celebration of Black life during the period of legalized racial segregation," is important in understanding engineered conflict.[17] While some Black people were able to move away from Chicago's Black Belt when de jure segregation was lifted, the hardships often deepened for those who could not, especially if they were living in mismanaged CHA buildings.* At the same time, we should understand that in different ways, no matter their social class, Black Chicagoans were catching their own particular type of hell. A comparative analysis of which group of Black people had it worse is unnecessary. We can discount neither the violent and traumatizing experiences of families who first attempted to integrate all-white areas in Chicago nor the state-sanctioned violence inflicted on communities that remained majority Black and poor. Where class privilege may have provided some buffers from white supremacy (home ownership, living-wage employment, health insurance, retirement plans, etc.), it is also clear that it did not make you

---

* The term *Black Belt* refers to the geographic location where over 80 percent of Black Chicagoans lived beginning in the late nineteenth century until 1948, when restrictive covenants were lifted by a Supreme Court case (*Shelley v. Kraemer*, 344 U.S. 1).

safe from its grips. And where it is true that for a brief moment in time Black CHA residents were provided with the supports needed to live and thrive, a realistic view acknowledges that that brief moment of sustainability was deeply nuanced and contested.

The prima facie example in the early years of CHA is the Trumbull Park Homes race riots, which ensued following the introduction of Black residents in the summer of 1953. Ironically, the disturbance took place because the person responsible for screening the families did not recognize the applicants (the Howard family) as Black, due to their fair skin color. Once word got out that a Black family had moved into the homes, white residents responded with riots and other random acts of violence for over a year, to the point where police escorts were required for Black families.[18] Instead of the displacement that takes place in the current moment of engineered conflict, the early years of CHA were marked by another inability to address issues of race and space. Instead of Black families being displaced, white racial terror often denied Black families affordable housing.

While residents were active in refusing their isolation, CHA, in concert with the mayor's office, moved in a way that minimally tolerated Black residents, though only in segregated communities. During the early years, the progressive board of CHA, led by board president Robert Taylor (who was Black) and CHA president Elizabeth Wood (who was white), had to fight city council for the approval of housing-development sites throughout the city. The efforts had some positive results with regard to integration, but it is more important to note the vehement resistance of the mayor's office and the majority-white city council to allow Black residents to live in the communities they governed.[19]

The early days of CHA may have been different for its Black residents, then, but they still faced racism and a strict opposition that allows us to bring some issues into focus. First is the structural relationship of CHA to the City of Chicago. Contrary to popular belief,

CHA is not an agency of the City of Chicago. Even though the commissioners are appointed by the mayor, CHA is a "municipal not-for-profit corporation" that is in compliance with the state to operate within the boundaries of Chicago.[20] As an agency, CHA has no taxing power and collects no annual appropriations from the city. Over the years, this relationship created a reliance on scant federal dollars, which turned CHA toward assigning oversight of certain housing complexes to private management firms. Their mismanagement then allowed government to argue for the irrelevance of public housing, missing the fact that much of the mismanagement was spurred by a refusal to commit to long-term affordable housing when low-income/no-income Black families became the primary tenants.* In the early days of CHA, only those Black families that had the financial means to pay rents high enough to subsidize maintenance costs were viewed as "acceptable." However, these families were also the first to leave public housing. Poorer residents who remained had limited access to economic and political resources and were left to their own devices as the infrastructure of public housing eroded by the late 1960s. As restrictive covenants were lifted throughout the city and high-rise public housing in CHA became the norm, the markers for disposability were set in stone.

In another instance of Jim Crow Nostalgia, early Black residents of CHA would often refer to the screening process of residents as the mechanism that kept CHA developments viable for low-income, working-class Black families. But a more accurate account

---

* In the first half of the twentieth century there were tensions between residents of Bronzeville in terms of what sets of Black people were deemed to be respectable. Messages were placed in newspapers like the *Chicago Defender* advised Black people migrating north on how to dress and make themselves "presentable." Often referenced as "respectability politics," the belief is that the compliance of privileged members of marginalized groups to mainstream, white, Western European norms would advance the collective concerns of a group. See Margot Dazey, "Rethinking Respectability Politics," *British Journal of Sociology* 72, no. 3 (2021): 580–93.

would be that it made them viable for *certain Black families*. If you were thought of as "deserving" of support and "qualified" for residence, you were granted access. If you did not qualify, there was little you had access to. In its earliest iteration in the 1940s, the process included an interview by a social worker, verification of employment, a criminal background check, home visits, and a scoring formula based on an assessment for families with insufficient income to purchase homes on the private market.[21] A similar formula was revisited in the late 1990s for former CHA residents who were applying for affordable housing in mixed-income developments, which at the time were pitched to CHA residents as the future of the agency. In the modernized screening process, former CHA residents were required to complete a background check, could not have anyone in their household with a history of drug abuse, were required to have a family income of at least $30,000, and were also required to be "lease compliant."[22] Around the same time, an executive order from the Clinton administration revisited the screening processes of the 1940s, allowing public-housing agencies to screen and remove residents with criminal records.[23]

These requirements have a specific relationship to engineered conflict, particularly in how they demonstrate the intention of public housing. The historical progression of public housing in Chicago speaks to an "up and out" strategy by CHA.* In its early days, as shelter for working-class families who were experiencing economic challenges due to the Great Depression or families who were unable to find housing due to war shortages, CHA understood its housing as temporary and experimental, with the expectation that its residents would transition out of public housing.[24] Public housing in Chicago became permanent for low-income/no-income Black families, but this stood in stark contrast

---

* The "up and out" strategy was the idea that CHA would only be temporary, and families with means would soon move out of the development, making room for other families.

to CHA's original iteration. As low-income/no-income Black families often did not have the means to leave public housing, CHA began to make decisions based on a deadly combination of triage and disposability. For those who could leave, there was hope. Because CHA was not equipped or interested in providing for long-term residents, families who couldn't leave were resigned to fate.

In addition to the screening process, the early shifting leadership of CHA reveals early signs of the logic of disposability. Upon the resignation of board chairman Robert Taylor and removal of president Elizabeth Wood, the city moved to hire Korean War veteran and West Point graduate William B. Kean to steer the agency, which had become the largest landlord in the city of Chicago by 1954. Wood and Taylor, as Kean's predecessors, shared a humanistic approach to public housing that championed low-rise developments that were more expensive to build, but less expensive to maintain. Kean's hire represented the direct opposite, as CHA shifted to build large, high-rise developments that removed many of the community-oriented offerings. Unfortunately, these were early signs of the disaster to come. Similar to the hire of Tom Tyrrell in the transport of CPS through the "Safe Passage" program following the school closings of 2012, the survival of Black people was left to chance.[25]

Where disposability was not the sentiment of every early CHA official, it became the function of the organization when the structural supports were removed. The reality is that public housing in Chicago was never intended for the most marginalized. Even at its best it was a a transitory space, intended to serve those who would eventually leave. Restrictions like "whole family requirements" or income thresholds were early markers of who would be accepted and provided with resources. Coupled with the early requirements for residency, it was clear that the earliest iteration of public housing in Chicago was not for those who found themselves at the bottom of the economic, social, and racial order in the city. There were support workers that took it upon themselves to take care of Black residents, and some supports remained until the early 1950s, but it was not the rule. By the mid-1960s, the infrastructure to maintain public housing dwindled as its population swelled with Black residents. D. Bradford Hunt's example of the Ida B. Wells Homes provides an important perspective:

> The Chicago Park District built a small indoor field house to serve residents of Ida B. Wells, but by the early 1950s it had deteriorated under heavy usage. The park district proposed building a new, larger field house to meet recreational needs not only for Wells, but for the Wells extension, scheduled to open in 1955. For its part, the CHA also planned to build a small community center at Wells Extension, which would be leased to the park district and other agencies for youth programs. But the park district dropped its plans for the new field house and elected to cram its programming into the CHA's small community center, a completely inadequate space for indoor recreation.[26]

Under these conditions of overcrowded and overused spaces with minimal maintenance, it was nearly impossible for young people to engage in any sort of meaningful recreation. When cost-cutting decisions are made, the needs of those with the least are often bypassed. Over time, those who remained were often blamed for the plight of public housing, without consideration of structural concerns, particularly the diminishing and soon-to-be inadequate resources for Black families in CHA.

As an agency, architecture and financial funding models were central to the structural inefficiency of CHA. When federal and local public housing had white families as its central focus, it moved in a responsible way for its residents. While some concessions were made for Black people in low-rise public housing units in Chicago in the early years of public housing, it was the exception and not the rule. Still, although mired with racism, the reality of a different funding mechanism that provided resources for maintenance created a relatively sustainable form of housing for the first Black CHA residents.

Design Absent of Consideration: High-Rise Public Housing

When public housing transitioned to larger, high-rise dwellings, CHA's population began to permanently shift to one that was predominantly Black and deeply marginalized. Ignoring this fact is dangerous, as it wrongly places the blame on poor Black people for the failure of public housing. A structural analysis reveals the physical and administrative problems of CHA, showing that it was impossible for high-rise public housing to work sustainably. As explained in detail by historian D. Bradford Hunt, Black CHA residents actively resisted disposability. The issue, however, was the limited commitment from the state to provide sustainable resources for communities to thrive. Hunt's explanation provides a necessary consideration for understanding engineered conflict:

> Blaming the tenants or even "problem" families avoids the central policy decision that produced buildings with unheard of youth-to-adult ratios, resulting in environments where opportunity for destruction multiplied . . . . Passing judgement on either wayward youths or irresponsible adults would see social control as a problem of the individual, not a collective concern. Like any other urban dwellers, public housing residents searched for order in their neighborhoods, as times valiantly, and they pleaded for help from public officials. But the structural demographics created by policy decisions, coupled with indefensible high-rise designs, made both informal social control by residents and formal control by management or the police an

extraordinary challenge. High-rise projects for families like the Robert Taylor Homes and other conceived in the 1950s were doomed from the day they opened.[27]

Despite the myriad of community efforts to "make something beautiful and livable out of what they had," the work of public-housing residents to provide for young people and families often fell short, particularly in high-rise public housing.* Notwithstanding the numerous efforts of resident collectives and external agencies to keep young people engaged while building a thriving community, the sheer size and perpetual mismanagement of CHA consistently resulted in disappointment. During the transition to high-rise public housing by the mid-1960s, CHA promised residents supports similar to what was offered to families in low-rise public housing in the early years of CHA. However, when the existing funding mechanisms and mismanagement could no longer support the neediest of families, disrepair became the norm. Gone were the days of available social workers that advised families on living-wage employment opportunities and CHA on-site programs for job training. In their place were invasive social workers who threatened families with eviction if they did not comply with the stated rules of the housing development.

Despite CHA's lack of attention to the needs of its residents, people were still able to challenge state power while creating a sense of community among families. Community efforts in the Wentworth Gardens development and the Henry Horner Homes to develop tenant management organizations are tangible examples of the ability of community members to organize and determine viable living conditions for families

---

* Quote taken from Silvia Mendoza at the American Educational Research Association annual conference on April 16, 2023, in reference to the creative practices of Latinx communities despite harrowing conditions, specifically in San Antonio, Texas. This concept is often used in Black communities to demonstrate the willingness to work for change despite apparently insurmountable obstacles.

who did not have high incomes.* Nevertheless, the lack of building maintenance and repair, coupled with the pressures of late-stage capitalism on CHA residents (minimal living-wage employment opportunities, under-resourced educational options, high levels of surveillance by law enforcement, etc.) deeply contributed to the demise of public housing in Chicago.[28] The conditions were ripe for conflict between people experiencing marginalization and isolation in perpetuity.

It is interesting to note that some of CHA's leadership knew this early on. CHA's first director, Elizabeth Wood (1937–1954), offered an early warning to city government of what could result from inattention to housing in Chicago:

> Chicago is in a most violent though invisible state of war on the question of race; and every public servant must decide on which side he will enlist, whose enmity he will incur. Though he may seek with all his mind the safe way to play it, there really is no safe way .... [There is] a great overflow of Negroes out of their ghettos in all parts of the city. Because this overflow is against the official will [of the city] it takes place with desperation and illegality; and new slums are being created daily. The exploiters are having a field day; and the next generation will have to cure this generation's blindness.[29]

Wood's speech was delivered in 1948, but its connections to engineered conflict are clear. Her reference to "the exploiters" should be read

---

* See Fennell's 2015 discussion of the transition of the Henry Horner Homes to tenant management. Led by a group of Horner residents, tenants sued CHA to halt their relocation efforts. CHA was required as a result to keep families on site while new homes were being built. Roberta Feldman and Susan Stall, in *The Dignity of Resistance* (New York: Cambridge University Press, 2004), also document the efforts of the residents of Wentworth Gardens, which is now the longest-running tenant-managed development in the US.

as a dual indictment. While slumlords were the obvious culprits in the first half of the twentieth century, Wood's statement could also be interpreted as speaking to the actions of the mayor and city council, who moved to high-rise public housing as a cost-cutting measure. By the late 1950s, CHA's population was almost 90 percent Black. In keeping with Chicago's hyper-segregation, high-rise public housing was only built in historically Black and poor communities, deepening the isolation of these popula-tions.[30] With the exception of the high-rise buildings of Cabrini-Green, which were built as an extension to the original row houses built in the late 1940s, the State Street Corridor soon became the largest continuous set of public housing in the world. Soon after the completion of the State Street Corridor (which includes the Robert Taylor Homes, Stateway Gardens, Dearborn Homes, Harold Ickes Homes, and the Raymond Marcellus Hil-liard Homes), CHA high-rise developments peppered the South and West Sides of the city, often in areas that were already experiencing disinvest-ment and other forms of marginalization. The high-rise unit represented a cost-effective model in city council's efforts to curb the leakage of Black families into traditionally white areas. Critical geographer Rashad Shabazz succinctly locates the tragic consequences of high-rise public housing in CHA, clarifying the rationale for planned abandonment:

> [High-rise public housing] packed large numbers of people in less space, but such design isolated them from the rest of the city in the process. These failures were not simply mistakes of judgement: they were consequences of racist housing policies that worked to concentrate Black people into racially zoned sectors of the city. The tragedy of this story was how the city dealt with the failures. The general sense of instability that emerged within many high-rise projects as a result of failed promises gave rise to a set of practices to prevent leakage. These practices drew on the logic of prison.[31]

Linked to the racist vision of the "radiant city" of Swiss-French urban planner and architect Charles-Edouard Jeanneret (popularly known as Le Corbusier), the goal was to ensure that racial lines did not blur.[32] But the high-rise developments of CHA were anything but radiant. Instead, they became stark reminders of the reluctance of a city to tend to the issues and concerns of its low-income/no-income Black residents. Like in a prison, the idea was to isolate and contain. If you are cornered away and contained, you are soon rendered invisible. If you are made invisible, disposability is the close cousin you are destined to meet.

Shabazz's reflections on CHA high-rise developments are critical in my own reflections on the State Street Corridor. The State Street Corridor lined not only both sides of State Street, where the Taylors and Stateway were located, but also the Dan Ryan Expressway to the west. The auxiliary roads to the west of State Street were always unusual to me in that they were never through streets, but would cut off abruptly. This design had a practical purpose in the eyes of CHA and the Chicago Police Department (CPD): In case of an "emergency," Federal and Dearborn Streets could be easily blockaded. Police cruisers would in fact often block the streets if there was a shooting or any other disturbance in any of the buildings. As an onlooker, I would always think that it wasn't so much about stopping people from getting in as it was about not letting people out. Organizationally, CHA had spun so far out of control that it began to engage in strategies that infringed on the constitutional rights of its residents. As part of CHA's "Operation Clean Sweep," a specific high-rise building could be targeted by CHA and the CPD for what were called "emergency inspections." Despite the policy language of building inspection, these were really unannounced police raids (without search warrants) that would take place either late at night or early in the morning to search for drugs, guns, and "unauthorized residents."[33]

In addition to living under the stressful environment of unauthorized sweeps, residents often saw large swaths of land between buildings left barren, sometimes speckled with occasional, scantly equipped playgrounds. The combination of a lack of resources for young people and the lack of repairs created a situation where young people sought enjoyment from the few things they had at their disposal, like riding elevators. With a lack of constructive and creative outlets, the actions of young people became criminalized, heightening antagonistic relationships with law enforcement.

By the late 1970s, mismanagement of high-rise developments had created an untenable situation at numerous levels. First was at the level of employment, where CHA management jobs were distributed as patronage jobs to people seen as loyal to the mayor, despite the fact that the federal government designed local public housing authorities to be quasi-independent bodies that were free of local political pressure.[34] In Chicago, the direct opposite was true, all the way down to the naming of the Robert Taylor Homes after the first Black Chairman of the Board of CHA, who actually opposed high-rise public housing. The strange irony of the name of the CHA development was not resolved by the ineptitude of CHA management. The Chicago political machine, in making way for patronage jobs, did little to ensure that material resources ever reached CHA residents. Patronage employees of CHA did not have the wherewithal or skill to address the compounded needs of residents.[35]

CHA president Vincent Lane's Operation Clean Sweep, mentioned above, included strategies where people appeared to voluntarily surrender their civil liberties. The implementation of identification cards for residents, guarded entryways, and drug raids were pitched to residents as strategies to reduce violence, a "no-nonsense," enforceable approach to providing a sense of safety for residents.[36] However, the opposite quickly became true. Lane's interventions had some initial success in curbing drug sales, but that quickly faded as those who were targeted by the raids (mainly suspected gang members and drug dealers) figured out ways to shift their operations away from the buildings where the sweeps were taking place. Programs like Operation Clean Sweep would often only shift violent activity from one place to another, producing engineered conflict. As those involved in the illicit drug trade were displaced from their original place of operation to other areas, rival crews would battle for territory and violence would often spike.[37]

The issue of street organizations (i.e., gangs) is also deserving of a complex and layered discussion, provided in the following chapter. In short, though the presence of street organizations is overly simplified to issues of violence, the history of gangs in CHA housing is layered and rooted in segregation and containment. Popular imagery of the "hardened criminal" is more trope and stereotype than an accurate description of the residents in high-rise public housing. The point here is not to dismiss the violence that takes place and has unnecessarily took the lives of CHA residents. Instead, the point here is to understand violence through the formation of organizations that flourished in CHA largely because there were so few opportunities for positive youth development and avenues to attain full-time, living-wage employment. For young people who came into contact with law enforcement (particularly in the form of arrests and convictions), it was even more difficult to secure gainful employment or education. Lack of employment and educational opportunities often leave only the drug trade as a viable employment option for families struggling to make ends meet. If this situation continues on a consistent basis over decades, gang sets involved in the drug trade will naturally come into competition with other crews to recruit both workers and customers, and conflict is inevitable. Edward Goetz correctly frames the phenomena of crime and displacement:

> Crime reduction at the redevelopment site, however, does not mean necessarily a reduction in crime citywide. Indeed, the major effect of redevelopment is not to reduce overall crime in the city, but to push it into different areas . . . . In Chicago, the crime displacement effects were notable. The neighborhood where the

Robert Taylor Homes once stood saw a large drop in homicides from 2000 to 2008, while two miles south the murder rate tripled.[38]

When coupled with displacement, the stressors of precarious living conditions can create a situation where conflict quickly becomes the norm. Even for those who may have originally felt safe in their environment, the loss and disruption of social networks that provided emotional and material support return them to a state of fear.[39] If there is a loss of connection due to forced displacement, the opportunity for positive health and educational outcomes will decrease significantly. In these instances, disinvestment and displacement at the hands of the state have engineered the conflict.

Piecemeal Planning in Public Housing: Engineered Conflict and the Plan for Transformation

The Plan for Transformation sought to eliminate the majority of public housing high-rises in the city. Many of the CHA developments targeted in the plan are located on prime real estate. Ida B. Wells is a perfect example, given its proximity to interstate highways, the downtown central business district, public transportation, and the lakefront. Along the short drive from the Ida B. Wells Homes to the downtown area, developers were also in the process of gentrifying the South Loop neighborhood to make a continuous stream of middle-income and high-end dwellings. The State Street Corridor also provided rapid access to the downtown area and a major interstate highway to the west. On the West Side of the city, developments like Ogden Courts and the Jane Addams Homes also offered direct access to downtown by way of major streets and large highways. On the North Side of the city, the Cabrini-Green development and the Lathrop Homes were next to some of the wealthiest neighborhoods in Chicago. Lightyears away from their original distinction as public housing for those who temporarily lost their jobs or were working in the war effort, public housing had now become a nuisance to the city and developers eager to move in on spaces that were primed for profit making.

Where the demolition of the Cabrini-Green complex and the struggles in the Henry Horner Homes and Wentworth Gardens are well documented and often spoken of in the discussion of the Plan for Transformation, they actually predate the policy, which was in progress from 1999 to 2009.[40] The Plan for Transformation primarily rests at the intersection of mismanagement, neoliberal privatization, and disposability, evident in each part of the winding, multi-layered, and intricate relationship between CHA, the City of Chicago, and the federal government. CHA's inability to execute the version of the plan articulated to residents should not be considered a "failure," but an intention. Just as the "failing" school with insufficient resources and a crumbling structure is in fact doing exactly what it was intended to do under white supremacy,[41] so is the Plan for Transformation—to contain, isolate, and displace while blaming those with the least amount of resources for their suffering.

When we take this into account, we see that the popular narrative of the unconcerned, careless, and ignorant CHA tenant is problematic and ridiculous. The real issue is longitudinal neglect. If people are isolated for over a thirty-year period with limited access to viable education, recreation, and living-wage employment, the situation intensifies. Goetz is correct that

> no one knew the deficiencies of existing public housing in Chicago as well as the residents. Having been ill-used by the CHA for decades, residents easily envisioned the multitude of further harm that could befall them in a displacement and relocation effort managed by the same entity.[42]

In light of CHA's history of outright negligence, it was very difficult for residents to trust CHA to do right by them. Organizations
like the Coalition to Protect Public Housing worked in coalition with
academic think tanks like the Nathalie Voorhees Center for Neighborhood and Community Improvement to challenge CHA to act in
ways that were responsible to residents, but the high rises presented a
particular conundrum. CHA's unwillingness and/or inability to repair
the buildings, coupled with the increased violence in them, accelerated the physical decline of the structures.[43] As the high-rise project
became the default category for the containment and isolation of
low-income/no-income Black people, CHA continued to offer empty
promises to its residents, most of which remain unfulfilled to this day.

CHA was also faced with a contradiction. Internally, the agency had to
deal with the fact that their properties had become extremely valuable to
developers, but CHA also had to deal with the fact that mismanagement
at developments such as those on the State Street Corridor had become
too large to ignore. As the vast majority of CHA residents knew this, the
agency had to create the appearance that CHA was moving in ways that
were considerate of the residents' long-term housing needs. They also
wanted to be careful, as CHA had recently lost lawsuits filed by residents
in the Henry Horner Homes and Wentworth Gardens, who secured their
rights to remain in their complexes during redevelopment and to serve as
tenant managers.[44] Now CHA had Cabrini-Green as a target, due to its
proximity to one of the wealthiest parts of the city, Streeterville, whose
residents were in a fierce push to demolish the development.*

The implementation of Housing Opportunities for People Everywhere (HOPE VI) after the 1989 Congressional National Commission on
Severely Distressed Public Housing created another layer of bureaucracy

* The Streeterville neighborhood in Chicago is one of the wealthiest communities in the city, home to a stretch of Michigan Avenue known as the "Gold Coast,"
which has the highest retail sales in the city.

to contend with.[45] CHA had begun to rely heavily on a process of offer-ing families Section 8 (renamed the Housing Choice Voucher Program) vouchers to address persistent mismanagement and disrepair.* Section 8 vouchers could be used for housing in the private market. The list of peo-ple who qualified could have as many as forty thousand families waiting for a slot and could be backlogged as long as three years. Overall, the pro-cess was unsuccessful, with only around four thousand families relocated with vouchers, and those often to other high-poverty Black communi-ties in the city.[46] Where many families remained hopeful that the waitlist would open, few were able to secure housing on the private market in communities that were different to the ones they left.† Despite minuscule attempts throughout the 1990s to create mixed-income developments, the efforts of CHA paled in comparison to its longitudinal problems.[47]

The descent of CHA reached its lowest point with the federal take-over by the Department of Housing and Urban Development (HUD) in 1995. Directed by Housing Secretary Henry Cisneros, the national dialogue on public housing identified CHA as the pinnacle of misman-agement and neglect. Having been named the "worst of the worst" by HUD, CHA attempted to engage in some face-saving maneuvers in the form of services and security. A separate police force created for CHA was positioned as a friendlier, more community-minded form of public safety. Like "Operation Clean Sweep" before it, this did little to curb violence in the high rises. Relocation services were also offered to fam-ilies in complexes that were scheduled for demolition, but to no avail. CHA needed a more significant plan to change the public narrative.

---

* The term *Section 8* is in reference to section 8 of the Housing Act of 1937, which granted families housing relocation vouchers.

† Lake Parc Place consisted of two CHA high-rise buildings that were converted into a "mixed-income" development. It was unusual, in that the entire devel-opment was Black, and the residents from the lowest income bracket were the smallest group of tenants.

Federal control of CHA ended after four years, on June 1, 1999, and the Plan for Transformation soon followed.[48] Originally shared as a draft plan in the fall of 1999, the full Plan for Transformation was introduced on February 5, 2000, with great fanfare. Housing secretary Andrew Cuomo was present, along with Richard M. Daley and a host of public officials to announce CHA's new direction. Vincent Lane was out as CHA director, and Phillip Jackson was selected to take the helm. As a former public-housing resident, he readily fit the bill as someone to redirect the agency. HUD committed $1.5 billion to the effort of moving CHA in a new direction, with another $1.5 billion needed to complete the plan's original projected cost of $3 billion.[49] The hefty price tag is important to engineered conflict in that it points to the neo-liberal rationales behind the decisions made by CHA along with the federal government. Like charter schools, public housing under neo-liberalism is repurposed as a public good managed by private entities.

Central to the Plan for Transformation was CHA's pivot from pro-vider to "facilitator" of the housing process. The transition only further pushed poor people to the margins. In classic neoliberal fashion, the pri-vate market was understood as the best solution to a social problem that had fully spun out of control, as it had been when HOPE VI's voucher system was accepted as policy. CHA hoped with the Plan for Transfor-mation to make mixed-income developments attractive to renters and buyers on the private market, a win-win for public housing authorities and private developers. As HUD pushed public housing authorities to "explore" mixed-income strategies by adding income tax credits for "moderate" income and market-rate housing, the most marginalized were removed from the equation.[50] Former CHA residents who did not meet the minimal requirements for the newly built or refurbished mixed-income developments were unable to secure housing. Shifting responsibility solely to the individual, the neoliberal mechanisms in the Plan for Transformation and the application for mixed-income housing hardwired exclusion of CHA residents who historically had the least. Leaning on the private market allowed CHA to slowly get out of the business of providing affordable housing, now that over 50 percent of their properties were privately managed. The title of "facilitator," however vague it may be, is accurate now that CHA has found a convenient off-ramp from its duties as a public housing provider.

At the same time, as the largest public housing–restructuring project in the history of the US, the Plan for Transformation needed to appear as if it was doing right by CHA residents. Task forces, citywide public meetings, and opportunities to provide public commentary gave the impression that CHA was moving responsibly in the rollout of the plan. However, residents were not fooled. The demolition of several developments predating the Plan for Transformation demonstrated that CHA was not an honest broker. So did the experience of residents from the Harold Ickes Homes, who were held in limbo for almost three years on the state of demolition of the complex. Tenants were given a forty-eight-page memorandum from HUD and CHA outlining their options regarding length of residency and availability of housing vouchers. CHA went back and forth between being "undecided" as to whether the Ickes Homes would be demolished and outright telling residents that it was not scheduled for demolition.[51] Meanwhile, in the Lathrop Homes, residents were provided housing options that were completely different from those discussed in the Plan for Transformation. All of the new scenarios described by CHA drastically reduced the number of available public housing units. This process deepened the fragility of housing conditions for existing residents on a plot of land that was known to be extremely valuable, given its proximity to the expansively gentrified neighborhoods of Bucktown and Lakeview.[52]

Language of the actual Plan for Transformation revealed that the number of demolished units and rebuilt/redeveloped units didn't match. CHA was looking to demolish "upwards" of 18,000 units of housing, while rehabbing/redeveloping around 25,000 units. The report recognized that it would be 13,000 housing units short, but the disrepair of high-rise buildings supposedly left "no alternative."[53] A great amount of dubious language can be located throughout the final proposal. One example is in CHA's explanation of the 14,000 units of high-rise housing that they did not have enough money to rehabilitate. Referenced as "Section 202" housing, this included eight high-rise and five low- or mid-rise housing developments. In reference to the demolition of Section 202 housing, the language of the policy draft is blunt, stating that:

> The Agency does not have sufficient resources to redevelop each of these properties. To determine which of the Section 202 sites will receive redevelopment funding, and to encourage additional private financing sources, the Agency will solicit proposals from development teams. It has also requested flexibility under the Section 202 rule to allow for the rehabilitation of the mid-rise and low-rise properties. Resident representatives and community partners will be involved in both establishing the criteria for selecting developers and in the actual selection process.[54]

The solicitation of proposals from "development teams" is the most problematic aspect of this section, in its reliance on the private market to subsidize the plan. The thirteen developments in the mandated demolition of Section 202 were essentially the most depopulated buildings (with vacancy rates of over 10 percent), and also those in the worst state of disrepair. Where it is true that many of the high-rise buildings were not recoverable and residents agreed that they needed different housing options, reliance on the private market would not guarantee that those residents would be tended to. Equally problematic was the fact that CHA could offer up a plan where half of the project was unfunded at all.

This fact provides insight into the desperation of the city to show that it was doing something, no matter how insufficient its projections were. In retrospect, even with the bold claim to be doing right by the most marginalized residents in the city, the language of the plan does not read as if it is prioritizing their concerns. The initial CHA research on a survey of rental properties in the region showed that the only available housing would be in similar segregated neighborhoods on the South and West Sides of the city, a dubious sign for the plan's success.[55] Because residents were well aware of this, they understood the Plan for Transformation as yet another half-baked CHA proposal, albeit this time with a federal guarantee for at least half of its proposed budget.

As housing scholar Janet Smith has noted, the Plan for Transformation was more a description of desired outcomes than an actual plan.[56] The agency's inability to reach residents before the rollout of the plan, coupled with its inability to secure the remainder of funds, kept residents sensibly skeptical. What happened most often was that residents were relocated into communities where they would be viewed as unfamiliar, once again increasing the likelihood for conflict to arise, just as happens when young people are forced to move schools in consecutive academic years. Often referenced as "mobility rates," the academic performance of students can suffer when they are consecutively switching educational environments.[57] The same is true in housing if families are forced to move without the necessary supports. If young people and their families are in a situation where supports are minimal and the stressors of educational and housing insecurity loom large, the stage for conflict has been set.

To provide a sense of the massive upheaval brought forward by the Plan for Transformation, the following table identifies the housing developments that were completely demolished as part of the plan, with the current state of the land where the CHA buildings once stood.

DEMOLISHED CHA DEVELOPMENTS IN THE PLAN

CHA Development	Apartment units
Ogden Courts	140
Rockwell Gardens*	1,136
Stateway Gardens*	1,644
Robert Taylor Homes (A&B)*	3,784
Harold Ickes Homes	1,006
Jane Addams Homes	1,027
Grace Abbott Homes	1,200
Washington Park Homes*	468
Washington Park Homes (low-rises)	488
Madden Park Homes	812
Ida B. Wells Homes	1,600
Clarence Darrow Homes*	479
Le Claire Courts	300
Randolph Towers*	155
Frances Cabrini Extension North	926
Frances Cabrini Extension South	597
William Green Homes*	968
1230 N. Burling (Cabrini-Green)*	134
TOTAL	**16,864**

*The Demolition of the Cabrini-Green Homes predate the original Plan for Transformation but are included in CHA's total of demolished homes. This list does

FOR TRANSFORMATION

Current State
Parking lot scheduled for mixed-income development
Vacant
Mixed-income development (Park Boulevard)
Vacant/mixed-income development (Legends South: Savoy Square, Coleman Place, Gwendolyn Place, Hansberry Square, Mahalia Place, Pershing)
Vacant/mixed-income development (Southbridge)
Vacant (scheduled for mixed-income development with Roosevelt Square)
Mixed-income development (Roosevelt Square)
Mixed-income development (4400 Grove)
Mixed-income development (4400 Grove)
Mixed-income development (Oakwood Shores)
Mixed-income development (Oakwood Shores)
Mixed-income development (Lake Park Crescent)
Vacant (scheduled for mixed-income development with The Habitat Company and Cabrera Capital)
Vacant
Mixed-income development (Parkside of Old Town, River Village North, River Village South, Renaissance North, River Village Pointe)
Mixed-income development (Parkside of Old Town, River Village North, River Village South, Renaissance North, River Village Pointe)
Mixed-income development (Parkside of Old Town, River Village North, River Village South, Renaissance North, River Village Pointe)
Mixed-income development (Parkside of Old Town, River Village North, River Village South, Renaissance North, River Village Pointe)

not include housing complexes that were refurbished or converted to buildings designated for senior citizens.

The intimate connection between housing and schools epitomizes the colossal upheaval of community space. Considering high-rise and mid-rise buildings on the State Street Corridor alone, almost 6,500 apartment units were demolished. Along with those demolished apartment complexes along the State Street Corridor, the elementary schools Edward Hartigan, John Farren, Amos Colman, Helen J. McCorkle, Daniel Hale Williams, Mary Church Terrell were either closed permanently or repurposed as schools with significantly smaller student populations. Crispus Attucks Elementary, one of the only schools to remain open on the State Street Corridor, was moved into the building of John Farren Elementary School, which was closed. In 2016, Attucks, by then with under 200 students, permanently closed. The original Attucks building was demolished in 2021. In 2024 DuSable High School, the only high school left on the corridor, had under 200 students from two co-located schools in a building built for over 2,000. Except for Williams Elementary, all of these schools were on the *same street*. Hartigan has been repurposed as Bronzeville Classical Elementary, which is now a selective enrollment school that primarily serves the new (and wealthier) gentry of the State Street Corridor and the South Loop. Terrell was taken over by a charter school called ACE Tech, which left the Terrell building in 2017, merging with another charter school in a neighboring community. Currently, Ludwig Van Beethoven is the lone neighborhood elementary school serving the State Street Corridor, with 265 students in a building that could serve just under 1,000.[58]

To claim the Plan for Transformation as a success is nothing short of ridiculous. Almost a quarter century after the drafting of the plan, the downsizing of CHA to its self-proclaimed "facilitator" status has primarily resulted in the mass upheaval and dispersal of people living in the most precarious housing conditions. Less than 10 percent of former CHA residents were able to secure housing in mixed-income

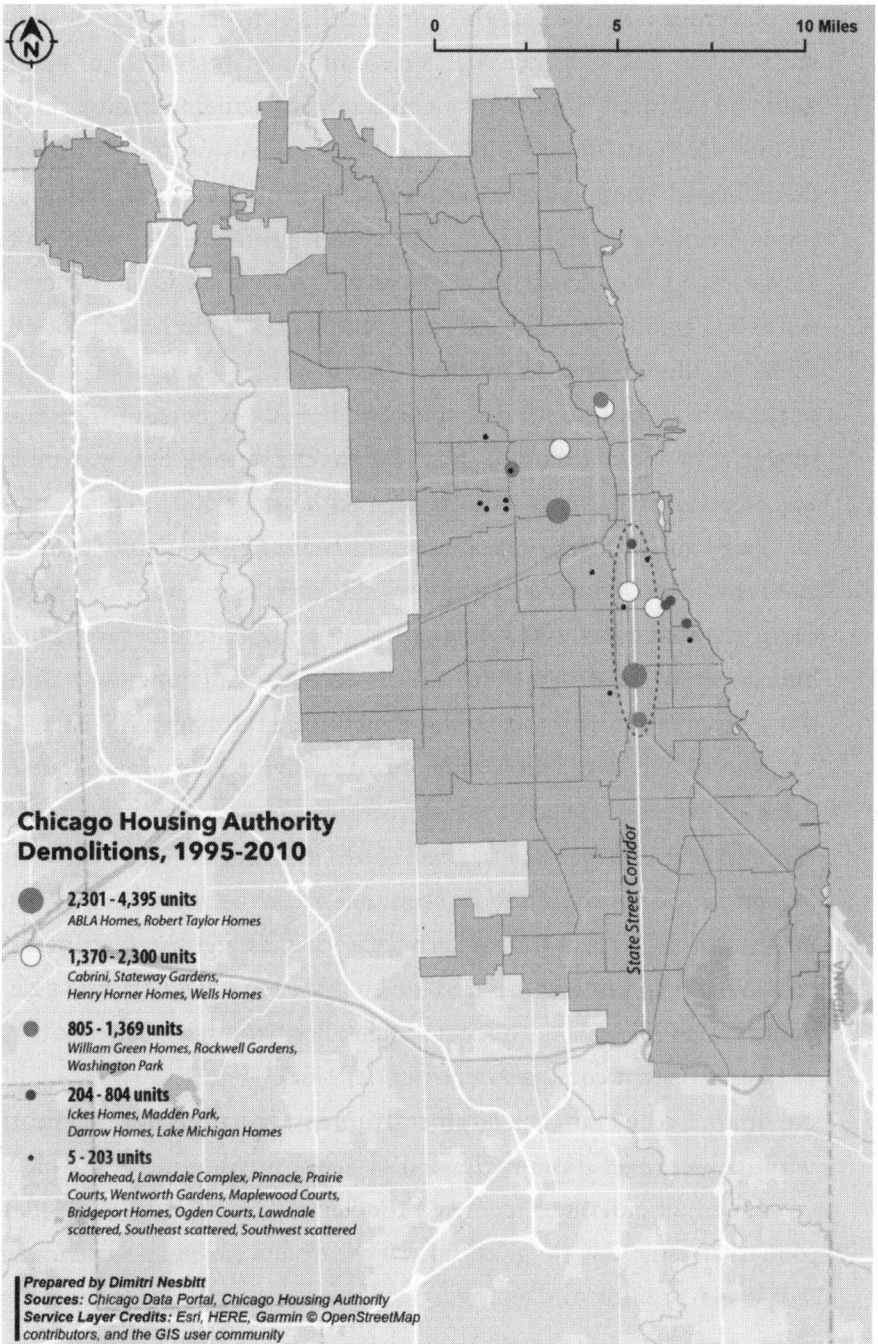

**Chicago Housing Authority
Demolitions, 1995-2010**

● **2,301 - 4,395 units**
ABLA Homes, Robert Taylor Homes

○ **1,370 - 2,300 units**
*Cabrini, Stateway Gardens,
Henry Horner Homes, Wells Homes*

● **805 - 1,369 units**
*William Green Homes, Rockwell Gardens,
Washington Park*

● **204 - 804 units**
*Ickes Homes, Madden Park,
Darrow Homes, Lake Michigan Homes*

· **5 - 203 units**
*Moorehead, Lawndale Complex, Pinnacle, Prairie
Courts, Wentworth Gardens, Maplewood Courts,
Bridgeport Homes, Ogden Courts, Lawndale
scattered, Southeast scattered, Southwest scattered*

Prepared by Dimitri Nesbitt
Sources: Chicago Data Portal, Chicago Housing Authority
Service Layer Credits: Esri, HERE, Garmin © OpenStreetMap
contributors, and the GIS user community

developments, which was the purported purpose of the plan. Less than 20 percent of former CHA residents live in traditional public housing. By 2016, almost 12 percent of residents had been evicted. In the same year, close to 10 percent of CHA residents that lived in developments targeted by the Plan for Transformation had died waiting for housing in the new developments. Just under 21 percent of former residents were using a Section 8 or Housing Choice Voucher. Since the public reveal of the plan, the largest grouping of former CHA residents (over 33 percent) are still living without any housing assistance by local or federal public housing agencies.[59] The only objective that came close to fruition was the demolition of close to eighteen thousand units of housing.

The Plan for Transformation has deepened the conundrum for former CHA residents by leaving swaths of vacant land where housing complexes once stood. In a city that is woefully short on affordable housing, former residents have been placed on the same waiting list of over forty thousand families, mentioned earlier in the chapter. Twenty-five acres on the former Robert Taylor Homes site remain vacant. Twenty-three acres of CHA property near the Abbott, Brooks, Loomis, and Addams development (ABLA) have been questionably loaned to the Chicago Fire professional soccer team, on land that is designated solely for public housing.[60] CHA has taken its "facilitator" role to heart and deeply marginalized its former residents, who've historically had the least resources to secure housing. In the process, they are sitting on property, providing first bids to developers who are fully committed to economically attractive mixed-income developments while privileging housing sold at market-rate prices.

When considering engineered conflict in the aftermath of the Plan for Transformation, it is important to note that with the destruction of distressed and ill-maintained public housing units, crime throughout the city did not decrease. In the early years of the plan (2000–2008), in the spaces where CHA housing had once stood, violent crime decreased by 60 percent, property crime by 49 percent, and gun crime by 70 percent.[61] It should be noted, however, that the neighborhoods that saw those types of reductions were those where over half of the housing in a community is demolished and not replaced. Throughout the city, violent crime only decreased by 1 percent, property crime by .03 percent, and gun crime by 4.4 percent.[62] Instead of a citywide reduction in violence, the data in the first decade of the Plan for Transformation demonstrate that violence only shifted along with the masses of people who were displaced throughout the city and adjacent suburbs.

Disposability as Explicit Intention

The layers of public housing are tangled and complex, however, and it is too simplistic to ascribe CHA's failure solely to the Plan for Transformation. In retrospect, the failure of CHA to replace disinvested housing in perpetual disrepair is only part of the issue. If we consider the same historical and temporary issues in education, we see that the City of Chicago has rarely provided viable quality-of-life entities for Black people. Nostalgic stories are also incomplete, particularly because the moments of support for Black residents of the city were so brief. There were fleeting episodes where both the housing and education systems had the appearance of providing people with what they need. Engineered conflict reminds us that Black people's ability to do what they needed was never a result of the benevolence of the system. Instead, it was the result of Black people who were not afraid to refuse and interrupt white supremacy *in spite* of the empty commitment from the city. Immediately following the brief moments of respite for Black residents, as soon as public education and public housing were returned to the controls of the Richard J. Daley administration, poor Black communities were quickly disinvested and marginalized. For these reasons, the Plan for Transformation, though an abject failure, should only be viewed as a reiteration of an old process. The next chapter will speak to how the "old process" of disinvestment and marginalization led to the creation and splintering of street organizations throughout the city, deepening conflict.

CHAPTER 3

THIS IS NOT A GANG PROBLEM—

IT'S A WHITE SUPREMACY PROBLEM WITH POLICY AND SPATIAL IMPLICATIONS

Chicago emcees Common and G Herbo have a song called "The Neighborhood," where they reflect on their experiences as people from nearby neighborhoods but two different generations. As I hail from Common's generation (and neighborhood) that grew up in the late 1970s into the early '80s, I am more familiar with the larger sets he names in the song,

like the Blackstones (sometimes known as the Almighty Black P-Stone
Nation or "Stones" for short), Gangster Disciples (GDs), Four Corner
Hustlers (4CHs), and Vice Lords (VLs). G Herbo, who is twenty years
younger than us, has a different frame of reference. Although we're from
the same side of the city (the Southeast Side, sometimes referenced as
"over east"), Herbo grew up in a moment when the commonly known
large street organizations were already splintered. The sets that G Herbo
mentions like No Limit, 300, 600, Funny Boy, and O-Block are the result
of the fracturing of large, traditional "gang" hierarchies with a particular
order and structure. The traditional gang hierarchies, while problematic
in their relationship to violence and drug distribution, were critical in
their ability to squash internal conflicts and beefs between rival organizations. When the Chicago Police Department (CPD), along with the
federal Drug Enforcement Agency and the Cook County State's Attorney's Office, targeted "gang" leadership beginning in the late 1990s,
much of the organizational structure and loyalties within the large organizations were largely diminished.

The displacement that resulted from things like CHA's Plan for
Transformation and over two hundred school closures put people who
were unfamiliar with each other in the same space. With larger sets no
longer in power, smaller crews like No Limit, 300, 600, SuWu, Black
Souls, and O-Block emerged amongst Chicago's Black youth on the
South and West Sides of the city. These formations may have loose affiliations with the older and larger sets, but many operate independently.
None of the new formations cover broad swaths of land like their early
predecessors. They are not "gangs" in the historical sense of the word.
Many do not have ties to the large hierarchies and leadership of the
larger, older sets. Their groupings instead have loose, non-hierarchical
structures. Some sets or cliques operate from an area as small as a single
city block. Gone are the days where "gang" chiefs called shots that low-
er-ranking members of the set had to obey or face violation. The vacuum

left by the loss of traditional chain-of-command structures in the older, larger street organizations created an instance where the cliques emerging had no loyalty to the old guard. In relation to engineered conflict, we must consider the chain of events that have alienated the members of these new sets at numerous levels, particularly with regard to public housing, education, and disproportionate interactions with law enforcement.[1] The most important thing to consider about these conditions is that when the structure and order of an organization is lost and people from one neighborhood are placed into unfamiliar communities in a hyper-segregated city, violence has the greatest chance to escalate. Instead of attributing the problem solely to members of street organizations that were dispersed and fractured, we must also consider the policies and actions by the state that activated the tensions among them.

For the remainder of this chapter, I use *street organization* or *set* in place of *gangs* because it is accurate to the history and formation of these particular groups of young people and their predecessors. Although *gang* is popularly used and considered to be an accurate descriptor, the term has been morphed into an imaginary that does not speak to the historical structure and function of these organizations. What is now interpreted as tensions between warring factions is often first a spatial conflict, only later affiliated with the stereotypical assumptions about "gangs." Current violence on the South and West Sides of the city, while primarily considered to be "gang related," is intertwined with a broader collection of policy moves and strategies that make the use of violence more common in certain neighborhoods. Urban studies scholar Roberto Asopholm is correct here that "to frame these relationships simply in terms of promoting deviance and criminality is to completely miss and/ or disregard" the actual dynamics of the situation.[2] Where the point here is not to belittle or excuse the activities of street organizations that have resulted in physical harm, death, and other traumas, it is important to understand these groupings as organizations with specific structures.

Like public housing, issues of violence among people who may (or may not) be affiliated with street organizations in Chicago are complex and deserve a nuanced discussion in the context of the city. Making sense of the spatial and policy relationship of street organizations to housing, education, and law enforcement allows us to further understand engineered conflict.

I also recognize the fact that it is misleading to wax poetic around my relationship with members of street organizations in my youth. It would be irresponsible to discount the lives lost in violent conflict in Black communities throughout Chicago. Many of my own friends were lost in conflicts between street organizations. Considering these contradictions, engineered conflict challenges us to contextualize violence and its relationship to perpetual disinvestment, containment, and other forms of subjugation. Instead of solely locating issues of violence at the level of individuals affiliated with street organizations, we should make a more nuanced analysis. Returning to Eisen-Martin's epigraph in the introduction, violence is the end result of a process that makes it easier for people to turn at each other, wrongfully interpreting fellow community residents as the sources of conflict. Circling back to the epigraph from Tongo Eisen-Martin's essay in the introduction chapter, in a city where some people were already hitting each other, engineered conflict only makes the hitting easier and more intense. This state of being makes it increasingly difficult to see the primary role of the state in your frustration.

When mainstream media magnifies rhetoric of "gang-related" homicides, it is often without detail or context, a problematic misinterpretation of current clashes between Black youth on the South and West Sides of the city. Absent are the multiple ways that conflict is engineered in Chicago, pairing the displacement and isolation of former public housing residents, the conditions of public schools, and law enforcement's efforts to maintain the containment of Chicago's most marginalized residents. In the same conversation, we also miss the roles of deindustrialization, mass incarceration, and disinvestment.[3] Coupled with informal illicit economies and the role of law enforcement, we must also contend with the complexities of the organizations commonly characterized as "gangs."[4] Instead of traditional conflicts between large-scale factions, the current moment should instead be considered a conflict between splintered neighborhood cliques that have loose or minimal connections to traditional gang structures in Chicago.

Reducing the current moment of conflict throughout Black neighborhoods in the city to beefs between large rivaling gang sets does not take into account the long-standing structure of Black street organizations in Chicago and the strategies used by government to fracture those structures, resulting in heightened conflict in certain areas. The response by law enforcement to street organizations is the third and culminating component of engineered conflict, solidifying the relationship between disposability and value in the city.

Value and disposability are intimate bedfellows in Chicago. If we understand the dynamics of place and race in Chicago and consider the historical and contemporary moves of a city steeped in white supremacy, marginalization, and containment, the relationship between value and disposability becomes clearer. Street organizations are key to this relationship, as they are used by law enforcement as the linchpin by which to position community members as the problem instead of the solution. I refer to this as a white-supremacy problem because value and disposability in Chicago are determined by a totalizing system that normalizes the assumed beliefs of white, Western-European, cis-gender, able-bodied, Christian, heterosexual males as normal, right, and good. When white supremacy becomes the default value system, it becomes easier to declare some groupings of people (i.e., residents of public housing and people who may be affiliated with street organizations) disposable. Racial capitalism, positioned by abolition scholar Ruth Wilson Gilmore as "the state-sanctioned or extralegal production and exploitation of group-differentiated vulnerability to premature death" is also critical, as many members of street organizations have experienced displacement and fracture by way of gentrification.[5] Revisiting Harvey's concept of "accumulation by dispossession,"* engineered conflict presses us to consider the splintering of historical Black street organizations as a predicament fueled by white supremacy and racial capitalism.[6] As Black people are dispossessed of housing on land that the city wants, their removal is coupled with the city's (and private developers') accumulation of the property. Once the property is accumulated by the city, it can be sold to developers that have established relationships with government, creating the opportunity for the new gentry to move in. Because this happens primarily by way of policy implementation in the city of Chicago, the fracturing of large street organizations is also indicative of a city making its declaration on who is valued and who is discarded in the making of the "new Chicago."

Splintered to Confederation, Back to Splintered

Many of the large Black street organizations started as smaller, splintered factions in the 1950s and '60s, similar to the smaller iterations of cliques and crews in the current moment. The Blackstone Rangers are named after the street (Blackstone Avenue) where the majority of the members used to congregate in the Woodlawn neighborhood. Groups like the Four Corners (later to become the Four Corner Hustlers), Deacons, and the Destroyers were South Side street organizations, which soon became members of the "Main 21" conglomerate, later to be known as the Almighty Black P-Stone Nation. Moving further west

---

* As land, property, and other financialized capital is accumulated by the state, it is soon sold to private entities who are already in relationship with the state. The people who do not have access to such capital are discarded.

on the South Side of the city, the Black Disciples originated as a small faction in the community of Englewood. When they became the Gangster Disciples (GDs), it was by forming a collective with organizations like the Devil's Disciples, the Egyptian Cobras, the East Side Disciples, and the Supreme Gangsters. On the West Side, the Fourteenth Street Clovers and Imperial Chaplains collectivized to become the Vice Lords (VLs).[7] The shift from splintered groupings to large confederations back to splintered groupings is important in understanding the current situation, as what is deemed to be "gang beef" between large sets has rapidly become a relic of the past.

Growing up, I was most familiar with the Four Corner Hustlers (4CHs), Vice Lords, and Blackstones (Stones). At that time I wrongly thought the Vice Lords originated on the South Side. I was unaware of the history of the organization, particularly its West Side origins and the work of a smaller faction who called themselves Conservative Vice Lords (CVLs). I was familiar with the name CVL, but had more contact with Insane Vice Lords (IVL) and later with Traveling Vice Lords (TVLs or Travelers). My limited understanding of the 4CH, Mickey Cobras (MCs), the Stones, VLs, and GDs contained some knowledge of the leadership (Jeff Fort and Eugene "Bull" Hairston with the Stones, Mickey Cogwell with the Mickey Cobras, and Donise "King David" Barksdale, Orthis "O.G." Commander, and Larry Hoover with the Gangster Disciples), but not of the organizations' functions and day-to-day operations. Where I was used to the larger affiliations of the "five" (in reference to the five-point star, the operative symbol of Blackstone affiliates, also known as "Stones," "People", "All-Is-Well," "Moes") and the "six" (the six-point Star of David, operative symbol of Gangster Disciple Affiliates, also known as GDs or "Folks"), I was unaware of the history of Black street organizations as smaller factions, some of which united under larger collectives that were popularly known throughout Black communities in Chicago and nationally.[8] I knew of the loose affiliations between some of the formations as a young person, but I didn't know until later, for example, that the Stones and Disciples were both conglomerates of smaller sets across the South Side of the city.

Some of the original members of the "Main 21" for the Stones originated in neighborhoods throughout the South Side, as restrictive housing covenants were lifted. These were all brought under one flag by Jeff Fort and Bull as the "Main 21." As a young person, I only knew that one of the insignia for Stones was a moon over a pyramid that had to be drawn with twenty-one bricks in it. At the time, I had no idea of the significance.* It later came to my knowledge that the twenty-one bricks symbolized the twenty-one organizations that united under the Almighty Black P-Stone Nation. Structurally, the organization had a more corporate conglomerate understanding of traditional hierarchy. "Chiefs" were the upper echelon of the organization, with rankings under them from "princes," "elites," and "foot soldiers." One person who lived on my block had the ranking of "prince," and most of my friends who were affiliated were at the rank of "elites." At the lowest ranking were the "foot soldiers."

I also had no clue of the organizational history of the Conservative Vice Lords and Gangster Disciples, particularly their overlooked attempts to participate in community development in the neighborhoods of Englewood and North Lawndale† in the late 1960s and early

---

* Because of the conglomeration of organizations, abbreviations might bring some confusion. The Blackstone Rangers were a single independent organization before they became the Almighty Black P-Stone Nation, which is an amalgamation of the "Main 21" sets. "Stones" is an abbreviation for the collective of organizations that united under the Almighty Black P-Stone Nation.

† The Almighty Black P-Stone Nation, Conservative Vice Lords (CVLs), and the Gangster Disciples participated in community-development efforts. CVLs' efforts were focused on the neighborhood of North Lawndale and the Gangster Disciples' in Englewood. Supported by federal grants, local religious organiza-

'70s.[9] Although their efforts were split between legitimate enterprises and the underground economy (particularly in the case of the Gangster Disciples, beginning with the numbers racket and extortion, soon morphing into prostitution and eventually drug sales), the community efforts of both organizations largely go unnoticed.

Living on the South or West Sides of Chicago could provide you with an intimate knowledge of street organizations. In my own experiences, I noticed that some groupings were only loosely affiliated with specific neighborhoods, while others had a more concrete relationship to space and region. In my neighborhood of Calumet Heights in the late 1970s and throughout the '80s, there were Four Corner Hustlers, Vice Lords, and a small grouping of Mickey Cobras, all of which were members of the Main 21.[10] The upper echelon of the Stones, known as the El-Rukns (whom we sometimes called *L-Rods*), was mythical to us. Their headquarters were in my parent's old neighborhood of Oakland in an old movie theater called the Oakland Theater. Renamed "The Fort," older members of street organizations from my neighborhood would wax poetic about how they had the best parties. I knew nothing more of the structure of street organizations or any connection to illicit drug sales. Members in the organizations were simply people I knew from neighborhood. These were the same people I played sports with, cracked jokes about, and hung out with.

---

tions, civil-rights groups (primarily the Southern Christian Leadership Conference), and Black Power organizations (primarily the Illinois Chapter of the Black Panther Party), the three factions were able to create legitimate entrepreneurial endeavors (gas stations, corner stores, ice-cream parlors, art galleries, etc.) that employed members from the large sets and other community members. Through the work of the Coalition for United Community Action (CUCA, led by C. T. Vivian) and Operation Breadbasket (under Jesse Jackson) there was also a moment where the Gangster Disciples, Vice Lords, and Blackstone Rangers created a coalition called LSD (Lords, Stones, Disciples) that protested the construction industry.

I was even less familiar with the structure of the Gangster Disciples, which was actually a conglomerate of groups from the South Side, originating in the Englewood neighborhood. Groups like the Devil's Disciples, East Side Disciples, Supreme Gangsters, and Egyptian Cobras were brought under one flag by Donise "King David" Barksdale and Orthis "O.G." Commander. In fact, I never even knew the name *Gangster Disciples* was actually a byproduct of an arrangement between the Black Disciples and the Supreme Gangsters.[11] They were viewed as the sworn enemy of the Stones (under the Main 21 conglomerate) in my days, so few of us could have imagined that there had been coalitions formed by Stones and GDs in the late sixties aimed at community development, employment, and education. None of us knew about the Conservative Vice Lords and their business and art galleries on the West Side. We were ignorant of the short alliance LSD (Lords, Stone, and Disciples) that had fought for union contracts for Black workers. By the time I was in fourth grade, all we knew in our neighborhood was that you did not venture in GD territory without a neighborhood "pass," which was usually acquired through athletics or being with a family member. Even with one, small conflicts could arise depending on the situation (a fight about a basketball game, arguments about intimate relationships, long-term neighborhood tensions, etc.). By the time I got to high school, I played sports with classmates who were GDs or lived in neighborhoods that were affiliated with them. Following the sacrosanct general rule in Black Chicago that you don't go anywhere where you don't know anyone, we learned how to navigate each other's neighborhoods, understanding what times to visit, what colors not to wear (Stones primarily wore some combo of black and red, Vice Lords often wore black and gold, GDs primarily black and blue) and who to talk to. Sometimes these tensions were deeply intense, resulting in large skirmishes that resulted in serious injury and, in the worst cases, death for members and non-members.

It is important for me not to reminisce on some idyllic period where things were "better." More accurate is that things were *different*. They were still intense in those times. Even though many of us figured out how to make it work, there were many others who did not make it through, either due to incarceration or death.* None of us were immune to the effects of the War on Drugs or the War on Crime.[12] Despite inter-conflicts (usually affiliated with personal beefs, neighborhood tensions, or the drug trade), the street organizations in my neighborhood were descendants of the Main 21, affiliated with the larger conglomerate of the Stones, and under that historical structure, if there was any tension between groups that rode under the five, leadership had the responsibility to squash the beef. Very few people were willing to challenge leadership in the hierarchal structure. The goal is not to glorify violence, but to remember the configuration of leadership, whose most important power was to keep smaller conflicts from escalating. It was the combination of law enforcement's targeting of street organization leadership within the larger sets, coupled with the destruction of public housing and the closing of schools, that made for the genesis of engineered conflict.

Taking this into consideration, the neighborhood of my youth, like many other communities in Chicago, is layered and nuanced. For many Black Chicagoans, the operative word in understanding the layers of conflict is *could*. Depending on who you talked to, conflict *could* be affiliated with poverty and a number of street organizations. For others, it *could* be associated with tensions between Black middle-class and working-class factions. The point is that conflict in certain communities often rests under the surface of daily life. You

---

* The "War on Drugs," originally rolled out by the Nixon administration, had devastating effects on Black communities experiencing disinvestment and deindustrialization. Coupled with the "War on Crime," the incarceration rates in the US multiplied, giving birth to the era of mass incarceration. Chicago was hit especially hard, as the drug trade, which at one time was controlled by larger traditional gang sets, proliferated in public housing.

could be in conflict with someone because they are from another neighborhood and are affiliated with a rival street organization. When those people move into that new neighborhood, conflict *could* occur with someone because you don't know much about them and make assumptions about where they live, or vice versa. Likewise, conflicts *could* arise because the city and/or developers have displaced you into a new community. A series of events or one policy maneuver *could* engineer conflict at a moment's notice.* All is connected to the legacy of hyper-segregation, whether it be along the lines of race, class, or place.[13] While many people associate conflict in the city primarily with street organizations, history reveals a more complex situation. Before we can blame the phenomenon of engineered conflict solely on street organizations, we must first consider the idea that neighborhood tensions between Black residents in Chicago sit at the intersection of regional segregation, city policy, rumor, and assumption. When people find themselves living under these conditions, the chance for conflict is at its greatest.

---

* Some of the tensions among Black people are affiliated with historical tensions between South Siders and West Siders. Whereas the South Side was the first port of entry for Black people migrating north during the first wave of the Great Migration (1919–1929), the West Side didn't get significant numbers of Black residents until the second wave began in the late 1940s. There was also an urban and rural tension, as many of the Black people in the first wave of the Great Migration were from urban areas in the South, while the second wave came from rural areas. Potential tensions deepened, as few residents that lived on the South Side would venture to the West Side. This continues to this day, as some South Siders are viewed as members of an elite bourgeoisie in contrast their West Side counterparts. A more accurate depiction shows a mix of Black people along class lines in both communities.

The Second Splinter of
Street Organizations in Chicago

As a Chicagoan, the "Hang Up on Bad Guys" pay phone policy discussed in the introduction chapter was one of the first alarms in conceptualizing engineered conflict. When large street organizations gained wider entry into the drug market in the 1980s with the introduction of crack cocaine, they were able to wield power in some areas of the South and West Sides, particularly in public housing. As CHA's Plan for Transformation began to raze public housing buildings, the market for drug sales in those neighborhoods quickly waned. Younger members, who at one time had looked to move up in organizations via "putting in work" to protect and expand drug markets, demonstrating loyalty through their capacity to earn for the organization, now no longer possessed the ability to do so. Along with increasingly draconian strategies employed through federal and local law enforcements' "War on Drugs," enhanced sentencing in the form of mandatory minimums and "truth in sentencing" legislation incarcerated thousands of residents, some of whom were leadership in large street-organizations.

This development is critically important when thinking about the structure and power of leadership throughout organizations. Because many of the street organizations that operated in public housing were part of large conglomerates, the hierarchy of leadership was the central mechanism by which they handled internal and external conflicts. When these social and economic ties were lost, it became impossible to regain control of the large-scale operations, because the allegiances that held them together (mostly money and organizational hierarchy) are impossible to regenerate. If there is no drug market, there is no money to be made. If there is no money to be made, and key members of your hierarchy have also been incarcerated with long sentences, it is difficult to hold a large grouping of people together. When this is paired with displacement into unfamiliar communities, there is a great chance that conflict will occur. Roberto Aspholm explains the process with clarity:

> Lacking leaders who possessed the authority and legitimacy to media and settle disputes between sets, gangs increasingly lost their capacity to maintain organizational cohesion across neighborhoods. These internal conflicts, then, whether based on money, power, or personal animosities, increasingly spun out of control and fueled further organizational erosion. . . . Loyalties might have been determined by not only generational allegiances but also by personal relationships and, within larger sets, geographic considerations. Indeed, in some cases, bigger sets splintered simply due to the growing inability of gang leaders to maintain formal cohesion among relatively large memberships with sizeable geographic territories.[14]

In addition to the realities of the deteriorating drug market, consider the following series of events: The city creates intolerable conditions in public housing and education in certain neighborhoods while using its police force to move in ways that maintain carceral conditions. Those who can move do so, while those who can't are left to suffer until they are displaced to another community, where conflicts arise between the displaced and long-term community members. For this to take place, a number of policies and practices needed to be activated. CHA's Plan for Transformation and CPS's Renaissance 2010 laid foundational policy groundwork. The connective tissue lies in the geography of where these events take place. The spatial relationship between demolished housing, closed schools, and containment actions by the police allow us to visualize the spaces that have been targeted as "valuable" by the city, while also marking the spaces that are designated as disposable.

Police Power in the City of Wind

Police are, for citizens, the most visible agents of the American criminal justice system, if not of the state itself. They are, first and foremost and by occupational definition, the front line of whatever criminal justice initiatives politicians and policymakers decide to push.[15]

—Simon Balto

In Chicago, one of the functions of police is to operate as the on-the-ground muscle to activate the city's desires to clear and revitalize space for its valued residents. From the moment that large street organizations moved their operations to drug sales in public housing on the South Side, the Chicago Police Department engaged in maneuvers that attempted to give the appearance of addressing the problem. Unfortunately, the opposite was true. From the early days of CPD's Gang Intelligence Unit in the mid-1960s, to Operation Clean Sweep in the late 1980s, to the federalization of the police force in public housing in the 1990s, to Operation Headache in the same decade, most police actions yielded few results in relationship to curbing violence.

Continuing its problematic approach, CPD commissioned a gang database in the early 2000s to collect intelligence on suspected members of street organizations, with the youngest person being one year old and the oldest person being one hundred.[16] The Chicago Crime Commission had already produced a questionable publication called *The Gang Book*, which claimed to provide a "detailed overview of street gangs in the Chicago metropolitan area."[17] Their assessment of street organizations makes no mention of the fact that CPD had operated a black site for decades on the West Side of the city (Homan Square), where over seven thousand people were interrogated and tortured. A sworn police deposition revealed that no booking records were kept at Homan Square, nor were there any records of arrests or detainments before 2004, though the warehouse was purchased by CPD in 1995.[18] Many West Side residents were familiar with the practices of CPD in Homan Square, but they were not revealed to the public until 2015. Before Homan Square, there was John Burge and his fifty-three-member midnight crew of the second and third police districts. From 1972 to 1991, hundreds of Black men were tortured into false confessions, with many sentenced to death.[19] The actions of CPD are not those of "bad apples," and are not confounding when we consider the function of police departments as the first line of protection for the state and the ruling class.

Since the early days of the Chicago Democratic machine in the late nineteenth century, the police have always been beholden to the will of the mayor. Originally used to curtail the capacity of workers to organize and certain immigrant groups to engage in leisure activities, public safety was also the rationale used for the actions of CPD that resulted in harm for residents in certain (read Black or new immigrant) communities.[20] In the days of Daley machine politics (1955–1975 and 1989–2010), the police continued to operate as either the containment or clearing arm of the mayor's office. While "serving and protecting" has always been a selective process along the lines of race and space, many Black Chicagoans experience the police in the manner documented in the US Department of Justice's *Federal Report on Police Killings*:

> We found reasonable cause to believe that CPD has engaged in a pattern or practice of unreasonable force in violation of the Fourth Amendment and that the deficiencies in CPD's training, supervision, accountability and other systems have contributed to that pattern or practice.[21]

The pattern DOJ "discovered" is not due to the shortcomings of CPD, which has operated under a consent decree since the 2017 report and has been out of compliance with it since it was established in 2019.[22] Understanding engineered conflict allows us to identify CPD's function, more than an agency of public safety, as the forceful, militarized arm of the state, prioritizing the city's will to clear and protect space for those who have been deemed valuable. Corruption, use of deadly force, codes of silence and immunity from accountability have been problems with law enforcement since police have been police.[23] The same way as scholars Jeffrey Duncan-Andrade and Ernest Morrell never consider a deteriorating school building a "failing school," I've trained myself to understand that when we see any extreme or confounding behavior by individual officers, including the nationally publicized shooting deaths of Black Chicago residents, it is not the product of "bad apples."[24] Instead, *it is what police departments are structured to do.* The DOJ report simply serves as a reminder that the primary function of a police department is to protect the property and well-being of the powerful.

What makes CPD particularly valuable to the city is its capacity to act with relative impunity. I make the point of accountability being "relative" given the fact that the City of Chicago has paid over half a billion dollars since 2010 to residents to settle police misconduct claims. At the same time, it is important to note that the claims are settled *after* the wrongdoing by CPD, and that CPD's budget still accounts for over 40 percent of the city's budget.[25] Given the lengths that the Fraternal Order of Police will go to in defending officers for the killing of residents, it allows me to understand the police power in Chicago even when officers are found to be in the wrong.*

---

* The shooting deaths of Laquan McDonald and Rekia Boyd are of particular importance given the national spotlight that was placed on police shootings in Chicago. Officer Jason Van Dyke was convicted of second-degree murder and sixteen counts of aggravated battery with a firearm for killing Laquan McDonald.

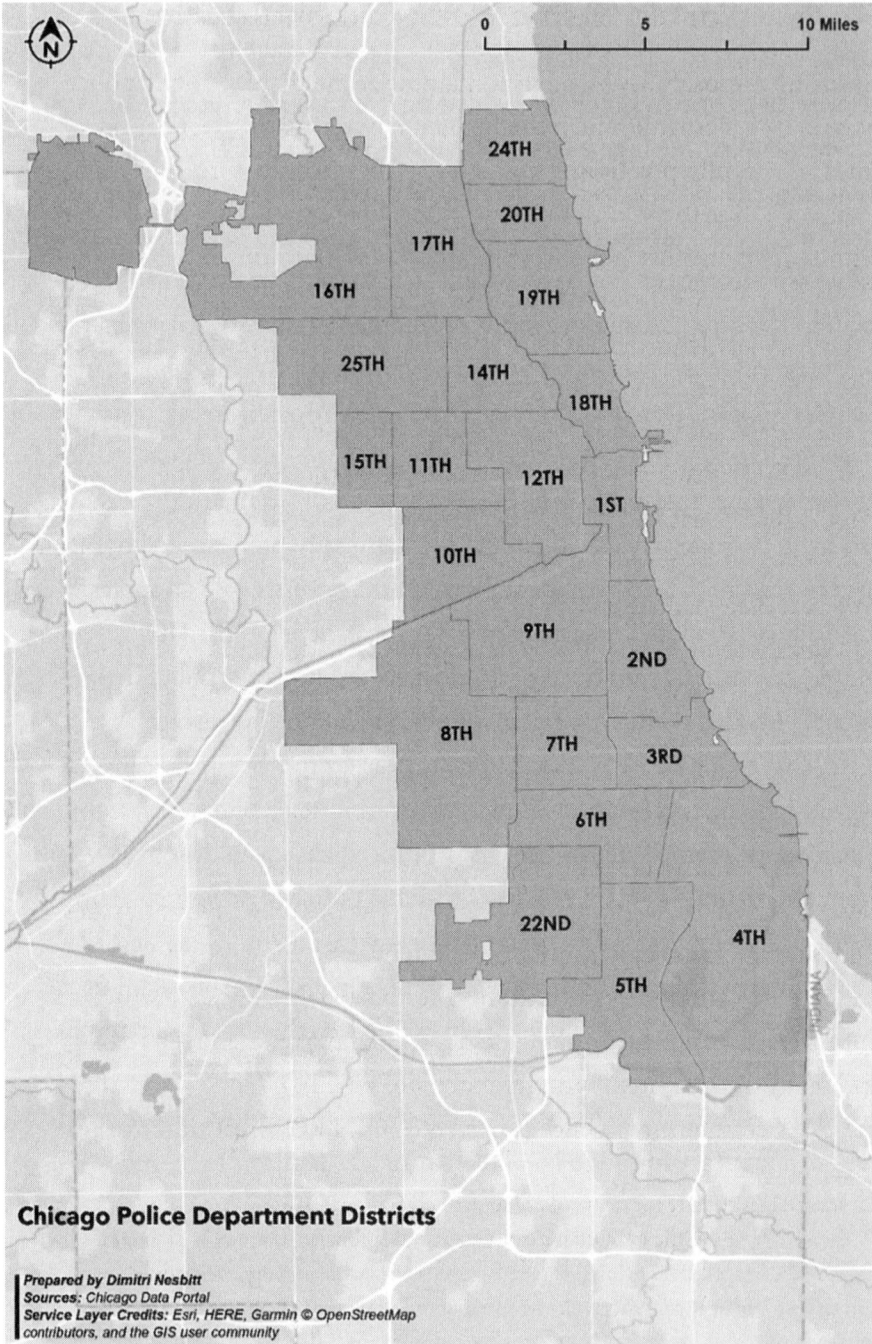

Chicago Police Department Districts

Prepared by Dimitri Nesbitt
Sources: Chicago Data Portal
Service Layer Credits: Esri, HERE, Garmin © OpenStreetMap
contributors, and the GIS user community

A "War" to Ensure Black Criminalization

Ensuring disposability through containment and displacement, police have played a critical role in the further splintering of street organizations. Originally positioned as a strategy that would curb crime and "gang" activity, there have been instances where CPD has paired itself with federal entities (most commonly the FBI) to disrupt the activities of street organizations internally (usually through infiltration) and externally (through raids, unwarranted arrests for minimal infractions, fabricated charges, or torture). Many of these approaches were ill-conceived and primarily resulted in the deepening of the criminalization of Black people in Chicago. Since the days of the second wave of the Great Migration, the last eighty years of police strategies have produced few results beyond the increase of incarceration rates amongst Black Chicagoans.

Taking their charge from the Radical Squad, commonly known as the "Red Squad" of the late 1880s under police captain Michael J. Schaack, and as the Industrial Unit of the Intelligence Division in the 1920s under Michael Mills, CPD's Gang Intelligence Unit (GIU) aimed at infiltration, disruption, and suppression. The original targets of the Industrial Unit were anarchists, and later individuals who were assumed to be communists ("red"). The tactics employed by the Red Squad were deeply problematic and overreaching. Local political and justice-centered organizations like the Black Panther Party, the Young Lords, and the Young Patriots were infiltrated and surveilled, and many of their members were tortured by CPD. Often assisted by the FBI's counterintelligence program (COINTELPRO), the goal of

---

He served less than three years of his sentence of six years and nine months. See Don Babwin, "Ex-Chicago Officer Convicted of Murdering Laquan McDonald Released Early," PBS News, February 3, 22, https://www.pbs.org/newshour/nation/ex-chicago-officer-convicted-of-murdering-laquan-mcdonald-released-early.

law enforcement was to "actively restrict a target's ability to carry out planned actions (prevention) or to encourage acts of wrongdoing."[26] In the process, hundreds of thousands of Chicagoans were surveilled, thousands were subject to wrongful arrests, and hundreds were killed in the almost century-long campaign of the Red Squad.[27] When they adopted the official name of the Subversive Section and later the Subversive Activities Unit in 1971, their actions overlapped with the work of the GIU (as some street organizations were surveilled under the Subversive Unit). They are often even confused as the same unit, but the distinction is important, as the GIU's attempt to suppress and eradicate Black street organizations has specific relevance to engineered conflict.*

Police superintendent Orlando Wilson created the GIU in 1967. Upon its formation, the tactical unit did not take into consideration the origins or structures of gangs, many of which were first formed for community protection from police or to address the lack of substantive recreation and job opportunities in poor communities. Because they did not understand these origins, CPD's strategy and policy for the suppression of gang activity was to increase arrests, with the hope of heavy police activity operating as a deterrent. When Wilson left CPD six months after the formation of the GIU, CPD superintendent James Conlisk appointed a Black lieutenant named Edward Buckley, who continued the hard-line approach to gang suppression. One year after Wilson's departure, Cook County State's Attorney Edward Hanrahan

---

* The Conservative Vice Lords (CVL) and Gangster Disciples moved into legitimate businesses and teamed with Black Power organizations in the late 1960s. Many of their members were surveilled, and sections of the organizations were infiltrated by CPD's Red Squad. See Natalie Moore and Lance Williams, *The Almighty Black P Stone Nation: The Rise Fall and Resurgence of an American Gang* (Chicago, Illinois: Lawrence Hill Books, 2011); and Lance Williams, *King David and Boss Daley: The Black Disciples, Mayor Daley and Chicago on the Edge* (Essex, Connecticut: Prometheus Books, 2023).

declared a "War on Gangs."[28] All of this despite the adamance of members in the Black community that police presence was not the solution. Community members advocated instead for education, recreation, job training, and arts programming.*

By ignoring the needs of community members, and their understanding of what would actually work, GIU grew its numbers, expanding from thirty-eight to two hundred officers in its second year, [29] and became a quasi-political force with support from the State's Attorney's Office and the Cook County Jail. GIU operated with few checks or balances, particularly due to the speed with which members of street organizations were arrested and processed. In the worst-case scenarios, GIU's operations resulted in the death of members of street organizations, with relative impunity. The situation eventually grew so serious that the FBI began an investigation to ascertain if CPD officers were intentionally killing Black people on the South and West Sides of the city.[30]

The early strategies of the GIU are important in understanding engineered conflict for several reasons. First, the infiltration of gangs and political organizations was a strategy to maintain control for the Daley regime. Taking his cue from the early days of the "Radical

---

* In addition to the legitimate businesses of CVL and the Gangster Disciples, there was also a federal intervention, when the federal government gave money to Jeff Fort and members of the Almighty Black P-Stone Nation in 1969 for job training and education. The money was squandered largely because the program was unsupervised and only loosely connected to the work it was chartered to do. By 1972, Jeff Fort had been convicted of misuse of federal funds. This led to the belief by many in law enforcement that members of street organizations were corrupt and ill equipped to address the needs of the community. Law enforcement did not take into account the work of CVL before they were infiltrated and surveilled by the GIU. See Natalie Moore and Lance Williams, *The Almighty Black P Stone Nation: The Rise Fall and Resurgence of an American Gang* (Chicago, Illinois: Lawrence Hill Books, 2011); and David Dawley, *A Nation of Lords: The Autobiography of the Vice Lords* (Long Grove, IL: Waveland Press, 1992).

Squad," Daley's office moved on any political or social formation that was viewed as infringing on the mayor's power. The thinking was that if these groups could be suppressed, it would demonstrate that the city was under control, and there would be a greater chance for the mayor to secure the favor and money of business and civic leaders. From the late-nineteenth-century "threat" of communism during Carter Harrison's mayoral term to the mid-twentieth century's manufactured "threat" of political upheaval and gang violence under Richard J. Daley, Chicago mayors have always moved to secure power. Rationales centered in decreasing violence are magnified, often invoking fear and frustration in residents. What is not discussed, however, is the fact that violence can be heightened when the needs of the marginalized are not met. Second, after numerous demographic and economic shifts in parts of the South and West Sides of the city, poorer Black residents were further marginalized and subsequently targeted by CPD. As conflict became deeply concentrated in certain areas of the South and West Side, the resources needed to address youth violence (education, recreation, job training, housing, health care) were increasingly difficult to attain. Discussed in detail in the next two sections, the specific timing and convergence of housing, education, and law enforcement policy at the local, state, and federal levels create a cataclysmic event in the development of engineered conflict.

RICO Statutes and the Error of Imitation

When G. Robert Blakey created the Racketeer Influenced Corrupt Organizations Act (RICO) in 1970, the idea was to prevent organized-crime factions from infiltrating legitimate businesses by way of extortion or fraud.[31] The initial tactics of RICO investigations produced few results; as the Department of Justice realized, tracing the proceeds of the criminal organization in the legitimate business would do little to take down the organization. Contrary to popular belief, nothing in the original legislation was intended to punish low-ranking, subordinate members of mafia rings. However, by 1984 the original narrow definition of RICO was broadened by Congress with the intent of ensnaring mafia leadership, in addition to their subordinates. The shift offered broad power to federal prosecutors. Where the original statute had allowed them to punish mafia members for the acquisition of a legitimate business, its expansion allowed them to prosecute members for the daily activities of a legitimate business, and to prosecute mafia leadership of running the business of the crime family, even absent of any contact with a "legitimate" enterprise. In short, RICO allowed DOJ to charge mob families with running any enterprise, whether it was legitimate or illegitimate. In later iterations, RICO could also create a dragnet where organized-crime leadership could be targeted due to the criminal activity of their subordinates. Where most criminal infractions are defined by either a physical act or concrete result, RICO does not define or prohibit any specific type of conduct. The definition of "enterprise" broadened to encompass a structure of relationships between individuals or groups, while a "pattern of racketeering" is codified as the relationship between multiple crimes.[32] Gerard Lynch offers an important understanding of the abstraction of RICO prosecutions and its relationship to engineered conflict:

> Because RICO is such a broad and abstract crime, it is capable of application to a number of different types of conduct in a wide range of circumstances. Because each type of conduct to which it is applied exists in its own unique context of pre-existing substantive and procedural rules, the effect of superimposing RICO on the remainder of the criminal code varies according to the type of conduct involved.[33]

Even though the RICO Act has its critics, and the broad reach of the legislation brought about problems regarding enforcement in government corruption cases and white-collar crime cases, the strategy was instrumental in limiting the reach of the mafia. The criminal enterprises of the five major crime families (Bonanno, Colombo, Gambino, Genovese, and Lucchese) were significantly damaged by RICO cases.[34] Seeing the success of DOJ in limiting the capacity of these international crime syndicates, law enforcement throughout the US looked to mimic its strategies to curb gang violence. In Chicago, CPD joined forces with DOJ and the Cook County State's Attorney's Office to ensnare what they considered to be the city's largest street organization at the time, the Gangster Disciples. However, the process did not produce the same results as its RICO predecessors.

Operation Headache: A Problematic RICO-Like Approach

The splintering of large street organizations in Chicago was not immediate. Instead, its gradual progression came from a series of legal strategies and law enforcement policies aimed at targeting leadership. One example of importance was Operation Headache.[35] Although the defendants targeted in this operation were not charged with RICO violations, the tactics used were RICO-like, in that it involved a large, fifty-count drug and weapons conspiracy indictment against thirty-eight named defendants. Also differing from RICO cases was the fact that it was not one case but three.[36] Otherwise the approach was similar to those used to stifle organized crime through RICO statutes, a large dragnet strategy thought to be the most effective tactic to immediately curb the reach of street organizations in Chicago. The timing of the case is of particular importance to engineered conflict, in that it aligns with the destruction of public housing and school closings. As street organizations had a significant presence in public housing developments, the dispersal of membership to other neighborhoods throughout the city, coupled with the absence of leadership, made many neighborhoods fertile for new conflicts.

Nicknamed "Operation Headache" by staff members in the Office of the Attorney General of the Northern District of Illinois, Eastern Division, the sting operation was the largest case on record that can be directly connected to the fragmentation of large street organizations in the city. Led by Ronald Safer, the case sent shockwaves throughout the city, given its heft and breadth. When Safer joined the US Attorney's Office in Chicago as an assistant attorney in 1992, he was assigned to lead a federal investigation of the Gangster Disciples (GDs) in Chicago, although he had no operating knowledge of street organizations or structures.[37] Even though it was a drug conspiracy case, Safer approached the GDs in a way that mimicked the DOJ's approach with the mafia in RICO cases. Federal prosecutors similarly took a page directly from RICO cases at the federal level, because GDs were attempting to move into legitimate enterprises.

By the time Ronald Safer came to lead Operation Headache, he had begun to observe the neighborhoods where GDs controlled the majority of the drug sales. The first thing he noticed was the young age of the people who were running most of the drug sales. He began to think about the workers as being victims of a leadership structure that would exploit their youngest members. He also realized that CPD's strategy of arresting those workers was deeply ineffective in curbing drug sales. As he built his case, his office alleged that GDs had created a massive criminal enterprise, largely through the sale and distribution of powder cocaine, crack cocaine, heroin, and marijuana. It was true that by the late 1980s, GDs controlled a significant proportion of the drug trade on the South Side of the city.[38] Although thirty-eight defendants were named across the three cases, Larry Hoover was the main target. As the undisputed leader of the Gangster Disciples since the early 1970s, Hoover was accused of running the GDs' criminal enterprises from prison, despite the fact that he had been serving time on a separate murder charge in 1973.

Given the earlier harm inflicted by the GIU on members of street and political organizations by way of torture, wrongful convictions, and state-sanctioned murder, there was a consent decree in Illinois that information on so-called gangs could not be collected.[39] However, this consent decree did not account for investigations at the federal level. By way of confidential informant evidence, eyewitness testimony, and wiretapping, federal attorneys were able to unearth an elaborate and intricately designed leadership structure. Hoover (often referenced as "King Larry" or the "Chairman of the Board" in the case files) ran a top-down organization that had officers (listed as Board members, governors, regents, coordinators, and soldiers) with particular duties and responsibilities for each position.[40] Within this structure, members working in drug sales were required to pay dues to leadership (referenced as "street tax," "the weekly," "count money," or "the personal"). Internally, members were required to buy narcotics from leadership at inflated prices, with the proceeds going back to leadership of the organization.[41] To control drug markets throughout the city and suburbs, no one outside of the GDs could sell drugs in areas controlled by them unless they paid a tax to the organization. Anyone found in violation of these rules could be severely harmed or killed.[42] The GDs scheduled regular meetings, often centered in planning and expansion of their enterprise.

Central to the indictment was the accusation that GDs had developed legitimate enterprises in the form of a community-based organization (Save the Children, Inc.) and a political action committee (21st Century V.O.T.E.). These were part of a larger organizational decision to use means sanctioned by local, state, and federal governments to make profits legitimately. Hoover even claimed that the name of the

"Black Gangster Disciple Nation" had changed to "Growth and Development" in 1987. In the eyes of many on the South Side (including my own), eyebrows were raised when we heard that GDs were "going legit."* I remember driving as a young person, playing the radio in my car, when I reached the corner of 79th and Stony Island and heard an advertisement for a party that was being held by Growth and Development Productions. I remember saying out loud to myself: "Damn, GDs are throwing parties and got commercials on the radio?" I imagine others had similarly perplexed reactions.

21st Century V.O.T.E. (Voices of Total Empowerment) was an organizational strategy utilized by GDs that garnered national attention and began to get local support, with politicians pushing for Hoover's release from prison. At the time, tensions between large traditional gang structures were high around the country, and Hoover was thought by some politicians and community activists to be a possible conduit to curb the conflict between rival factions.[43] At the same time as the 1992 conflict between street organizations in Los Angeles received national coverage, there was a truce announced between the larger street organizations on the South and West Sides of Chicago. Following the truce in Chicago, there were a series of "gang summits" facilitated by civic and political leadership (most notably Jesse Jackson of Operation PUSH and Louis Farrakhan of the Nation of Islam).[44] Around the same time, Hoover released his "New Concept" to launch GDs into legitimacy.[45] The main premise of the New Concept was to gain political power through the electoral process. Once political power was achieved, Hoover posited that membership could move into sectors that would uplift Black residents experiencing multiple forms of isolation and marginalization. Citing the "Blueprint of a New

---

* "Going legit" is a euphemism for the process whereby a person who was once engaged in criminal activity makes the decision to disassociate themselves with that activity or the organization that they once held membership in.

Concept—From Gangster Disciple to Growth and Development," the passage below provides insight to their thinking:

> The Vision is that we dedicate ourselves to a war on illiteracy; that we pursue professional business careers such as accounting, drafting, computer science, business management, etc.; that we master the trades of industry such as brick masonry, building and road construction, textiles, machine shop, surveying, welding, etc., that we acquire knowledge and expertise in areas that are needed in our community, such as plumbing, carpentry, building management and maintenance, auto body repairs, auto mechanic, etc., that we prepare ourselves to become small business administrators in areas such as grocery stores, clothing stores, hardware's, entertainment (lounges and dance halls), distributors of general household merchandise, etc., that we amass credentials such as certificates, diplomas and degrees as a statement to our desire to excel positively; that we expand our views to include the educational, economical, political and social realities of society; that we began to value the positive implications of righteous endeavors.[46]

Similar to the calls of civil-rights and Black-power organizations thirty years prior, it would be difficult to argue that the things mentioned in the New Concept would not be beneficial to working-class and poor Black people throughout the city. The platform appeared to take a page from earlier attempts by CVLs under Bobby Gore on the West Side, Blackstones under Jeff Fort in Woodlawn, and GDs under the leadership of "King David" Barksdale in the late 1960s on the South Side to develop infrastructure in disinvested Black communities. However, the difference between Hoover's attempts and the ones of years prior was that the federal government could directly connect his operations to drug sales.

At its height in the early 1990s, 21st Century V.O.T.E. had begun to run political candidates and criticize Chicago's political machine. Walter "Gator" Bradley, a former high-ranking member of the GDs, was a candidate for the third ward's aldermanic seat. He and Hoover grew up in the same neighborhood and were both incarcerated in Stateville Prison. Like Hoover, Bradley believed that the electoral process was the best means to secure empowerment. Before Bradley's campaign, 21st Century V.O.T.E. had supported a candidate (Jerry Washington) in a primary for a statewide seat.[47] This might have been an miscalculation by Hoover, due to the local and national attention given to 21st Century V.O.T.E. As a powerful street organization sought to legitimately move into electoral politics, the racialized skepticism of the federal government drew federal prosecutors to get a wiretap investigation approved. This was especially problematic in a state like Illinois that has convicted hosts of public officials dating back to the early twentieth century. In Hoover's Operation Headache trial, wiretap evidence and eyewitness testimony provided damning evidence against Hoover's efforts to get released.[48] Jurors heard wiretap conversations between Hoover and high-ranking GDs on how Hoover ran drug sales and enforced violations of GD policy from prisons in Vienna and Dixon, Illinois. Even though he revealed contrition in some of the evidence, it was clear that Hoover was mistaken to believe he would be granted the same graces of lenience by law enforcement given to members of the Daley political machine upon their arrest, conviction, and sentencing.[*]

Despite the convictions it leveled, Operation Headache failed to identify the real reasons that drug sales became the most lucrative

---

[*] Hoover stated in one of the recordings that he knew the problems of the drug trade, but it was a cold reality that the organization had to deal with. The idea was to move away from the sale and distribution of drugs, but the money was still needed to finance the legitimate operations of the GDs. See Ann Scott Tyson, "The Many Faces of a Reputed Gangster," *Christian Science Monitor*, May 6, 1997.

enterprise in disinvested neighborhoods. Safer and his team of federal prosecutors did not assess the broader structures of capitalism, uneven development (gentrification), and other forms of marginalization and isolation that deeply impact the illicit drug trade. Where some may think this critique to be unfair, it is important to bring the function of policing/law enforcement into focus. In mainstream framings of the criminal legal system, the job of law enforcement is to assess and punish criminal infractions by way of arrest and prosecution. Those who are found to be in violation of the criminal code are "breaking the law." Conceptually, the prosecution of criminal infractions is linear and ultimately positioned as being for the sake of "public safety." Absent from this analysis are the mechanisms driven by capitalism that can put people in "survival mode." When people do not have access to life-sustaining entities (housing, health care, education, living-wage employment, etc.), the struggle to exist in the world can become extremely difficult.

The prosecution for Operation Headache also did not consider the fact that if people are engaged in the high-risk activity of working in an open-air drug market, it is often a decision of last resort. Sometimes young people are fooled to believe that wealth will be attained through these means, but this often ends abruptly after a cycle of being in and out of the criminal legal system. Instead of placing blame on the individual, we should consider the fact that many of the people working under these conditions are trying to make ends meet. When people are participating at the ground level of hand-to-hand drug sales, contrary to popular belief, they are not getting rich. Instead, they are disenfranchised people experiencing exploitation, who cannot access living-wage employment, education, health care, or housing through "legitimate" channels.

At the same time, the point here is not to exonerate the actions of the Gangster Disciples outlined in Operation Headache. Underneath the call for Black uplift and self-determination, the upper level of the organization operated and maintained an enterprise that was structured around the exploitation of its own members. GDs were able to capitalize on the fact that the lower levels of the organization were willing to work and be taxed at high rates for their labor. Structurally, an understanding of engineered conflict calls into question a system that allows this to happen. The only difference between the GDs and large corporations is that the products the former were producing and distributing were "illegal" substances to fund legitimate organizations. The structure and practices of the organization were identical to "legitimate" corporations. Simultaneously, engineered conflict pushes us to consider that the people oppressed by racism and capitalism are the easiest to exploit. Akin to the practices of many Fortune 500 corporations, GDs took a page from late-stage capitalist exploitation and used it on their own membership. The issue is that the limited scope of the criminal legal system only allows these instances to be interpreted as the fault of a group of individuals. Engineered conflict pushes us to understand that exploitation, like violence, is a structural concern. It is the product of a system in which it is normalized. The actions of the exploited are racialized and framed as "criminal" while access to life-sustaining entities are severely limited and removed from certain communities. Many actions deemed to be "criminal" are therefore often "crimes" of survival, another fact that CPD and the US Attorney's Office did not take into consideration in Operation Headache. Their idea was that if they took out the leadership, the power of the organization would be diminished, as had been the case with other organized crime outfits. In this case, their thinking that "the chain would be broken" was woefully shortsighted.[49]

Proponents of law enforcement state that its primary job is to get criminals off the street, the sordid concept of "catching the bad guys." We need to consider this as a ploy by government to give the (white) general public a stronger sense of safety and trust in law enforcement.

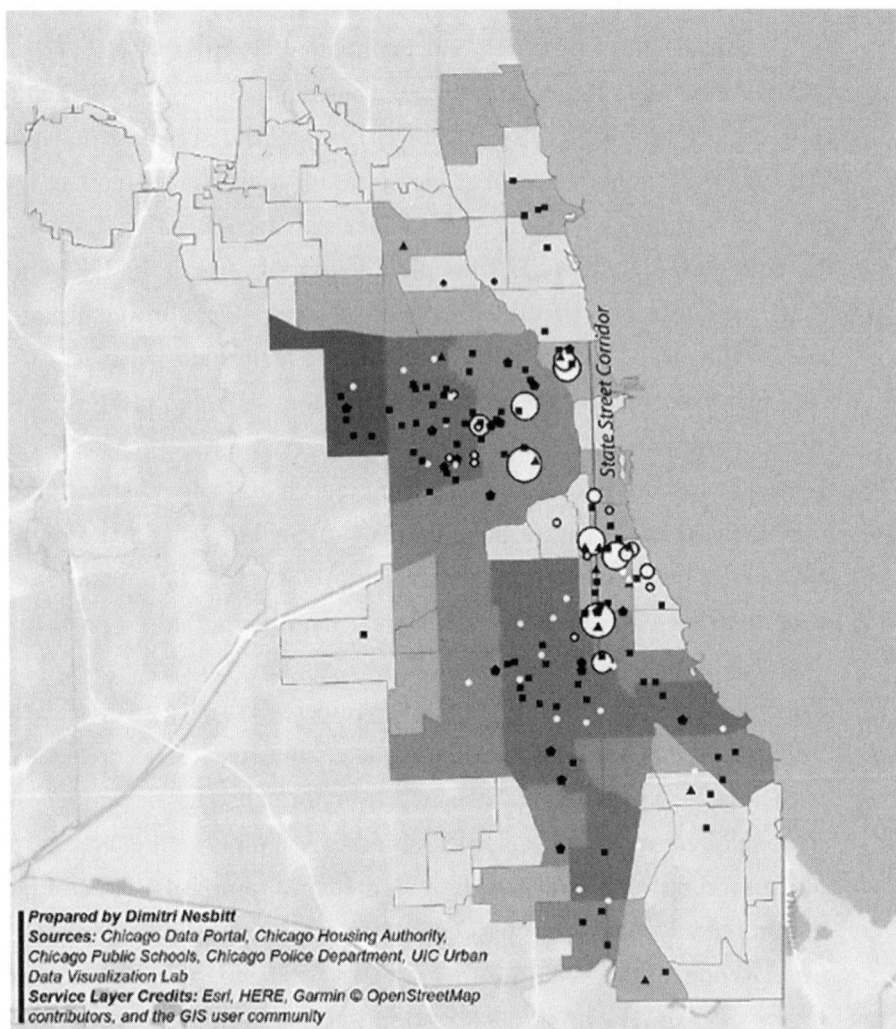

Prepared by Dimitri Nesbitt
Sources: Chicago Data Portal, Chicago Housing Authority,
Chicago Public Schools, Chicago Police Department, UIC Urban
Data Visualization Lab
Service Layer Credits: Esri, HERE, Garmin © OpenStreetMap
contributors, and the GIS user community

I offer that it is not that simple. Given the racialized history of policing and the criminal legal system, a structural analysis of the conditions that intimately impact the lives of poor and working-class Black people *was never the concern of law enforcement in the first place.* To this end, carceral solutions are never solutions. They are only rationales used to further disenfranchise and alienate the exploited.

Mapping Engineered Conflict

157 Chicago Public Schools affected
- ■ Closure
- ▲ Closure & Consolidation
- ● Consolidation
- ♠ Phase-Out
- ○ Reconstitution ("Turnarounds")

24 Chicago Housing Authority developments *(units demolished)*
- ◯ 2,301 - 4,395 units
- ◯ 1,370 - 2,300 units
- ◯ 805 - 1,369 units
- ○ 204 - 804 units
- ∘ 5 - 203 units

784 Homicides in 2016 by Community Area
- 0 - 5 homicides
- 6 - 12 homicides
- 13 - 43 homicides
- 44 - 65 homicides
- 66 - 94 homicides

0   5   10 Miles

The Lingering "Headache" of Law Enforcement Policies for Black Chicago

Following what was thought to be the initial success of Operation Headache, CPD, along with state and federal agencies, began to employ its myriad strategies to ensnare members of other street organizations in Chicago. Beyond the categorical denial of what actually works to reduce violence (access to quality education, living-wage employment, health care, and affordable housing), the GIU's tactics in the "War on Gangs" resurrected themselves by way of enhanced policing strategies. Due to the consent decree of 1981 denying local police the capacity to collect evidence on gang operations by way of infiltration, policing strategies were rooted in suppression or arrests by undercover officers posing as either drug buyers or distributors. As Operation Headache slowed street organization activity only for a brief moment, similar tensions were unearthed as had been with the destruction of public housing and school closings. This iteration of tensions between Black youth did not involve the large, corporate structures of historical Black street organizations, but were instead between splintered factions with only residual ties to larger organizations.

A few years before 21st Century V.O.T.E. appeared as a political organization on the South Side, the City of Chicago created a "gang loitering ordinance" to stop groups of young people from congregating on street corners and commercial thoroughfares in 1992. Under the official name of "Gang Congregation Ordinance," the policy stated that if "apparent gang members" were congregating on a street "for no apparent reason," police could ask them and anyone with them to disperse or detain them if met with resistance. Not knowing if this would stand constitutional muster, lawyers for the City of Chicago admitted in the Supreme Court that the law was a "guinea pig." By their own account, they had no idea how to write a constitutional antiloitering law.[50] Still, the city maintained that so-called gangs were menacing in presence alone, and that a policy was required that would not allow them to pose threats to the community at large.[51] Noting the problematics of the policy, the Supreme Court held that the Gang Congregation Ordinance was constitutionally vague and essentially criminalized daily human interactions.[52] The decision was a temporary victory for young people of color throughout the city, but the mayor's office and CPD did not let it deter their efforts.

Another strategy employed by CPD and other police departments throughout the nation was the tactic of "focused deterrence." Here the idea was to engage in a series of interactions with members of street organizations involved in drug sales in order to keep watch on people who had been convicted of drug felonies, and to let them know that they were under close watch. Where few focused-deterrence strategies have produced results, the idea is that because no one wants to go to prison, if they know they're being observed they will not engage in activities that would put them there. Where the first half of this assertion is correct, the second is not necessarily, because it does not consider what people feel like they have to do in situations where there are few options. In the early 2000s, CPD employed focused-deterrence measures through gang tactical units, under the name of "Operation Double Play," where CPD officers would pose as buyers. "Operation Disruption" was another strategy that deployed the placement of digital cameras in supposed drug "hot spots." "Operation Closed Market" was the attempt to put more officers on the street to curb drug sales.[53] By 2003 CPD had employed a policy of collecting "contact cards," where police would collect demographic information from people they thought "could assist in investigations."[54] The vagueness of this strategy led to unnecessary harassment and unwarranted arrests. Compounding the issue, Illinois developed its own "Street Gang RICO Act" in 2012, aimed at curbing the activity of larger organizations that might have been participating in underground drug sales.[55]

Where these efforts may have increased arrest rates, they were not effective in addressing the core needs of poor Black residents on the South and West Side. As the large, corporate-structured street organizations became further splintered, conflict moved to other areas of the city, continuing the concentration of violence to specific areas of the South and West Sides. Once again, the issues stand boldly in the face of law enforcement and elected officials. What is missing is the political will to shift priorities and engage in strategies that require different thinking and different people. The next chapter offers an explicit example of what the splintering looks like in a particular neighborhood, and of what engineered conflict looks like at the community level.

CHAPTER 4

WHEN IT ALL COMES TOGETHER

RACE, PLACE, SCHOOLS, AND POLICING IN WOODLAWN

No love for the Black American . . . you know the lick
They orchestrate our demise, we go and promote the shit
We openly offin' each other bogusly over shit
Shit that ain't even worth it
Imagine lookin' in the mirror but you ain't seein' purpose
Gotta tend to your garden so it's easy to see the serpents
We ain't lookin' hard enough to see what's beneath the surface
I see us and see a circus
What the fuck is a safe haven when your own is your
opposition
No pot to piss in, no optimism, we locked in prison

And killing each other, like it's incentivized
You ain't no bro of mine if you partake in genocide.
                                        —IAMGAWD, "Civil War"

Along the lines of the epigraph from the introduction, lyrics from Chicago emcee IAMGAWD provide a stark reflection on loss and frustration. Without using the phrase *engineered conflict,* IAMGAWD succinctly captures how the process works in "Civil War." His ability to unearth a process where "your own" becomes "your opposition" alerts us to the reality that when life-sustaining resources are low, the risk of violence can be high. His metaphor of tending the garden to see "beneath the surface" unearths the "serpents" of interpersonal violence, displacement (gentrification), school closings, police abuse, and other forms of state-sanctioned violence. In the South Side community of Woodlawn, the process of not being able to see the serpents is a steady one that can make it extremely difficult to see the people you might be in conflict with as potentially holding solutions to your problems. The bottom line remains: If you are struggling to secure housing, quality education, health care, and living-wage employment, the layers of marginalization can wage a war of epic proportions on the body and mind.

I offer this chapter specifically to provide a window into what engineered conflict looks like in the neighborhood of Woodlawn. To many long-term residents of Woodlawn, the layers of contradictions, frustration, and loss are visible. The intensity of the moment is heightened through the confounding twists and turns of school closings, public housing, and law enforcement strategies. From my own perspective as a resident, it's one thing to talk about them separately, but another to see how they work together. Woodlawn provides an example of what the remnants of engineered conflict look like in real time. In a space that is

preparing itself for a "new" gentry along the lines of race and class, gentrification places Black residents already on the margins in deeper precarity. In my reflections, the events taking place in the neighborhood have
reminded me of my conversations with critical educational policy studies scholar Pauline Lipman about gentrification. She always reminds me
that gentrification can look different in different places under the same
set of rules. The educational, housing and law enforcement parameters
of engineered conflict may look different in Woodlawn than they do in
other communities in the city, but the same rules apply—one group is
in, another is out, and those that are out are never to return.

Spatial Reflections on Woodlawn

Even though I grew up about four miles south of Woodlawn, my parents had to remind me that the neighborhood had a booming nightlife
in the late 1950s and '60s. The Woodlawn I remember from the days
of my youth (specifically in the 1980s and '90s) was very different, in
that the economic downturn had deepened by the time I was able to
move around the city independently. Standing almost vacant from
the late 1970s to the early 1990s, Sixty-Third Street between Cottage
Grove and King Drive had become so barren that film location scouts
decided to use it as a film site in the Cuba Gooding Jr. and Emilio
Estevez movie *Judgment Night*.[1] Gone were my parents' days of the
jazz and blues clubs that lined Cottage Grove Avenue and Sixty-Third
Street, stretching from Woodlawn Avenue to the east and South Parkway (now Dr. Martin Luther King Jr. Drive) to the west. Nightlife
beacons like the Tivoli Club, Grand Ballroom, Trianon Ballroom, Bud-
land, Basin Street, the Crown Propeller Club, and the Hotel Pershing
were gone by the 1970s.[2] Most of the buildings had been demolished,
and the memories of these places remain only in the recollections of
my parents and their generation. Only the Grand Ballroom and Daley's

Restaurant (currently the longest continuously operating restaurant in Chicago) serve as remnants of a distant age.

To understand Woodlawn's relationship to engineered conflict, I am guided by scholars who engage in Critical Race Spatial Analysis (CRSPA) who "want to understand the processes constructing whiteness but establish a means of resisting its effects."[3] Woodlawn provides a specific example of the ways race and space impact education, housing, and law enforcement policies. Geographically, the neighborhood is a lakefront community on Chicago's South Side; its physical borders are Dr. Martin Luther King Jr. Drive to the west, Lake Michigan to the east, Sixtieth Street to the north, and Sixty-Seventh Street to the south. Once a prairie that was home to Dutch immigrant farmers in the mid-nineteenth century, the neighborhood was annexed by the City of Chicago in 1889.[4] It is bordered by the communities of Greater Grand Crossing (to the south), South Shore (to the southeast), Washington Park (to the west), and Hyde Park (to the north). Woodlawn was one of the first neighborhoods that Black people could move to outside of the historic area formed by restrictive covenants known as the "Black belt."[5] Once restrictive covenants were lifted throughout the city, due to the efforts of Carl Hansberry, the community that was once home to recently arrived European immigrants and their affluent white neighbors became almost entirely Black in less than a decade.*

---

* *Hansberry v. Lee, 311 U.S. 32* (1940) was the landmark case where Carl Hansberry (father of award-winning author Lorraine Hansberry) sued the State of Illinois to lift restrictive covenant laws to purchase a home in Woodlawn, at 6150 S. Rhodes Ave. The case and experiences of the Hansberry family were the inspiration for Lorraine Hansberry's groundbreaking play *A Raisin in the Sun.* The "Black Belt" or "Bronzeville" was an eight-square-mile area on the South Side of the city where 80 percent of all Black people lived from the late nineteenth century to the late 1940s. See Michelle Boyd, *Jim Crow Nostalgia: Reconstructing Race in Bronzeville* (Minneapolis: University of Minnesota Press, 2008).

Soon after the departure of white residents, deindustrialization left Woodlawn void of city services and infrastructure, as the city began to isolate the community as undesirable. One of the more pronounced frictions after the departure of white residents was with the University of Chicago (U of C). Even after restrictive covenants were lifted, there was an explicit plan to prevent Black residents from encroaching on the university's property by numerous means. At one point, the university contacted the Chicago Plan Commission to see if the area that bordered U of C and Woodlawn could qualify for a development project to "serve as a buffer between the university and the deteriorating neighborhood to the south."[6] U of C administration also suggested that the "problem of restriction might be avoided by the wrecking of undesirable buildings and the development of attractive quarters that would be occupied by university faculty and employees."[7] Steeped in the politics of "urban renewal," U of C administrator and Chicago Plan Commission chair Julian Levi* was blunt in his assessment of Black residents of Woodlawn:

> If we are really serious about the next generation of teachers and scholars, lawyers and doctors, physicists and chemists, then we have got to worry about the adequate housing of the graduate student; about the clearing of land for a new laboratory; about the closing of streets to divert traffic from campuses; about the development of a "compatible environment" including substantial slum clearance. . . . We cannot have it both ways. We are either going to have graduate students, who produce leadership for the next generation . . . or we are not going to achieve these results because we are unwilling to disturb existing owners and populations.[8]

* Julian Levi, inaugural director of the South East Chicago Commission, directed an urban renewal project that constructed 2,100 new buildings while displacing almost four thousand families in the Chicago communities of Hyde Park and Woodlawn.

The border between Woodlawn and U of C, on Sixty-First Street, has historically stood as the racialized border between the university and community. The code words "deteriorating" and "undesirable" are racial dog whistles that spatially marked Woodlawn as the site of both displacement and possibility for the university. Ironically, this earlier contestation has since been eased, as the "buffer" is no longer needed in the northeastern quadrant of the neighborhood. U of C has fulfilled its promise by providing "attractive quarters" that are occupied by university faculty and other new white residents of the neighborhood. In the eyes of some, the border that once sat as a hard line between Woodlawn and the university has become more porous, expanding to the southernmost border of the neighborhood (at Sixty-Seventh Street). U of C has emerged as one of the primary beneficiaries of this expansion, which occurred by dispossessing Black poor and working-class residents of affordable housing in Woodlawn and marketing it to faculty, staff, and students. The U of C shuttle bus currently makes stops throughout the Eastern corridor of Woodlawn beyond Sixty-First Street, marking space for a new class of settlers. To "protect" this space for the new gentry, U of C has grown its police force to the largest private security force in the city, second in size only to the Chicago Police Department. These not-so-subtle developments continue to fuel gentrification/displacement throughout the neighborhood, particularly in the eastern corridor of the neighborhood, stretching east to Lake Michigan and west to Cottage Grove Avenue.

A Presidential Center for the "New" Neighbors

Deepening the concerns of long-term residents of Woodlawn is the building of the Barack Obama Presidential Center (OPC). While President Obama has touted the center as a space that will support education, job development, and the training of civic leaders, he has also rejected the prospect of a community benefits agreement (CBA). In most cases, a

CBA is developed by a community organization or a coalition of groups to ensure that a new development will not operate as the catalyst for future displacement of long-term residents in a neighborhood. If there is no CBA around a central development hub, the results often come in the form of either the displacement or increased isolation of working-class/ poor residents. In the case of the OPC, a coalition of groups who refer to themselves as the Obama Community Benefits Agreement Coalition (OCBAC) has made a set of concrete asks of Mr. Obama and his collection of developers. These demands include commitments to employment, economic development, education, housing, transportation, and sustainability for existing Black residents.[9]

Designed in the form of a city ordinance, OCBAC has proposed a list of demands, including the mandate that 5 percent of revenue generated for the center be used to develop a community trust fund to support neighborhood development initiatives. Another demand is for the OPC to operate as a library with a full-time librarian and staff, to be open every day that Chicago Public Schools are open, with full access for neighborhood schools. The ordinance also specifies that the high school across the street from the proposed center (Hyde Park HS) should remain a neighborhood public high school without selective enrollment or other special designations that would limit significant numbers of Woodlawn youth from attending. In concert with responsibility for the employment of South Side residents, the ordinance demands that "35% of the apprenticeships and 20% of journey workers, across all trades, hired by the contractors must come from the Southside and their demographics must reflect Southside communities."[10]

In light of Obama's work as a community organizer fighting against environmental racism on the South Side of the city, one would think these demands to be in concert with the stated goals of the presidential center. Instead, OCBAC has been met with staunch opposition from OPC staff and Mr. Obama himself. In the past, his rationale for rejecting a CBA centered around the idea that if the presidential center abided by the agreement, who's to say that others wouldn't come and make different asks? To some, this may appear to be rational in the spirit of free-market capitalism and neoliberal expansion of the private sector, but to others, Mr. Obama's expectation of droves of other organizations pushing for a CBA borders on the ridiculous. It would be extremely unlikely for another coalition to try to usurp the terms and conditions of the original CBA. More importantly, if another group attempted to secure another CBA, the Obama Presidential Center administration could politely refuse, stating that there was already a CBA in place. The tensions that Mr. Obama speaks of do not exist. Nevertheless, other tensions do remain, as some support the building of the presidential center without a CBA (a small collection of city council members, a group of local Woodlawn clergy, and real estate developers) while OCBAC members hold steadfast to the necessity of a CBA.

The OPC is touted by many homeowners and real-estate developers as a development that will concretize gentrification in Woodlawn. Another is the proposal of an adjacent golf course to be designed by professional golfer Tiger Woods.[11] There is already a golf course in the Southeast corner of Woodlawn, a vestige of the days when the South Shore neighborhood (adjacent to Woodlawn to the southeast) was the playground of the wealthy. Once a private golf course, it is currently owned by the Chicago Park District. To sell the "promise" of Woodlawn, Woods's development of a PGA-level golf course in the neighborhood, along with the Obama Presidential Center, is projected to serve as a significant revenue generator for the community. As a "consolation" offer to the community, Hyde Park Academy High School was given $40 million to improve programming and the physical plant of the building.[12] Where the naked eye would view this as a windfall for the school, we need to consider another set of questions: Particularly, are these "innovations" intended for the students that currently attend, or are they part of a larger plan to attract the children of the new gentry in Woodlawn to eventually attend the school? To some, my questions may appear paranoid, but these tensions are ever-present in Woodlawn as the push for quality education and housing continues to come at the expense of the marginalized.

It is obvious to most that the proposed new golf course is not for the historically marginalized Black residents of Woodlawn. Likewise, Obama's rejection of a CBA is connected to Woodlawn becoming a desired community for real estate developers. Though many still think of displacement/gentrification in Woodlawn as a recent development, historical and spatial analysis reveal that it is only the last stage of forty- to hundred-year plans of urban renewal. Where the presidential center and golf course are developments stemming from the mid-2010s, the larger plan dates back to the late 1940s. I take Michelle Boyd's warning against waxing poetic about the halcyon days of Black Woodlawn. But it is critical to recognize how demographic and spatial shifts in the neighborhood are connected to broader structural components that gradually wage violence on community members who find themselves at the margins. Where some may view the Obama Presidential Center as one of the "needed improvements" to the area, missing is the question, "Improvements for whom?" This is especially important given the fact that the first million-dollar home was sold in the neighborhood in March of 2023.[13] The narratives of race and class remain intimate partners in the layered story of engineered conflict and the dispossession of Woodlawn's long-term working-class and low-income Black residents.

A View from My Front Door

Upon moving to Woodlawn in 2012, one of the first things I noticed was a police cruiser parked on the end of my block every night, usually with a ranking police officer (or "white shirt") sitting by themselves in the driver's seat.* During the day, a group of police officers on bicycle patrol would congregate on the block west of me and hold makeshift roll-call meetings. Sometimes officers, usually in groups of three, would patrol my alley on foot. This was especially concerning as I would always think about the number of young people that take out the garbage at night. I feared that if a loud sound came from garbage falling into a trash can, police officers could mistake it for a gun and tragically end a person's life. Fortunately, this never happened, but the presence of three police officers, maybe new to CPD, patrolling in a dark area where they are potentially nervous, does not bode well for residents.

There was deep skepticism in the community regarding the intent of the new patrols to the area. The police attention given to the area during this time was officially connected to a recent rash of shootings in the neighborhood, but many people, including myself, wondered: "What is this in preparation for?" We would soon find out, when the announcement for the Obama Presidential Center was released. As a critical component of engineered conflict, the eastern corridor of Woodlawn had been marked as an area to be protected, while some portions of the neighborhood west of Cottage Grove Avenue were designated as areas to be contained. Although this has shifted drastically since my move to Woodlawn, there was a moment where the spatial lines between value and disposability were stark and evident.

There is a contradiction in my own personal relationship to Woodlawn, complicating matters further. A material analysis of my home purchase in the spring of 2012 could see it as a factor contributing to the uneven development (gentrification) of the neighborhood. Despite me being Black and a person committed to justice struggles in housing, education, and abolition, it would be irresponsible to overlook the role played by my purchase of a home in an area experiencing multiple

* The term *white shirt* refers to police officers over the rank of sergeant, who wear a white shirt to identify their rank to other officers.

levels of engineered conflict. This was brought into focus for me when I first moved to the community and a neighbor who lived across the street told me the story of my home beyond the narrative that had been offered to me by the realtor. From my neighbor's recollection, a Black woman had owned the home from the 1960s until the mid-2010s. Unfortunately, when she passed away, her children couldn't keep up with the mortgage payments and were forced to sell the home. A developer bought the home for less than $15,000 and sold it for nineteen times more on the open market. Since 2012, the house has almost doubled in value, while the property taxes have quadrupled from the time of the sale. Across the street from my house are three homes that were built by a developer in 2001. At the time, each three-bedroom, two-and-a-half-bathroom home sold for under $170,000. Currently, each of the three homes is valued at almost $300,000.[14] On the corner of my block stood a house that was owned by a Black family who found themselves in a similar situation to the former owners of my home. The children who had lived there moved to Mississippi, the home was placed into foreclosure, and a developer purchased the property and built four three-story apartment buildings where the house once stood. Each building has one two-bedroom apartment per floor, each renting for over $2,000 per month. Depending on one's income bracket, this may seem affordable given today's inflated rents, but we should take into consideration that the average rent for a two-bedroom apartment in Woodlawn in 2010 was $1,020.[15] In 1997 the median income for the neighborhood was less than $14,000.[16] Currently the median household income in Woodlawn is $69,619.[17] This does not seem exorbitant, but the increase is significant given the fact that Woodlawn was once one of the poorest neighborhoods in Chicago in the 1990s.[18] Since I have been in Woodlawn, land has also been cleared across the alley from my house where another three-story condominium has been completed. Another open lot on my block was sold in 2018 for $95,000.[19] Since the time of purchase, a local developer has built a six-unit condominium building on the same parcel of land, completing construction in the spring of 2024. Each condominium unit is currently valued at $466,000.[20]

Many would consider what I've described to be a "normal" situation, where the day-to-day moves of financialized capital manifest themselves through real estate. In response, I offer that nothing about this situation should be normalized once you consider the realities of race, class, city, and neighborhood. Contrasting traditional rules of capitalism that note only the goals of profit and growth, the human element of displacement in Woodlawn cannot be ignored. Where those who have access to capital are able to maintain and increase that access, there are also thousands of Black residents in Woodlawn who have been permanently displaced from their neighborhood, simply because they can no longer afford to live there. Recognizing my own participation in this process by way of the purchase of my house, the harsh reality is that is nearly impossible to escape the reign of late-stage, racialized capitalism. The "rules" of the market (buy low, sell high, accumulate assets and sell when their value increases) deeply advantage the developer and quickly dispose of residents who do not have access to capital. Woodlawn pushes us to take a page from Critical Race Spatial Analysis and consider the power of "race-based ideologies and other ideologies of power to produce the highly textured, power-laden aspects of space."[21] I use the example of my block and the home I live in to understand the texture and layers of accumulation by dispossession in an epicenter of uneven development.

Deepening the conundrum is the contradiction that my presence in the community stands in contrast to what I actively fight against (gentrification). Unfortunately, my commitments to justice-centered efforts in my neighborhood and throughout the city do not exclude me from being included in the category of the "haves" (homeowners) in a situation where the "have nots" (Black working-class/poor residents who are primarily renters) are moved further into the margins. There are hundreds of geographic blocks in Woodlawn that are experiencing similar shifts as mine. It is not difficult to envision on all of them an extremely difficult experience for Black residents who have been marginalized and isolated. For those who were not able to purchase homes or afford rents, displacement became inevitable. For those who remain, it has become increasingly stressful, as they are subject to the unsustainability of rising rents, exorbitant home prices, and increasing property taxes.

The Struggle for Quality Education in Woodlawn

From the early years of Black residents moving to Woodlawn in the 1950s, schools have been contested spaces. By 1960, when the neighborhood had shifted from 86 percent white to 90 percent Black, the city focused its educational attention elsewhere.[22] Given the rapid influx of Black students to the neighborhood, many of the schools found themselves overcrowded and without resources. Woodlawn, a small community area that covers a little over a square mile, had expanded to over seventy thousand residents.[23] As Chicago Public Schools superintendent Benjamin Willis sought to prevent white flight from the South and West Sides by stalling attempts at integration, students and community members in Woodlawn were subject to state-sanctioned violence and marginalization. Because Black residents began to organize themselves early in their arrival to Woodlawn, they were well versed on how they were viewed by U of C, along with its plans to encroach on the community.

    One of the ways residents organized themselves was through the Woodlawn Organization (TWO). Documented extensively by historian Elizabeth Todd-Breland, TWO united community residents and advocated for community control of education. Under the leadership of pastor Arthur Brazier, TWO exposed the politics of integration as deficit-oriented and unrealistic. Much of the popular desegregation rhetoric and research in the mid to late 1960s stated that Black children could

not achieve educational success without the presence of white students.[24] Brazier, along with the like-minded educator Barbara Sizemore,
rejected this claim. Collectively, they agreed that "the power to improve
Black educational achievement already existed within Black communities in the collective energies of community members, administrators,
teachers, parents and students who believed that Black students could
succeed academically in predominantly Black schools in Black communities."[25] Together, these shared beliefs became the Woodlawn Experimental Schools Project (WESP).

WESP is important to understanding twenty-first-century school
closures and engineered conflict in Woodlawn, as it represents an organizational shift from community control to neoliberal school "choice."
Where community control promotes the belief in the collective efficacy
of community members to self-determine, neoliberalism plays on the
desperation of families that have been denied access to quality education. Both TWO and the University of Chicago are central in facilitat-
ing the shift in Woodlawn. Where WESP originally positioned itself
as an unapologetic advocate for Black children, it was also paired with
TWO's desire to participate in American democracy by way of economic empowerment and political participation.[26] Taking their initial
strategy from non-conformist Black-power organizations, WESP and
TWO supported Black self-determination and self-reliance, but only
to the extent that it would allow for access to the resources of the mainstream. While some Black-power organizations advocated for minimal
support from the state, TWO and WESP made it a priority to seek positions by which to influence the state to achieve their stated goals.

By the time WESP ended in the early 1970s, TWO had shifted its
interests to economic development, particularly in the business sector
and housing, through offshoots of TWO that became the Woodlawn
Community Development Corporation, the Woodlawn Preservation and
Investment Corporation, and the Fund for Community Redevelopment

and Revitalization. Brazier's combination of religion, housing, and business is still visible in the community through these entities.[27] This becomes important in understanding closings, as TWO and U of C have maintained an antagonistic relationship regarding land and schools. Despite the tensions, they have become contentious partners during the development of the Obama Presidential Center, maintaining the facade and aspiration of a thriving neighborhood that is "mixed" both racially and ethnically. To the contrary, as poor Black residents continue to be pushed out, their displacement and the depopulation of certain sections of the neighborhood continue to be rationalized by TWO and U of C as "the problem." Discussed specifically in the next section, the same rationale has been used with schools in the neighborhood.

Setting the Stage: "School Choice" as the Precursor to School Closure in Woodlawn

The Small Schools Initiative (SSI) represented an interruption to the strife between TWO and U of C in the late 1990s and early 2000s, but closure remained a central theme throughout the neighborhood. In Woodlawn, SSI supported the creation of the Woodlawn Community School in 1996.[28] The school originally operated inside the Wadsworth Elementary School building, as a "school within a school," but by 2003, it had its own building on Sixty-Seventh Street, occupying the former location of the Nikola Tesla Alternative School for Pregnant Girls. The small-schools movement was short lived in Woodlawn, and only pro-duced the one school, but it came at a time when the precursors of school closure and gentrification were beginning to reveal themselves. By the late 1990s, the rhetoric of "choice" and "community control" had been usurped by the charter school movement.

In 2006, the University of Chicago Charter Schools (UCCS) pitched itself to residents of Woodlawn as a viable education option for potential students from the community. As UCCS sought to expand its network to Woodlawn (they were already operating in the Bronzeville area to the north), there was pressure from community members to make sure the school would be for students who lived close to the school. Given the historical contentious relationship between U of C and the community, UCCS quickly acquiesced to the community's demand for quality education. The newly minted U of C Woodlawn High School (UCWHS) positioned itself as a college preparatory high school for grades seven to twelve. This was attractive to a certain set of community members, as college prep was not the central focus of Hyde Park High School, which historically served Woodlawn students. Once the tension was settled around the new school's attendance boundaries, UCWHS began its occupation of the Wadsworth building in the fall of 2006.* Because Wadsworth was underpopulated at the time (the building had space for 1,500 students but had less than 350), the argument was made that there was enough room for the new group of students to co-exist.[29] Already using a school-within-a-school concept when Woodlawn Community School used to be in the building, the school was prepped for co-location. By 2013, UCWHS had taken over the entire building, while Wadsworth students were displaced to the former Alexandre Dumas School building a few blocks away.[30]

Woodlawn residents were placed in a common predicament for Black families throughout the country, where their desperation for quality education was exploited. Because the educational options for families often come by way of disinvested schools, many families are willing to consider the pitch of charter school networks. Their approach

---

* Charter schools traditionally have citywide admissions, meaning that students in any part of the city can attend a charter school of their "choice." Charters use a lottery system for admissions. The UCCS Wadsworth campus was unique in that community members were able to negotiate an attendance boundary that solely included Woodlawn.

usually operates on the rationale that families have experienced decades of ineffective education. If this is the reality, the charter school network steps in and offers families a "choice" as part of a last-ditch effort to get them to enroll their children. The Woodlawn of the early 2000s was in this situation, as many of the public schools in the neighborhood were under-resourced and disinvested. UCCS keyed in on the desperation of families and gave them the familiar charter school pitch that what UCCS were offering couldn't be worse than what they already had. Once again, where this may look to be true on the surface, there is no collective data set demonstrating that charter schools outperform neighborhood public schools. Unfortunately, this set of events, coupled with depopulation, neoliberal housing policy, and policing strategies ushered a calamity of school closings, renamed buildings, and shifted students. Heightening existing conflicts throughout Woodlawn, a significant portion of poor and working-class Black families were shuffled throughout the neighborhood by way of educational and housing realities.

A Subtle Start:
Uncontested Renaming and Closings

School closings and renaming in Woodlawn started with little fanfare in the early 2000s, when the Tesla School for Pregnant Girls was closed and taken over by the Woodlawn Community School in 2003. Because Woodlawn Community School had been operating in the Wadsworth building years before Tesla's closure, the takeover of the building was not met with community opposition. Similarly, there was community support when a corrective measure was taken in 2006 to rename James McCosh Elementary School to Emmett Till Math and Science Academy, in honor of slain Chicago teen Emmett Louis Till, who had been a student at McCosh Elementary before his untimely death by lynching in Money, Mississippi, in 1955. Originally named after the

eleventh president of Princeton University, the move to rename the
school came by way of a community-driven effort.[31] In the years before
the renaming, McCosh had a robust student population of over 1,300
students. The building was overcrowded to the point that an extension was built in the 1960s that would soon house the primary grades,
holding the original building, built in 1896, for the upper grades.[32] By
the late 1980s the extension had closed, but McCosh held steady with
a student population of over 1,000. This is a drastic difference from
the current moment: The student population at Till in 2024 was 335.[33]
Discussed in later sections of this chapter, depopulation is a central
driver when considering the violent shift in school closings throughout the neighborhood. It is key in understanding engineered conflict
as long-standing communities are placed under triage and constantly
subjected to the will of the state.

Wadsworth and Dumas: Shuffling Names, People, and Emotions

One of the first noticeable signs of triage was the closing of Dumas and
the shuffle of Wadsworth Elementary. While some school administrators and district officials hold the idea that young people are inherently
resilient to traumatic experiences, students in fact experience great
emotional strain from school closings. The city ignored the concerns
of Woodlawn residents and took a neoliberal approach to the closures,
assuming they would not have significant impact. CPS's thinking was
that, in an area with such a small geographic footprint, young people
walking a few blocks would have no significant impact on their educational experiences. Missing from this analysis, however, is the fact
that there are numerous spatial boundaries *within* a neighborhood. No
matter how small the area, if these boundaries are not taken into consideration when schools are closed, there is a great chance that conflict

will arise. Given CPS's intentional ignorance, school closings in Wood-lawn were disorienting and confusing. When all was said and done, the result clearly stands as a testament to who is valued and who is considered disposable in a gentrifying community.

It is difficult to imagine the level of upheaval that young people had to deal with as schools shifted and closed throughout Woodlawn and the ground was being pulled from under their feet. For long-term residents, these shifts over time can play tricks on the mind. When the school building you know under one name now exists with another, the identity of the original building is discarded. I can only imagine Woodlawn residents' struggle with what Eve Ewing called "institutional mourning," as a series of "devastating event(s) that leave an indelible emotional aftermath" occurred.[34] For those who are able to remain in the neighborhood, the closing and renaming of schools plays a malicious game on one's memory. The layers become even more confounding for families with school-aged children, who are forced to choose the school that is the least devastated.

One of the most contested school spaces in the neighborhood is James Wadsworth Elementary School. Originally named after a Union Army general who was killed during the Civil War, the school has been in numerous stages of flux since its completion in 1926.[35] When the neighborhood shifted to a primarily Black population by the 1960s, the school maintained a predominantly white teaching staff. This was soon interrupted by the efforts of TWO through WESP. Recent developments in the Wadsworth building include closure, co-location, relocation, and renaming. These developments began a series of closings and shifts in the neighborhood that are directly connected to the city's interpretations of depopulation and underutilization.

One of the primary reasons that the Woodlawn Community School was housed in the Wadsworth building was the size of the building, with a capacity for almost 1,200 students. After Woodlawn Community School moved to its own building in 2003, UChicago Charter moved into the Wadsworth building in 2006. Wadsworth, still the neighborhood public school, continued to share the building. By 2013, UChicago Charter Wadsworth Campus argued they had outgrown the space they were occupying and needed more classrooms to accommodate students. Less than five blocks away, Alexandre Dumas Elementary, which had just received a magnet technology designation in 2008, was closed as part of the 2013 CPS closures, under the rationale that it was "underutilized."[36] Wadsworth was the higher-performing school, while Dumas was the building with the best physical plant. Wadsworth staff and students were moved into the Dumas building, which was given the name Wadsworth STEM Elementary School, leaving Dumas teachers in a precarious situation. The science and technology title stayed with the building along with the Dumas students who chose to remain. The staff situation was different as the front office staff of Wadsworth replaced Dumas staff. Teachers and staff at Dumas either had to leave or apply for new openings at the "new" relocated Wadsworth.[37] As an outside observer, I tried to imagine what this would mean to a family that got the news of the closure in the mail. Some parents and families attended the hearings held by CPS on the Dumas closure in April, but there were other families that were unable to go.

The announcement for the closure came late in the school year, in June, making it difficult to plan for the start of the following school year. The neoliberal rationale for this move by CPS purported that there was no problem with the move because the school buildings were only four blocks apart. However, student mobility rates (the number of times students transfer schools over a given period of time) deeply impact student performance, and there is also the problem of tensions between students who may be from different parts of the neighborhood. In many instances, this is wrongly interpreted solely as tensions between "gangs."

In reality, these tensions are fueled by layers of long-term segregation, coupled with historical tensions that easily manifest themselves in schools. CPS tried to address the shift through various means (restorative justice circles, trust-building activities between new and current students in the building, "office hours" for families with questions regarding the closures, discretionary funds to address student needs, etc.), but these did not last beyond the 2013–2014 school year.[38]

UChicago Charter Schools fully moved into the Wadsworth building, but you could get a sense that the location was temporary. Even though the land in front of the building was redeveloped, there was little investment into the physical plant of the Wadsworth school building. For the entire time that UChicago Charter Wadsworth Campus occupied the building, between 2006 and 2017, there was always the sense that they were preparing for something else. When plans were finally revealed to move, officials from UChicago Charter School explained them by stating that there were too many repairs needed in a building that was almost one hundred years old.[39] By January 2018, the new U of C Woodlawn High School (UCWHS) building was completed, at the cost of $27.5 million. Currently the UCWHS stands as the only K–12 school building in Woodlawn, populated at over 50 percent of its capacity.[40] The original Wadsworth building lay vacant from 2013 to 2023, until it was converted to a temporary shelter for migrants from South America (primarily from Venezuela).[41]

Most importantly, the shifts to Wadsworth occurred in concert with changes in housing and law enforcement strategies throughout the city. Ren 2010 was rolled out by CPS in 2004, shortly following the beginning of CHA's Plan for Transformation. Charter schools were placed in the mix of CPS policy on reinvigorating schools throughout the city. As community members brokered for a specific attendance boundary solely for Woodlawn residents, their request paralleled significant shifts in Chicago's attempt to establish itself as a global city.

When high-rise public housing became the target of the Plan for Transformation in 1999, it was coupled with a beautification effort across the city, focusing on public parks. Wadsworth was targeted in this effort, with abandoned houses cleared to make greenspace.[42] This became the Wadsworth Campus Park, a collaboration between CPS, the Chicago Park District, and the Public Building Commission of Chicago.[43] Similar to CHA's plan for public housing, the dedication of Wadsworth Campus Park is an important marker of time and space, in that it sits in the epicenter of uneven development (gentrification) in the neighborhood, in the area that is experiencing the most drastic changes in rent pricing, property taxes, and home purchases. It is also close to the Obama Presidential Center and the proposed golf course.

Sexton, Fiske, and the Invisible Boundary of Cottage Grove

Northwest of Wadsworth and Dumas, Austin O. Sexton Elementary presents another story of closure as another large school building experiencing depopulation. Discussed in chapter 1, the spatial relationship between Sexton and its neighbor three blocks to the east, John Fiske Elementary, placed the two school communities in danger of perpetual conflict. Just as the combining of Wadsworth and Dumas perplexed many families, the closing of the Fiske building and its relocation to Sexton bordered on the ridiculous. Yet again the neoliberal rationale, that problems would be minimized because the two schools were only three blocks away from each other, was tragically incorrect. Throughout the closings in Woodlawn, CPS did not consider historical boundaries across space and class. Despite community concerns around the merger, CPS moved forward with its decision, rooted in the rationales of utilization and student performance. Missing was the analysis that the depopulation of both schools was due to a long struggle for housing in a neighborhood that was targeted for redevelopment by the city and the University of Chicago. In addition to the struggle for housing, school closings dispossessed community members of stability and safety. Though community members expressed that Sexton was beginning to turn the corner in terms of its performance due to the efforts of their new principal, it would still be closed due to its inability to improve performance metrics under the CPS rubric for improvement.[44]

The central spatial boundary between the two schools is Cottage Grove Ave., with Fiske on its east side and Sexton on its west, its northern corner facing Washington Park. One of the oldest streets on Chicago's South Side, Cottage Grove also serves as the boundary between East and West Woodlawn. This has significance due to the "new" amenities of the university and the neighborhood, as the east is favored for its proximity to Lake Michigan and the major street DuSable Lake Shore Drive, which provides direct access to downtown. To the east of Cottage Grove, the Fiske building is practically on the campus of U of C, less than half a block away from two university buildings, including the headquarters for the University of Chicago police. Historically, the corner of Sixty-First Street and Cottage Grove geographically represents the hard start of the U of C campus. Once standing as an explicit boundary between Woodlawn residents and the university, the presence of U of C has now extended into the area south of Sixty-First Street.

The closings are related to Woodlawn's housing problems too, as the Sexton and Fiske buildings were both in proximity to the affordable housing units then known as Woodlawn Gardens, the name of which was changed to Grove Parc Plaza in 1987. Its buildings straddled Cottage Grove, with some on both the east and west sides, stretching from Sixtieth to Sixty-Third Street. The majority of students that attended Sexton lived in Grove Parc Plaza, whereas the majority of Fiske students lived in apartments or single-family homes in east Woodlawn. Over the years, the reputations of both schools began to reflect a class divide, though they were only three blocks away from each other. Adding to the divide was the performance metrics of both schools, with Fiske designated as the "higher-performing" elementary school. Irrespective of the fact that both buildings were significantly depopulated, Sexton's building was also in better physical condition than Fiske. Because of the physical plant of Sexton, the school was designated as the receiving site for Fiske students. This was extremely disheartening as Sexton had just received a new principal in the 2012–2013 school year who had started to make significant strides at the school.[45] Returning to the neoliberal rationale that there wouldn't be problems in a school transfer with schools less than three blocks away from each other, CPS made another drastic mistake.

Once again, one building was physically shuttered (Fiske), while the neighboring school was closed (Sexton) and officially given the staff, students, and name of the school from the "higher-performing" shuttered building. Sexton teachers could reapply for positions at the "new" Fiske, but much of a school's culture is lost when its administration and staff is terminated when a school is closed. Sexton students were asked to suffer through the mourning of their upward-trending school while staying in the same building with a new name, new students, and new staff.

To their credit, many of the school principals in Woodlawn schools, including those of Fiske and Sexton, understood community tensions and made use of the resources provided by CPS for welcoming schools in the first year.* At the newly named Fiske, principals reported fighting between students, in addition to Sexton students and families being treated harshly by Fiske staff. Given the perceived class divide, much of

* Schools that took students from closed schools were given the name of *welcoming* or *receiver* schools. Depending on the neighborhood, tensions could be high in welcoming schools, especially if they did not receive the resources to authentically welcome students into the building.

the initial strife was blamed on students from Sexton (the lower-performing school).[46] With the resources provided by CPS, they had some success in calming some issues. The real issue, however, was that few of those resources lasted beyond the first year. There was programming at the newly renamed Fiske, but there was a strangeness to it. Students of the former Sexton were positioned as the "strangers" in the same land. Along with the new set of students, they were being "welcomed" into a building they had already been in. The situation is complex, and it also pushes us to come to grips with the fact that even the receiving school is positioned precariously if it is also significantly depopulated. Eve Ewing's point is salient, in that,

> We should understand that all of these schools exist within an ecological matrix that created barriers to them optimally functioning as sites of excellent instruction. Though their challenges may differ, these schools are all struggling under the weight of closures—past closures, threatened closure, nearby closures, actual closures, responding to closures— and the possibility that they might very soon be on the proverbial chopping block once again.[47]

If we consider the closings, renaming, and depopulation of schools in Woodlawn collectively, it is impossible to look away from another potential problem. As the community gentrifies, there is also the issue that there will be fewer school-aged children in Woodlawn for a considerable time. In line with engineered conflict, a worst-case scenario in which these trends continue has the potential to create another round of closures.

MAP OF WOODLAWN SCHOOLS AND CLOSURES

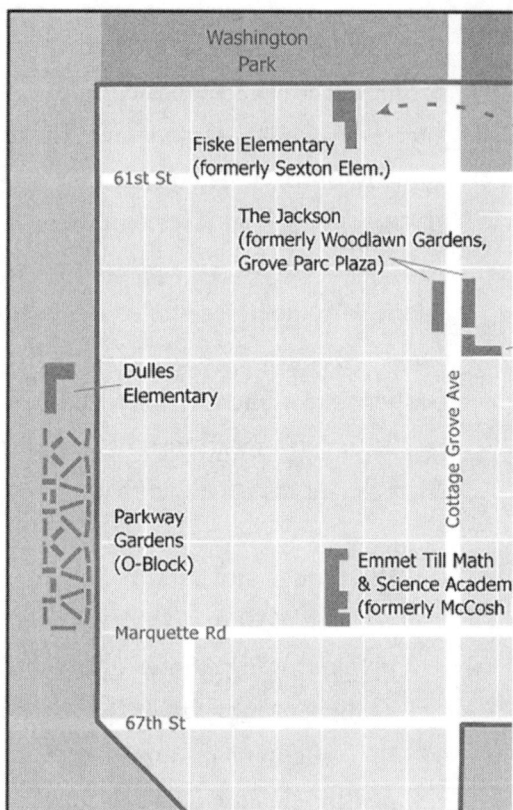

Washington Park

Fiske Elementary
(formerly Sexton Elem.)

61st St

The Jackson
(formerly Woodlawn Gardens,
Grove Parc Plaza)

Dulles
Elementary

Cottage Grove Ave

Parkway
Gardens
(O-Block)

Emmet Till Math
& Science Academ
(formerly McCosh

Marquette Rd

67th St

TABLE 3 CURRENT WOODLAWN SCHOOLS

Name of School
Emmett Louis Till Math and Science Academy (formerly James McCosh Elementary School)
James Wadsworth STEM Academy (formerly Alexandre Dumas Math and Science Academy)
Woodlawn Community Elementary School (formerly Nikolas TeslaSchool for Pregnant Girls)
John Fiske Elementary (formerly Austin O. Sexton Elementary)
Hyde Park Academy High School
U of C Woodlawn High School (charter)
Andrew Carnegie Elementary School
John Foster Dulles Elementary School

The current population data is from cps.edu. Capacity data is from the Quest Center of

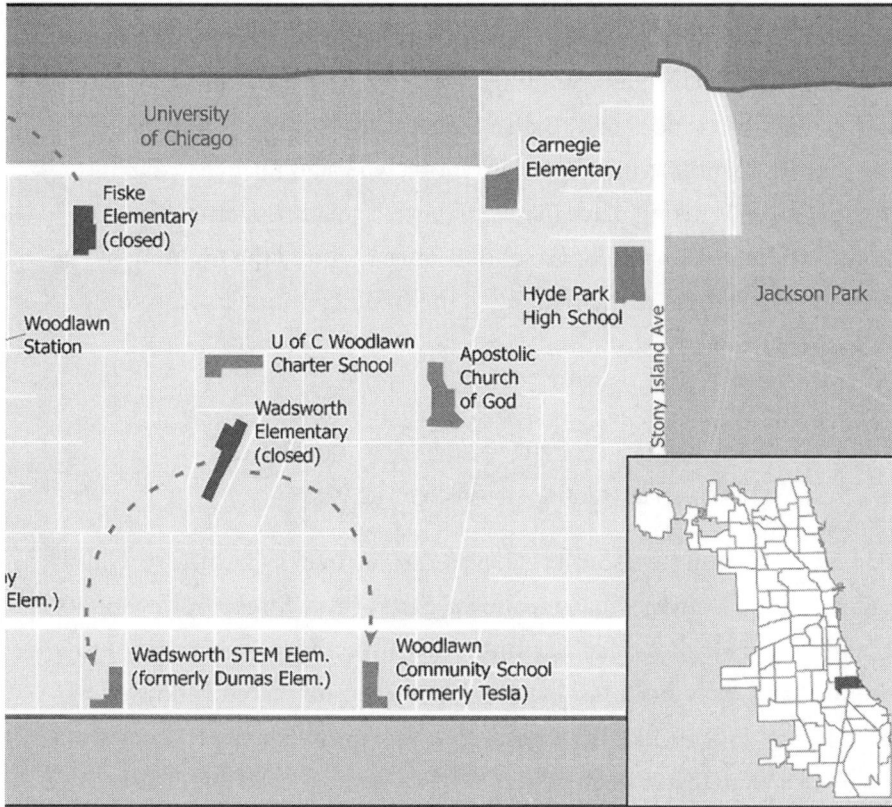

Percent Black	Current Student Enrollment (2023–24 school year)	Estimated Building Capacity (in students)
86.3	335	1,800
90.4	449	1,200
96.8	154	420
92.6	366	1,200
96.8	867	1,800
99.2	625	650
95.8	361	900
94.5	655	700

the Chicago Teachers Union.

If we consider the table above, we see that there are only two schools at over 50 percent of their buildings' capacity. Ironically, one of these two (UChicago Woodlawn) is also the newest. In contrast to some of the schools identified in chapter 1, Woodlawn's significance is that its depopulation is taking place in an area with a small geographic footprint. Where some Woodlawn schools once required the building of additions to address overcrowding, if the trend continues, some could face further consolidation.*

Housing: A Perpetually Contested Struggle in Woodlawn

For me as a young person, the elevated train tracks (known to Chicagoans as "L" tracks) that ran down Sixty-Third Street from Stony Island to one block west of Martin Luther King Drive (King Drive) to Stony Island were both fascinating and eerie. The rusted yellow support beams looked like the opening to a magical labyrinth. Because the tracks were lower than most, they blocked out the sun, making it dark underneath them no matter what time of the day it was. The area was even darker when the dim lighting that ran under the tracks wasn't working. In the seventies and eighties, sometimes I would stay with my aunt Julia and uncle Clarence, who lived around the corner, in the Parkway Gardens housing development on King Drive. I would always be excited to walk to the train station or grocery store on Sixty-Third Street with Aunt Julia. I would find myself excited by the activity at the intersection of Sixty-Third and King Drive. On the northeast corner of the intersection was Harold's Chicken Shack #1, a Chicago-based franchise of restaurants that served made-to-order chicken and fish that I

---

* Wadsworth, McCosh (currently Till Math and Science Academy), Carnegie, and Hyde Park Academy High School all had additions built to accommodate overcrowding at different times beginning in the late 1960s.

still love today. For South Siders in Chicago, you would be associated with the Harold's you were closest to. The one in my neighborhood was Harold's Chicken Shack #14, on Eighty-Eighth and Stony Island, but I still enjoyed either a half-dark or six wings with extra mild sauce from Shack #1.

What I did not know as a young person was that the intersection of Sixty-Third and King Drive was the dividing line between the neighborhoods of Woodlawn, Washington Park, and Greater Grand Crossing. Parkway Gardens, a cooperative development that was shifted to a collective of rental units under HUD's Section 236 Interest Reduction Program, had been given the name "O-Block," and became one of the more dangerous areas in the city in relationship to shootings and homicides.* O-Block is on the Greater Grand Crossing side of the boundary, while Washington Park is directly to the north of Sixty-Third Street. Given its proximity to the neighborhood, O-Block is often considered to be part of Woodlawn. At a similar intersection exactly one mile east, on Sixty-Third and Cottage Grove Avenue, used to be the development known as Woodlawn Gardens. Later renamed Grove Parc Plaza Apartments, it was a self-contained 502-unit development that I mistakenly thought was public housing as a young person.

Because *project* carries such a negative connotation, little did I know that neither Woodlawn Gardens nor Parkway Gardens were creations of the Chicago Housing Authority (CHA). Woodlawn Gardens was in

---

* *O-Block* was given the name after twenty-year-old Odee Perry was killed by a member of a rival set, Gakirah Barnes, who was also killed soon after Perry. See Frank Main, "'O Block': The Most Dangerous Block in Chicago, Once Home to Michelle Obama," *Chicago Sun-Times,* November 2, 2014, https://chicago. suntimes.com/2014/11/2/18458059/o-block-most-dangerous-block-in-chicago-michelle-obama-chief-keef-parkway-gardens-south-king-drive. It was taken over by HUD in the 1970s and sold to a series of management firms, the most recent being Related Midwest Realty. See "Parkway Gardens," Related, https://www. relatedmidwest.com/our-company/properties/parkway-gardens.

fact a collaboration "project" between the Department of Housing and Urban Development (HUD) and TWO that had at one time stood as an attempt of a community organization to create a project of self-determination.[48] By the time it had been renamed to Grove Parc Plaza, the complex, along with certain sections of Woodlawn, was depopulated and in disrepair.

Woodlawn's population decline had begun in the mid-1960s. As TWO was able to halt the majority of land clearance during the city's attempt to engage in the federal program of urban renewal, many of the businesses that once stood on Sixty-Third Street were slowly abandoned, as opposed to being shuttered rapidly. A number of buildings on Sixty-Third were then burned down in the rebellion following Dr. Martin Luther King Jr.'s assassination in 1968. This was soon to be followed by a series of arsons for insurance money, which lasted until the early 1970s.[49] This left large swaths of vacant land on Sixty-Third Street. Because the areas under the "L" tracks were so dimly lit, many traditional, large street organizations and others in the underground economy conducted business on certain pockets of Sixty-Third Street, including drug sales, street-based sex work, and number running. Originally called "Baby Skid Row," similar activities continued throughout the neighborhood well into the 1970s, '80s, '90s, and early 2000s.[50] Years later, in 1997, a segment of the "L" tracks that stretched from Drexel Avenue to Stony Island was torn down, as certain members of the community found them to be an eyesore and a deterrent for businesses.[51] Soon after this section of the "L" tracks was demolished, two blocks of traditional Chicago greystone buildings, along with six other blocks of apartment complexes and traditional two-flat buildings, were demolished in the eastern corridor in Woodlawn and replaced with homes that started at $199,000.[52] Although one-fifth of the housing stock was preserved for "affordable housing," the construction of the new homes set the stage for uneven development in the area.[53]

By the late 1990s, a significant portion of Woodlawn residents did not have access to living-wage employment. As many residents with means began to move out of the neighborhood, those with the least in Woodlawn could not afford to move. In the next decade, during the financial crisis of 2008, Woodlawn's foreclosure filing rate was eight per one hundred residential parcels, three times higher than the city average.[54] From its peak population in 1960 of just over 81,000 residents, by 2018 Woodlawn's population had dwindled to 25,000.[55] By 2019, the neighborhood had over one thousand vacant lots, with almost half of the vacant property owned by the city, making it prime space for developers.[56] Many of the schools were able to retain much of their student populations until the mid-2000s, but student numbers began to dwindle shortly after. As it was in the early struggles for quality education, TWO was in the eye of the storm.

Since its beginnings as a direct-action community organization, it is safe to say that the six-plus-decade-long existence of TWO has been complicated. When the neighborhood was a space where the oppression of poor Black residents was explicit and abject, TWO stood as a tangible example of economic community self-reliance. Its training by U of C criminologist–turned–community organizer Saul Alinsky provided deep instruction on the practice of focusing on issues that were "winnable." As Bishop Brazier, E. Duke McNeil, and Leon Finney took these instructions to heart, it became the long-term strategy of their organization. From early "wins" in halting land clearance and securing housing, TWO had become a formidable force in Woodlawn by the mid- to late 1960s. In addition to its housing initiatives, by the early seventies TWO had built a grocery store, gas station, and movie theater, and created a security service on Cottage Grove Avenue.[57] Already involved in education through the WESP, TWO also secured federal dollars through the Model Cities Program to develop infrastructure and to work with members of street organizations (specifically the

Blackstone Rangers) on job-readiness programs.[58] Serving in the capacity of community spokesperson, TWO was also able to hold off displacement by way of land clearance through deals negotiated with U of C, the City of Chicago, and HUD. In the days of "urban renewal," TWO was able to resist the state's effort to displace Woodlawn residents by securing resources to address community needs. Before its days of infamy, the creation of Woodlawn Gardens stood as an innovation in community-controlled housing. Never under the authority of CHA, Woodlawn Gardens was the result of a negotiated parcel of land between TWO, U of C, and the City of Chicago.[59] As the university was trying to clear land to build a set of dormitories, TWO was able to negotiate a deal where the university promised not to expand its development south of Sixty-First Street.[60] It was an important move, as the land between Sixty-First and Sixty-Third on both sides of Cottage Grove would be secured for the Woodlawn Gardens development.

Although the process of securing land and beginning construction on the development took almost three years (1966–1969), the development stood as a testament to Black economic development, as the buildings were primarily built by Black laborers, who had difficulty joining trade unions. In addition to the brickmasonry, TWO secured a contract with a Black electrical company, making sure that services were not outsourced.[61] The self-determination of TWO stood as a feat of epic proportions in the late 1960s and a beacon for the neighborhood. At the same time, there were a host of issues from the outset of the development of the housing complex. TWO wanted to make Woodlawn Gardens a mixed-income development, with part of the development operating as subsidized public housing. Because they had secured a grant from HUD, however, TWO would need the approval of HUD and CHA along with the federal government to make this possible. At the same time as TWO was attempting to secure low-cost public housing for Woodlawn residents, CHA was in a court battle on disparate impact and neglect. Because CHA was found to be in neglect of its tenants, it was not allowed to partner with TWO in its attempt to create affordable housing.[62] This dealt a heavy blow to TWO, because it could not provide for the neighborhood's most vulnerable residents without CHA's assistance. Instead, TWO became the sole landlord for Woodlawn Gardens, soon to have the responsibility for evicting tenants who were delinquent on rent. This problem has become a recurring one in Woodlawn, as its poorest residents are still the last to get what they need and deserve.

Mismanagement at Woodlawn Gardens became a theme for the next three decades. The golden years of the development were short-lived, as three years after its opening in 1969 TWO was unable to pay the mortgage. As financial troubles deepened, evictions, vacancies, and revenue issues sunk the complex $15 million into debt, ending in a bankruptcy filing by the mid-1980s.[63] Before a HUD takeover of the complex in 1986, TWO was charged with gross mismanagement of funds after Leon Finney (then executive director) diverted $818,000 to other TWO projects. During the HUD takeover, U of C and other community officials made a push to renovate the property, creating the Woodlawn Preservation and Investment Corporation (WPIC). Under WPIC, the name of the complex was changed to Grove Parc Plaza Apartments. Twenty years later, due to inattention and other forms of neglect, HUD took over the property for a second time in 2006.[64] By this time, evictions, vacancies, and disrepair had made the complex a magnet for illicit drug sales and activity from large street organizations. The situation had deteriorated to the point that HUD proposed to demolish the complex and give residents housing vouchers to use in other parts of the city.

Luckily, Grove Parc tenants didn't take this lying down and began to organize themselves to resist displacement. At the same time, Boston-based developer Preservation of Affordable Housing (POAH) saw an opportunity in Grove Parc Plaza. Because developers prioritize developments that are close to train stations, Grove Parc's location under the Green Line was considered prime.[*] Directed by Chicago Area Vice President Bill Eager, POAH negotiated with the Grove Parc Tenants Association to ensure that residents would not be displaced. To get the plan in motion, POAH secured a $30.5 million grant from HUD's Federal Choice Neighborhoods program.[65] By 2012, Grove Parc Plaza had been demolished. In its place now is the Woodlawn Park development, which includes Woodlawn Station, the Jackson at Woodlawn Park, the Grant at Woodlawn Park, the Burnham at Woodlawn Park, and Trianon Lofts. Where Grove Parc Plaza residents were given priority in the new development, some took housing vouchers to rent apartments in other parts of the city. If it were not for the strength of the tenants organization, the new development might have displaced a greater number of former Grove Parc Place residents.[66] As is the trend in new development, Woodlawn Station has retail on the first floor and rental units above. The hope is that this will attract other businesses to lease property in the building. POAH has dug its feet into the development of Woodlawn, with twelve properties throughout the neighborhood. Now that Woodlawn Park is complete, its crown jewel development looks to be Woodlawn Social, a seventy-unit, mixed-income development that features affordable housing and market-rate townhomes.[67] Recently, Daley's Restaurant, the longest continuously running restaurant in Chicago, was convinced to move across the street into Woodlawn Station, creating a destination site. Gone is the beauty-supply store across the street, replaced by a

---

[*] The City of Chicago refers to this as "transit-oriented development." See Natalie Moore, "Chicago Awards Grants to Spur Development Near Transit in Disinvested Neighborhoods," WBEZ Chicago, November 23, 2021, https://www.wbez.org/race-class-communities/2021/11/24/chicago-funds-11-transit-oriented-development-projects.

health clinic. As these things are viewed as needed amenities for the neighborhood, the question remains: *Who is this for?*

When TWO shifted from direct-action organizing to economic development, it also distanced itself from the larger justice-centered movements of its day and began to focus hyper-locally on economic development in certain segments of Woodlawn. By the 1970s, TWO had advanced politically and materially, but did so by beginning to mimic the entities it had once fought against. Although it was successful in creating infrastructure for the organization and for some Woodlawn residents, there was still a considerable number of people who could not take advantage of the programs offered by TWO. Even when TWO used direct-action tactics in their early days, however, it was only to secure an audience with city officials who had access to power. It had always positioned itself in the pragmatic tradition of Alinsky organizing, with a focus on securing tangible "wins." Since then, its ability to establish gains in workforce employment, housing, and development through its subsidiaries (Woodlawn Community Development Corporation, Woodlawn Preservation and Investment Corporation) has created a windfall for outside entities, at the expense of the most vulnerable residents of Woodlawn, who were, as always, the first to be displaced. In the present, the poorest residents are still blamed for Woodlawn's ills.

Like many spaces, Woodlawn has been "rebranded" by developers, with "walkability scores" and language of the neighborhood "turning around." All of the language around thriving communities is still centered around middle-class aspirations. TWO no longer attempts to hold off the project of urban renewal as it had in its early days, but switched course once it gained access to the material resources needed to position itself as a landlord and developer. Over time, because transformative work is difficult, the concerns of low-income residents were replaced by the concerns of people who could enhance Woodlawn's economic viability as a lakefront community in a rapidly shifting city.

This continues in the formation of Bishop Brazier's son, Dr. Byron T. Brazier, with his organization One Woodlawn, which advocates for the economic development that will come with the Obama Presidential Center, apparently in the hopes of replacing the most vulnerable for the sake of a "thriving community."[68]

When Your Own Is Your Opposition—Dro City, O-Block, and Years of Splinter

The police presence on my block mentioned earlier in the chapter was part of a citywide initiative where select Black neighborhoods were used as training grounds for first-year officers in CPD.[69] In a moment where homicide rates were climbing throughout the city, elected officials felt pressure to address shootings in "high crime" areas (specifically sections of the South and West Sides of the city). In Woodlawn, CPD's tactic was to demonstrate physical presence throughout the neighborhood. Police sergeants would hold meetings with tactical teams in public, sometimes in the middle of a block, as a demonstration of police power. More than a response to the requests of long-time residents of Woodlawn, the show of visibility was mostly for new residents, as the city and developers were concerned with Woodlawn's prospects as an "untapped" South Side gem for homebuyers and businesses. CPD's directives included both containment and exclusion: In the early days of the tactic, the idea was to exclude the criminal element from the eastern corridor of the neighborhood and to contain it west of Cottage Grove. Since gentrification in the neighborhood has spread west of Cottage Grove, some of the tactics have shifted, but similar ones continue throughout the city as Black youth are either contained or excluded, particularly from areas frequented by tourists or affluent whites.*

---

* In the current moment this manifests itself in the form of curfews or heavy police presence in tourist zones to protect Chicago's image as a tourist destination.

CPD's strategies of containment and exclusion in Woodlawn were an alert for certain (read low-income and Black) residents that they were being watched and had been deemed disposable. Seeing the continued presence of police did not make me feel "safer." What I did not know was that I was on the "Dro City" side of a conflict between the fractured remnants of the large traditional street organizations that once ran the neighborhood. At the time, the small crews of "Dro City" were in conflict with a set of small factions that operated in the Parkway Gardens housing complex (currently known as "O-Block," formerly "WIIIC City"). The conflict in Woodlawn, like the conditions in other parts of Black Chicago, is rooted in the layered and complex story of the fracturing of street organizations beginning in the late 1980s, as well as the shifts that have taken place in Woodlawn over the last seventy years. Traditional street organizations were splintered, schools were closed, and public housing for low-income Black residents was demolished in nearby areas, increasing displacement of families into Woodlawn. This is especially important to Woodlawn, a foundational neighborhood to early formations of Black street organizations on the South Side that began as small groupings, collectivized for a period of time, and splintered again.

At the same time, it is impossible to ignore the violence attributed to street organizations in Woodlawn and in other parts of Black Chicago, particularly in the forms of shootings and homicides. Although violence is a constant in the activities of many street organizations, engineered conflict challenges us to consider the conditions that make it more likely to occur. Pulling from the introduction chapter, it is hard to live without conflict if your housing is insecure, educational options are irrelevant, and there is little access to living-wage employment or health care. Considering the structural violence experienced by the community of Woodlawn in the form of disinvestment

---

Millenium Park, Streeterville, and State Street are all areas that are populated with significant police presence.

and marginalization, it is not hard to understand violence as a human response to despair. I am not condoning violence. Instead, I offer a challenge for us to begin to understand it. If people are unable to see their way out of a worsening situation, the chance for violence increases. If we understand the forces that generate structural violence (school closings, lack of affordable housing, violence at the hands of the police, etc.) the solutions we propose are much less likely to include punitive strategies rooted in the criminal legal system. Because police and prisons do not curb violence, engineered conflict serves as a challenge to consider a different set of preemptive solutions.

Although Woodlawn was the birthplace of the Blackstone Rangers (Stones), their presence had waned there by the early 1970s. Woodlawn was reeling from the lack of education and employment opportunities for its young residents in the late 1960s, when, for a fleeting moment, TWO teamed with the Stones to create a job-readiness program for Black youth in the neighborhood. Stones soon took their efforts north to Bronzeville, however, and reinvented themselves as the El-Rukn Nation, so that Woodlawn no longer operated as their stronghold. This was partly due to East Side Disciples, who always had a presence in the neighborhood. Refusing to join the Stones' "Main 21," the East Side Disciples maintained an oppositional stance. Over time, a mutual respect developed, and the two groups held a short allegiance when the Stones secured federal dollars from a War on Poverty initiative.[70] The rise and departure of the Stones in Woodlawn also takes place during a time where neighborhood schools were severely overcrowded, and the poorest residents of the neighborhood were being victimized by slumlords due to lack of affordable housing. As young people bore the brunt of the neighborhood's disinvestment and depopulation, the situation in late-1960s Woodlawn was one where membership in street organizations could fulfill the need for belonging, protection, or both.

Even then, because opportunities to access adequate housing, quality education, and living employment were low, the chances for violence to escalate remained high. When the Stones had their Black Power moment under the leadership of Jeff Fort, they also remained active in underground economies, specifically the sale of codeine (syrup), extortion, and taxing other organizations for drug sales in Woodlawn. By the time I moved to the neighborhood in 2012, Woodlawn had experienced over four decades of structural violence in the form of marginalization and displacement. With the Stones gone from the neighborhood, the Black Gangster Disciple Nation (BGDN) was in its third decade of splintering as a substantial rift between groups that were once under the same flag.

Returning to the discussion in chapter 3, BGDN originally formed by way of a truce between the Donise "King David" Barksdale's Black Disciples (BDs) and Larry Hoover's Supreme Gangsters. Rank-and-file BD members begrudgingly abided by the orders of Barksdale to honor the truce, but there were some BDs who remembered earlier conflicts with the Supreme Gangsters. It became a significant source of tension after Barksdale's untimely death in 1974. When Hoover went to prison for murder in 1973, a series of agreements were made between BDs and Gangster Disciples (GDs) in prison, who were now under the leadership of Larry Hoover. BGDN was a merging of one-time rivals, but on the streets, a small faction of BDs did not honor Hoover's leadership. Before BGDN's attempt to go legit through the efforts of "Growth and Development" and 21st Century V.O.T.E. in the 1990s, Hoover had moved operations solidly into the underground economy, primarily in the drug trade. Amassing significant power and wealth from drug operations, Hoover and his associates were able to grow the organization into a multimillion-dollar operation by the late 1980s. Though Hoover maintained official control of BGDN while incarcerated, there were factions in local prisons and on the street that did not agree with Hoover's directives.[71] A section of the BDs had already splintered from the conglomerate a decade before BGDN leaders were indicted and convicted in Operation Headache between 1996 and 1998. Following the convictions, the split deepened further. Because there was a void in leadership on the street, conflicts were no longer settled by high-ranking members. Because GDs were sizably greater in number and resources, only members or people in some proximity to members knew the difference between GDs and BDs. Although both are commonly referred to as GDs, the split between the two factions is significant.

One of the events that sparked some of the tensions between BDs and GDs in Woodlawn was the demolition of Randolph Towers. Standing across the street from O-Block on the Washington Park side of Sixty-Third Street, the set of two sixteen-story CHA buildings had become synonymous with drug sales, particularly the sale of crack cocaine and heroin. From the mid 1980s to its demolition in 2007, one of the buildings was known as the "Castle" and run by BDs who had a connection to other BDs in the Robert Taylor Homes a mile to the northwest. When the Randolph Towers were demolished as part of CHA's Plan for Transformation, BD members were dispersed throughout O-Block and Woodlawn. There were smaller confrontations between BDs from O-Block and the Castle, and a more sizeable conflict with GDs who had set up their drug operations in Grove Parc Plaza (formerly Woodlawn Gardens). As Grove Parc Plaza stood as GD territory, O-Block stood as a BD enclave. Even though Grove Parc Plaza straddled the east and west sides of Cottage Grove, GDs were primarily in East Woodlawn, east of Cottage Grove. During this moment of conflict between GDs and BDs over drug markets, the neighborhood saw its share of violence.[72]

The demolition of the Castle in 2007 and the subsequent demolition of Grove Parc Plaza in 2012 dispersed residents affiliated with BDs or GDs throughout Woodlawn or outside of the community.

When the Castle was demolished in 2007, the jobless rate for Black men between the ages of twenty and twenty-four in Woodlawn was 42.4 percent.[73] By this time, ties to larger street organizations were considerably muted because the corporate structure of the drug trade in public housing was abruptly interrupted by harsh sentencing policies in the form of mandatory minimums and truth-in-sentencing laws. Beginning with large drug busts in the 1990s to Operation Headache at the end of the decade, the claim to BD or GD varied depending on geography. Some would claim connections to BD or GD, but few were connected to the literature and laws of the larger organizations. By this time, the large-scale GD and BD factions were fractured into sets like O-Block, 600, 300, Bar None Crazy (BNC), Saint Lawrence/E Block Territory (STL/EBT), Mac Creek, Sawblock, Snowblock, and Row Life. Some groups had smaller allegiances with each other (O-Block, 300, 600), while others were in deep conflict (O-Block and Dro City). The names of the cliques have their own origin stories, and they are also fluid, as members from one grouping can leave one and team up with another or start their own clique.

As young people living under these conditions began to make their own way, many of the initial conflicts were intense. Lyrics in the hip-hop genre of drill from the early 2010s often reflect, and amplify, conflict between certain crews. Chicago had been given the name Chiraq in reference to the bevy of murders that took place beginning in the late 2000s. Drill emcees like Chief Keef, King Louie, Lil Durk, G Herbo, and Bibby began to receive national visibility for their unfiltered tales of struggle, suffering and aggression.* The lyrics are often intense, but there are also moments where drill emcees reflect the pain of living under precarious conditions. In Woodlawn, BDs affiliated with O-Block were

---

* Although drill is known for its aggression, there are some songs that are reflective of the struggles of daily life. See Lil Durk's "Shootout @ My Crib," King Von's "When I Die," and King Louie's "Live and Die in Chicago."

deeply entrenched in conflict, as emcees either affiliated with O-Block (King Von, affiliated with a BD set in O-Block) or in opposition (FBG Duck, affiliated with a GD set in Dro City) were murdered in violent, public showings. These public demonstrations of violence are often to let the opposition ("the opps") understand the intensity of the conflict.* As the murders were sensationalized in songs and news reports, what went missing was the story of how this type of violence becomes normalized when options for housing, education, employment, and health care are scant. As the inheritors of engineered conflict, the young people who experience the violence are constantly assessing imminent danger in the forms of violence from the police, violence from another grouping of young people, and the violence of displacement.

Still in the Struggle

In the midst of the structural violence waged against its poor and working-class Black residents, Woodlawn remains a contested space. In this moment, there is a necessity to raise public consciousness on what the intersection of education, housing, and law enforcement

---

* Both Dayvon "King Von" Bennett and Carlton "FBG Duck" Weekly were violently murdered in public places. Bennett was shot after a fight outside of the Monaco Hookah Lounge in Atlanta on November 6, 2020. Weekly was shot sixteen times in front of the luxury retail store Dolce & Gabana in Chicago's Gold Coast Neighborhood on August 4, 2020. Bennett had a BD affiliation, and ties with O-Block. Weekly was from Dro City and affiliated with GDs, who were in conflict with O-Block. Weekly mocked an O-Block affiliate who had been violently killed. His murder was thought to be retaliation for his actions. See M. Rodriguez, "The Story of King Von: The War in Chiraq," *Medium*, October 20, 2021, https://medium.com/@mrodriguez0/the-story-of-king-von-57b7ff2c78fd; Tom Schuba, "$100K Bounty Was Placed on Killing Chicago Rapper FBG Duck, Informant Told Chicago Police," *Chicago Sun-Times*, January 27, 2023, https://chicago.suntimes.com/2023/1/27/23569891/fbg-duck-king-von-drill-rap-carlton-weekly-oblock-chicago-gangs-gang-violence-parkway-gardens.

means for its current long-term Black residents. In addition to Brazier's One Woodlawn, organizations like Blacks in Green (BIG), Southside Together Organizing for Power (STOP), and Woodlawn East Community and Neighbors (WECAN) have supported efforts to interrupt displacement, while attracting businesses to the area. Although the views on the presidential center are not completely aligned, all are centered in the belief that sustainable economic development is key in halting the structural violence of displacement. The issue, however, is that when "development" is welcomed to a community, it is often followed by an eventual turn to displacement. As Woodlawn witnesses its new day, the larger question is still, *Who from the old neighborhood is allowed to stay?* If the same efforts to halt uneven development are not maintained, Woodlawn could face a future akin to communities like Williamsburg in Brooklyn, Silver Lake in Los Angeles, U Street in Washington, DC, and Brixton in London. As those communities currently stand as shells of their former selves, the Blackness of Woodlawn can easily be reduced to a tourist destination.

It should be noted that movements do not reflect a perfect world where all who come to the table agree with each other's decisions. Nevertheless, the struggle and role of community coalitions in the improvement of the living conditions of the marginalized is critical. It is also a perpetual battle. For the swath of community residents still experiencing marginalization, a hard-fought struggle was able to halt complete upheaval in Woodlawn by way of a housing ordinance. Positioned as a compromise between the Obama Foundation, the City of Chicago, and the Obama Community Benefits Agreement Coalition (OCBAC), the Woodlawn Preservation Ordinance was approved in city council on September 9, 2020.[74] Because staff from the Obama Presidential Center would not guarantee a community benefits agreement, they agreed instead to sit down with a local elected official (twentieth ward Alderperson Jeanette Taylor) and the coalition to hash out a number of strategies to ensure that Woodlawn's eastern corridor would not completely succumb to the will of developers.[75] The resulting ordinance identifies a number of supports, including a requirement that housing placed on city-owned lots in Woodlawn make at least 30 percent of apartments affordable to low-income households, defined as households making less than 50 percent of the median income in Woodlawn (around $45,000 annually for a family of four).[76] It also includes a loan fund for rehabbing homes, a fund for low- and middle-income families to purchase homes and a guaranteed "right of refusal" for renters if a landlord decides to sell a property. This right of refusal provides renters the option to collectively purchase the property before it can be placed on the open market.[77] Though the policy language is strong and intentional on guarantees, the struggle to hold the city accountable will be long and onerous. Like the initial victories achieved by TWO with Woodlawn Gardens in its early years, it will be a continual fight to ensure the policies of the city are enforced in word and deed. The next chapter engages with formations of Chicagoans who have made the decision that, despite the challenges faced by those who are willing to resist, the call to protect and build with Black people is something that *must* be done.

CHAPTER 5

BLACK FUGITIVE FUTURES

THE STRUGGLE FOR ABOLITION IN A CONTESTED CITY

[Abolition] means understanding that the value of our lives is not set by the amount of time a person spends in a cage for hurting us, but by the ways in which we organize to keep us safe.

—Andrea Ritchie[1]

If we don't cling to what makes us stronger, I fear we'll succumb to what aims to break us apart.

—Ayana Contreras[2]

Radio personality, cultural critic, and DJ Ayana Contreras reminds us that no matter what Black people have faced in Chicago, they have always been able to build and create. Her book *Energy Never Dies* bears witness to what Black people have done to resist the realities of disinvestment, marginalization, and the carceral state. These acts of resistance are as subtle as they are significant, representing the sheer determination of Black people to be seen and accounted for.[*] As a Chicagoan, despite the troubles, I am reminded by a term like *Summertime Chi* of the intentions of Black people to demand and create joy in the face of disposability. It is a task that should be commended and understood as the key to any resistance to engineered conflict.

I am also encouraged and challenged by the concept of abolition. Where most may think of the concept as an anarchist call to destroy, I read abolition as the collective call to determine something to be unacceptable. From the recognition of what is insupportable, there is the responsibility to build something different. Police violence is unacceptable. School closings are unacceptable. Lack of affordable housing is unacceptable. Engineered conflict is unacceptable. In recognition of these facts, abolition is the process that centers the questions of Mariame Kaba and Kelly Hayes: "What should we do?" "What should we create?"[3]

With this concluding chapter, my goal is not to leave you stuck in a depression about the realities of life for working-class, low-income Black people on the South and West Sides of Chicago. Instead, it is to understand that violence is not inherent to Black people, but is the result of a series of policies, circumstances, and other determinations. Sitting with this reality also pushes us to wrestle with the fact that engineered conflict doesn't have to be permanent. In Chicago's long

---

[*] The term *Summertime Chi* refers to the festivals and cultural events that occur throughout the summer months in the city. Many of these events take place in historically Black neighborhoods and serve as communal gatherings.

and well-documented history of organizing and collective struggle, certain segments of Black people have never ceded to the will of the state. The uprisings after the tragic deaths of Trayvon Martin in Sanford, Florida; Michael Brown in Ferguson, Missouri; Breonna Taylor in Louisville, Kentucky; George Floyd in Minneapolis, Minnesota; and Laquan McDonald and Rekia Boyd in Chicago moved masses of people to rethink their relationship to policing and the carceral state. Locally, these organizing efforts have resulted in permanently getting CPD out of schools and the "Treatment Not Trauma" campaign to encourage mental health treatment instead of the trauma induced by the state-sanctioned violence.* Although these campaigns have targeted the state, they do not originate from reformist rhetoric. Instead, they come from a progressive movement in the city, largely led by Black abolitionists and other abolitionists of color. While some would consider these efforts to be "nonreformist reforms," in that they use the mechanisms of the state momentarily, the purpose of the measures is to remind people of the possibility of abolition. As an example, the state of Illinois has enacted the Pretrial Fairness Act, officially titled the "The Safety, Accountability, Fairness and Equity—Today Act" (the SAFE-T Act) that has eliminated cash bail in any court hearing.[4] This was not birthed as a "reform" measure, but was centrally

---

* By pressuring local officials, student, teacher, and parent organizers mobilized the "Cops out of CPS" campaign that resulted in getting all resource officers and Chicago Police Department officers out of CPS school buildings. There have also been numerous activations around the "Treatment Not Trauma" campaign that seeks to reopen the eight closed mental health clinics in the city and to offer a mental-health crisis hotline that would send mental-health workers instead of police officers to respond to mental-health emergencies. See Reema Amin, "Chicago Board of Education Votes to Remove Police Officers from Schools, *Chalkbeat,* February 22, 2024, https://www.chalkbeat.org/chicago/2024/02/23/chicago-board-of-education-votes-out-police-officers/; Collaborative for Community Wellness, https://www.collaborativeforcommunitywellness.org/treatmentnottrauma for information on Treatment Not Trauma.

informed by a twenty-year struggle of abolitionists to keep people out of the throes of the carceral state.*

Resisting the pull of engineered conflict requires a commitment to act in ways that are, in the words of scholar-activist Michael Dumas, *fugitive*. Dumas told me that fugitivity is the recognition that you are "not free, but you have made a decision to run."[5] In my own thinking, I continue his thought with the idea that you are not running from something, but to something, with the people in your community. You have made the decision that the situation you're in is unacceptable and you must eliminate and replace the thing that you are suffering from. It is "fugitive" because the rules and orthodoxy of the establishment don't always apply. A Black fugitive future is a determination by Black people and their allies to create "life-giving" spaces, where people get their needs met while passing on the lessons of how to build similar things for others.[6] People can use the accepted rules to achieve their goals through fugitive means, but there are also spaces that are in between the rules, and moments that require you to intentionally go against the rules. Similar to maroon communities in the US and throughout the Western Hemisphere, fugitivity is a place where people "disappear" from the idea of relying on the state to meet their needs. As Fred Moten and Stefano Harney explain with their concept of the *undercommons*, the institutions and resources of the state are grounded in the logics of compliance and compromise, meaning that they will never lead to sustainability for those on the margins.[7] Fugitively, the resources of the state are fleeting, as they should only be used to the extent that we are able to meet our needs in the short term. In the end, the goal of fugitive work is to build pathways that are self-sufficient.

The point of Black fugitive space is not to demonstrate how well the system works when it is taken to task. Because fugitivity is not about

---

* The Coalition to End Money Bond was comprised of sixteen abolitionist and reformist organizations across Chicago and the state of Illinois that sought to end the practice of money bond in Illinois Courts. See https://endmoneybond.org/about-us/.

abiding by rules, we need to make note of the spaces that recognize that the state is neither prepared nor structured to address the needs of low-income, working-class Black people in a city that has declared them disposable. I agree with activist-scholars Zoé Samudzi and William Anderson that Chicago, like the United States, "cannot exist without Black subjection."[8] However, the role of Black people is not to sit and let white supremacy wash over us. Instead, there are lessons to be learned from the people who are actively identifying the needs of Black people and working to address these needs in real time. This communal nature of Black fugitive work is consistently up against the heavy contradictions of capitalism in the form of the non-profit industrial complex (NPIC) and racial capitalism. Nevertheless, commitments to fugitivity cannot be ignored if we are to consider a future where the hold of the state is eliminated.

A Black fugitive future is also abolitionist. Despite the concept's popularity in certain circles, I do not take abolition for granted. Central to the process is the idea that for the new thing that we build to be effective, it must be rooted in well-being and self-determination. The fugitive, aspirational, and experimental nature of abolitionist work requires a commitment to long and slow work that can be difficult at times. I agree with justice worker Kelly Hayes that rebelling against the "continued normalization of mass death, human suffering and annihilation" is a serious undertaking.[9] Because it is against the grain of the status quo, it is the type of work that challenges us instantly. Community builder and scholar Mariame Kaba, along with AirGo Radio, has created a film called *One Million Experiments* that documents how communities of color across the country work to create safety and spaces of well-being. Because these commitments have existed from time immemorial in Black communities facing white supremacy in the form of state-sanctioned violence and engineered conflicts, people in the present moment are building on lessons from history to demonstrate the possibilities of abolition. While not a panacea, abolition is a necessity as we exist in a world that attempts to render us disposable.

The remaining pages highlight the work of three organizations that resist engineered conflict by centering themselves in abolition and self-determination. I have included them in a conversation of Black fugitive futures because each formation is less concerned with the rules that govern traditional nonprofit organizations, and more concerned with their capacity to address the daily needs of the people they care about. They are "fugitive" because they are clear that the people who understand their work best are those who are marginalized by the state. Instead of being "palatable" to philanthropy, their concerns are centered in building collective power for the purposes of improving the practices that support well-being. Abolition is a site of struggle for all three organizations as they all attempt to move beyond the aspirational and into the material needs of community members. All three organizations are collectively resisting engineered conflict in their respective communities. Their work is intertwined through numerous venues, as members know each other and have worked together in various capacities. Where they are not the only organizations in the city that situate themselves in an abolitionist politic, they are reflective of a commitment to struggle in uncertain times. Instead of speaking "for" these organizations, the remaining pages are guided by their words, with only sparse commentary. The only "edits" I have made to their comments are for clarity.

Breathing a New World into Existence:
The #LetUsBreathe Collective

My first interaction with members of the #LetUsBreathe Collective was at a benefit concert for Palestinian freedom fighter Rasmea Odeh. In the back of the venue there was an area filled clothing racks and hat racks. When I asked if the items hanging on them were for sale, one of the people minding the area told me that it was a "free store," where people were encouraged to take what they need. My first thoughts were: "What is this?" and "Who are these people?" Where I was intrigued by the idea of a "free store," I was even more encouraged by the idea that people had taken it upon themselves to think about their work as connected to addressing a need with no strings attached. Because there was a lot happening at the benefit concert, I wasn't able to have a longer conversation with the people at the free store, but they stayed on my mind as I went to other activist and protest formations throughout the city. As I would run into them more frequently, I came to know that their name was the #LetUsBreathe Collective. They understand themselves to be an "alliance of artists and activists organizing through a creative lens to imagine a world without prisons and police."[10] Their efforts center an ethic of "love over capitalism, abundance over scarcity, and collaboration over control."[11] By shifting their efforts away from late-stage capitalism, their shared belief is that "people and communities are able to govern themselves peacefully when they have access to and sovereignty over quality education, housing, art, health care, nutrition, useful & prosperous livelihood, and skills for nonviolently resolving harm and conflict."[12] The following conversation is with founding member Damon Williams.

ORIGIN STORY

First time we found out about crowdfunding, GoFundMe, it was called the #LetUsBreathe Initiative. I was working on a song at that point called "Let Me Breathe," which was supposed to be like a dual metaphor for "get out of my face," social friction, and then structural oppression of the boot on our neck. Then collectivized it to #LetUsBreathe, went down for the trip, just thought we were going to bring those supplies down [to Ferguson, Missouri], cut a check to the organization, and have done our social-justice contribution, and was transformed by the experience. Came back the next weekend, and then two weeks after that, and within that first month, decided that this is not an initiative. This is something we want to continue to do. And so it went from the #LetUsBreathe Initiative to #LetUsBreathe Collective.

So again, the show we were doing with my sister was called Lack on Lack, and the notion that through a love ethic and abundance, we can address lack and create these different spiritual and material surpluses recognizing that the scarcity is engineered and that we have more than enough metaphysically, but literally there is more food being produced than is needed. There are more houses available than is needed. There is enough land. The resources of this planet are not scarce. It is the distribution of them. That was embedded. Then again, what we now would call the mutual-aid tradition and movement was something we were aware of.

So that was some of the spirit of "we got to go down there." Also, the emergence of Twitter, and so the images and communication being in real time, and then also having these dual channels of information. We have access in real time to what's happening on the ground, and we're seeing how CNN and the corporate news structures are framing the conversation, and so also wanting to bring photographers and videographers down to help document that distinction.

"What are the needs being named?" What came back first [in Ferguson] was gas masks because they were getting teargassed every night, first aid supplies, and water, because it was also August heat in Missouri. We come with this ethic of love, care, and contribution. And then from there, we enter into the political conversation. How do we create a space that's more accessible, allows for deepening of collective consciousness and relationship building, and is regenerative? And so the free store became a central part of this four-hour movement-building series that was intended to make our space more grounded and sustainable.

Marking their commitment to abolition was their forty-five-day occupation of an empty lot across the street from the black site maintained by CPD known as Homan Square. Upon returning from Ferguson, Missouri, after the uprisings protesting the execution of Michael Brown, there was a moment where members of the collective began to look at their world differently, asking themselves questions on how artists could contribute to the long struggle of liberation. The organization asked themselves the question, "Are we going to actually activate around these things that we write plays, poems, and songs about, or are we going to, you know, be passive, and still perform on the sidelines?"[13]

FREEDOM SQUARE

The intention was to pivot the direct-action muscles we had built toward a more love-facing intention because we were in North Lawndale. Now we're in the most incarcerated zip code, the space with the most school closings. All of the statistics and experiences are compounding right here. We don't want to come here and be shutting down traffic. We don't want to come here and just be talking about, "They're killing us, you're killing us." That model then was we used our little rig sound system and played cookout music and tried to have some love-facing chants.

I want to uplift the movement around torture justice in the city at large. When the idea of a black site gets named, it's not really a far jump, because we know the practice is happening everywhere, decentralized. But for me, for real, it was . . . I believe it came out in 2015, maybe 2014. It was an article that *The Guardian* did. That was the first of like Homan Square, black site, CPD. It's like, that's a thing that exists. It's like, "Bet, you don't got to tell me twice." I accepted that it exists.

We chose Homan Square because of that article. It was like, "Well, nobody's really done any activation around the space." There was this bullshit that just happened here a few, couple weeks ago that felt like a wound . . . This community needs to be re-engaged. It's ready. Kids are just coming out, ready to turn up. But that did not go well. That's not it and I don't want that to be what movement looks and feels like to this space. Between that article being published and then this experience that happened there, it was like, "Oh, well. Then this is a perfect site," because what we were . . . The main political demand at the time was the push against the Blue Lives Matter ordinance that Anne Burke was trying to pass, which had passed in Louisiana when Alton Sterling was killed.

Then we're going to basically deploy those efforts on Homan Square. We're going to have open mic, we're going to have an art-making station. We're going to have our free store. We're going to have different resource distribution like an employment network, and a way of community and movement activation. This is going to be the antithesis of that space [Homan Square]. So torture happens there, but now love and freedom making happens here.

The intention was to just hold it down for one day, but we bought these tents to be part of the activation. So we wanted the tents to represent, at the time, the divest/invest platform. That IACP (International Association of Chiefs of Police) action in

October 2015 was the first public launching of what became the Defund the Police campaign [Defund]. So people talk about Defund in 2020 as if it came out of nowhere. But really this platform was the divest/invest platform that was brought into space and action, and to invest into education, into housing, into youth development, restorative justice, health, so on and so forth, even community, infrastructure space. With that, we had the idea of, "We could camp out." At that point it was like, "Man, folks got to get arrested."

At the same time, we also are coming off the Laquan McDonald issue. The political flux, the reparations ordinance had just got passed. There were all of these defensive survival mechanisms you could tell the administration was going through at the time. Before Rahm [Emanuel—Chicago's mayor from 2011 to 2019] pulled out of that, they obviously had orders to not cross the sidewalk. We functionally had sovereignty.

It was using this space as a stage for engagement and for our political demands. Then within that first forty-eight to seventy-two hours, I had dozens of conversations with people just walking by who asked, "What y'all doing here?" mostly from a place of interest, not super skeptical, and we would try to talk about there's this Blue Lives Matter in the ordinance and trying to jumble, jumble, jumble through explaining this thing that's important but still trying to be a little discreet. Then in the middle of it, we get to, "Do you know what happens here?" Some people would say no. Then you explain it. So people say, "It's like a police station," or a lot of people would say, "I know exactly what happens in there."

Well, this needs to be the beginning of the conversation. It can't be our little coalition's interests come first, and then we talk about this, if we're going to be here in this community. It's now clear to me as somebody who slept through stats class a couple of times. If just in walking distance, the amount of people, the sample size of people that are walking by saying they had this experience, if you extrapolate that toward what this place must be, this is now an epidemic level of violence in the city, but particularly this local neighborhood, this community, and this healing, this addressing, this naming that this needs to stop within the first four to five days, then shift it to being this is our demand.

Because there was no physical building that we called Freedom Square, it was just the basic human problem solving that we have to do . . . Make sure there's a bathroom and garbage and porta-potty and making sure there's enough ice, that level of just literal space holding that, if we're saying we are creating a new thing, then we are responsible for it. Then to come here, the luxury is to have toilets and electricity, but that explicitly informed our vision and intention of what this is and what it means on that list of space agreements. On that sign that's behind you, the last one or the second to last one is, "I agree to have a conflict with love and respect without calling police."

That was initially crafted for an event that was originally scheduled for four hours. It became a moment that was utilized in a space across from a police torture facility for six weeks. After the Freedom Square activation, we had to ask, "What does it mean to uphold that same energy for years in a space?" Practically, we had to move to, "What happens when someone's cars get broken into?" and so on and so forth.

ON ABOLITION

But oftentimes, what I think abolitionists and transformative-justice practice teaches us is most of this abolitionist safety work is for things we don't call police for in the first place, or a lot of the things that police get called for are things that are not that serious. Most times it's about conflict or a disturbance. I forget the exact stat, but it's something like 70–90 percent of calls are not for a crime. They're for some type of disturbance. A disagreement, basically.

The responsibility required, of meeting people where they are and holding folks, and then, over time, learning how to have boundaries, which is like, a difficult thing to establish because folks can perceive any or all boundaries as replicating things that are carceral. You're always moving within it. Usually the struggle is not folks wanting more police, and this is abolitionist enough. We have it. Either you're not protecting the space with enough intensity or vice versa.

And we have to ask the question, "What's the relationship with police?" The issue with carceral justice is that it's an entity. Well, one of the issues. It is an entity that there is really no interaction with outside of entering from this place of authority, and that authority is only established through authorized violence and domination. The state and the cops are people that we do not have a relationship with. They come in with power over us when they enter a space. The only tool they really have is to detain, or to use force, or to kill. All of their negotiations are then through that. What happens, theoretically, or in practice, when our relationship with our community is one as collaborators, or as somebody who has fed you, or as someone who has provided clothing and childcare to you, or someone who has organized for you to have a stipend, theoretically, this establishes the trust and comfort to then incentivize behavior and/ or redress behavior. That is the superstructure we want to build. We want to have a public space that provides all those resources and then has a network of infrastructure that can proactively prevent harm and then respond to harm in a more healthy way. Some of that has happened. A lot of that has happened. I don't want to sound, like, too weary, but it's not that clean.

There's the vision and desires I have, and then there's, what will our capacity allow? What we have striven to do and have done in pockets, and it's been a struggle, is to more consistently build this cooperative economy of resources to activate and sustain folks. What does it look like to not have a tent for someone but actual housing? Or what does it look like to not have, not just have some hot dogs on the grill, but to have a farm and to be feeding folks with vegetables? What does it look like to have stewards of this space with stipends and to support their income, as opposed to only depending upon volunteer work? What does it look like to know how to practice that in order to build up a base to further the liberatory movement, to be stronger in our resistance, to be able to levy more grounded demands? Also, I think in practice, there's been a much deeper commitment to healing work.

We, through work and analysis, have challenged the language of safety and security. I think it's so much neoliberal violence, imperialism, and also sometimes aversion to struggle and how we use it within our spaces. The idea of safe space can be conflict avoidant and/or protect power for the people who already have it. So in challenging that move from safety and security to wellness and protection, what we call *well-pro*. Through our programming or through maintaining this space, an ethic of proactive, intentional modes of care and commitment to the health and well-being of everyone we are sharing space with.

How do we then build that out on a neighborhood level, where we're actually in folks' lives? Not just as a conflict-response space, but as one that is rooted in ecological and human relations. It's like, how do we fix your windows and also be the people you call if there is a domestic dispute before it gets dangerous? The hope always is to have been there already by now. But I think if all of these programs coalesce, that would be the ultimate contribution we would hope to be able to offer, or a legacy that we hope future generations pick up and carry.

We had this pivot from centering power and state and resistance toward more community-facing care and love. But the idea is to build up our capacity, because there is direct resistance that is needed, and so trying to figure out a way that, beyond what it looks like now, is like being in coalition and participating in the different iterations like legislative policies on Treatment Not Trauma or Bring Chicago Home now or whatever the local political thrust is.* But beyond that, how do we take that original frontline ethic and expand it to be in deeper resistance to state violence on a communal level?[14]

Ujimaa Medics—Skill Sharing for Our Collective Survival

As the city of Chicago experienced a rash of homicides between 2016 and 2018, I began to hear about the work of a group of Black women who were community organizers and healthcare workers teaching community members how to treat gunshot wounds. Soon after, I came to learn that the name of this group was Ujimaa Medics (commonly

---

* The "Treatment Not Trauma" campaign is a legislative push to reconfigure how the city responds to mental-health crises. It resulted in the return of city-run mental-health clinics that had been closed under the Rahm Emanuel administration. "Bring Chicago Home" was a legislative campaign that proposed a progressive tax on any property valued over $1 million, using the collected tax dollars to build affordable housing and offer treatment for homeless residents.

known as UMedics).* UMedics were intent on carrying on the traditions of their ancestors, the care workers that existed in Black communities before mainstream hospitals and clinics, in their day-to-day work in communities. Similar to the #LetUsBreathe Collective, their attempt to address human need reminded me of something I heard from a group of community members in Detroit that demolished abandoned houses. They were asked why they do the work that they do and the answer was simple: "The call has been made—ain't nobody coming—so what are you going to do?" As they were talking about how some communities in Detroit were experiencing blight and disinvestment, they were clear that they needed to make the decision to take care of themselves and the people they cared about in ways that might appear unconventional. For some, however, this work is not unconventional, due to the inability of Black people in large cities to address quality education, health care, housing, and employment. Collectively, UMedics addresses the question: "How do we care for ourselves when the state refuses?" In Chicago, because certain communities receive delayed ambulatory care or are denied it completely, UMedics have stepped up to fill in. The following account is from a conversation with founding member Martine Caverl.

ORIGIN STORY

I would say that the kernel of the idea for UMedics had been brewing for some time. In 2011 I was doing organizing on a volunteer basis and had a community around me of others who were doing a lot of different kinds of community work on the South and the West Sides. At that time I was actually with this collective that came together after the 2010 earthquake in Port-

---

* *Ujimaa* is a Kiswahili word that means "collective work and responsibility."

au-Prince, Haiti. But what we were trying to do was redirect people away from just giving money to the American Red Cross, the Clinton Foundation, and really big nonprofits. Foundations like that basically had control over Haiti through non-governmental means. We wanted to focus on fundraising on Haitian-led and Haitian American–led grassroots efforts. Also, we wanted to raise awareness, especially among Black people in the US, about the importance of Haiti for our freedom and our identity. Why we should be paying attention to what's happening there and why we should be supporting it, especially the rebuilding of Haiti and Haiti's continuing quest for self-determination.

That brought together a lot of different people. Two of us that were in that organization, we're pretty good friends. At the time, there was also this organization called STOP—Southside Together Organizing for Power. They were doing a lot of youth organizing. I had met some of the youth in STOP . . . I organized a delegation to Haiti a couple of years back, and some of the youth involved with STOP had gone to that. Through that, I met this young man named Damian Turner. I remember we had this campaign to get a Level I trauma center at the University of Chicago Hospital. University of Chicago had a Level I pediatric trauma center, but it didn't have one for adults. When Damian was shot, they did not have an adult trauma center. He was one year too old to go to the pediatric trauma center. They put him in an ambulance and then the ambulance drove to the North Side. He died in the ambulance. I think that the reason I gave that context is because the response to him dying was different from other situations. I don't think it was because of how he lived his life that people thought to respond in the way that they did, which was, "Oh, we need to organize in this situation. We need to think about what the root cause is, you know, for this."

Like, why doesn't University of Chicago have a trauma center that could have taken his case? He had cofounded a youth organization called FLY (Fearless Leading by the Youth), and then FLY, together with STOP, and then together with a whole bunch of other organizations, started organizing to put pressure on University of Chicago to open a trauma center. At the time we were talking about why we need to organize to put pressure on University of Chicago.

SHIFTING FROM PROTESTING
TO ORGANIZING FOR SELF-DETERMINATION

But we also need to recognize and see the power we have between us. Between the people right here on the street, right here in the living room, right here in the meeting, like between me and you. What can we do between me and you? There's a lot of power there to transform our conditions also. There's power there to transform how we see ourselves. There's power to actually make material change in the world through the saving of a life and through somebody witnessing that act too. The challenge for me and for others who were there at the time was: What if there was someone there who knew first aid for gunshot wounds? What could have happened?

We don't know for sure, but we know that it would have been powerful had somebody at least been able to try, you know, and the other assumption we had, a belief we had and still have, is that where people have skills and knowledge, they will be motivated to use them. You know what I mean? Our assumption is, had somebody been trained, oh, 100 percent, they would have done the best that they could to use that training in that situation. And across any situation. Any situation we faced in our neighborhoods, any situation we face as Black people, where somebody knows what to do they tend to want to do it. Especially when we see each other and we see ourselves as worthy and valuable. I have these skills, and I see this young person, or I see this neighbor, or I see this stranger as worthy of me using these skills on, you know what I mean?

We're in a situation where not everybody who is a professional responder sees it that way. If they're Black, they're more likely to. But not always. That's just the reality. We wanted to train bystanders, not professionals. We wanted to train youth, we wanted to train neighbors, we wanted to train grandmas. We wanted to train all. Because we wanted to train for this, we wanted to get involved from the beginning.

THE FIRST WORKSHOP

I knew some first aid, and I was getting ready to go to nursing school. One of my motivations was to create something that would . . . Some kind of institution, some kind of project that would be like a grassroots service to people, in emergency situations especially. When I got back to Chicago from nursing school, all that kind of stuff, there still was not an agreement for the trauma center (on the South Side) yet. The campaign was still ongoing. Then what? We piloted a workshop in my living room. It was me and my husband, Makalani, who, you know, we hosted the workshop. We invited family and friends that we wanted to, first of all, share the skills with. You know, like, "I would like to help you. I assume you would like to help me. Let's learn together."

I was under the mentorship at the time of somebody who had been working for the fire department as a paramedic for thirty years. This is a person who had been sharing openly what he knew with the community for more than thirty years. Actually . . . he always made sure that he paid it forward. I was one of the beneficiaries of his mentorship. I was able to take some of what he taught me and filter it through organizing lists to say we're going to do a skill share. We're going to examine the question, "Why do we even have to do this in the first place?" What are some of the other contexts around responding to a shooting in your neighborhood? We had family, friends, there were even children at that first workshop.

From there, me and Amica in particular started just talking to people like, "Hey, are you interested in learning this?" Once we figured that people were interested in learning this, we began to ask, "Is anybody doing this, like, widespread? Is anybody teaching this?" We did our homework to try to figure out if there were other efforts that were scaling up and spreading the information.

It didn't seem like there were. This was, I think 2014, I remember that summer Mike Brown was killed in Ferguson. There was all this energy around, facing up against violence coming from the state, violence coming from police, Black Lives Matter. That fall, we were asked to teach a public workshop. It was us teaching gunshot-wound first aid. Then we were partnered with a group that was teaching cop watch. At that very first workshop, actually, it was me and a teenager, we were teaching together. That person is now the training coordinator in UMedics, that's Joey.

We taught that first workshop together. But we still weren't really . . . We were still kind of this family and friends thing. We were still a loose, informal thing, at that time. I think there were about maybe seven or eight people that were just kicking things around like, "Let's teach whenever we're asked to."

NATIONAL SOLIDARITY AND CREATING UMEDICS

Then we ended up meeting these sisters from Oakland, like a couple of months later who were doing very similar work, called People's Community Medics. They came together after Oscar Grant was shot by BART police. They did an investigation about how long it took for the ambulance to respond and said, "Oh no! We got to take this into our hands."

We started talking and building with them, talking about what they were doing. We formalized our work in Chicago and came up with a name, and we became an actual organization in 2015. Then we started training, using the work we did in 2014 to develop a "train the trainer" workshop where we taught our peers how to deliver this training too. Now, it wasn't like a quick thing, but it was more like an initiative. Then we started just talking to people and telling people we were available. We didn't have any money. We didn't write the grants. We just took stuff from around the house to train with, because that was what we were focused on. We were like, "Look, you know, you might not have a first aid kit. We barely have a first aid kit. But like, there's stuff that you carry in your wallet, the clothes you have on, the stuff in your diaper bag, stuff you fix your hair with, that you can actually use to save somebody's life."

We wrote up the principles of first aid, that we still teach now . . . One of our current board members now, he has retired from the fire department himself. We talked to him about, from their end, what are some of the things that we need to make sure people understand, especially like about calling 911. It could be with some firearms instructors and folks who do know-your-rights trainings around, how to deal with police because when you think you're there saving somebody's life, and the police roll up, they might see something else. How do you keep yourself safe when they pull up? Especially if they are the first to the scene? How do you negotiate to get access to that person to see if you can actually help them?

PUBLIC HEALTH AND SELF-DETERMINATION

The thing about it is we say that this organization is related to public health and self-determined health. Then safety, and a community's ideas about what creates a safe place where you want to live, a safe place where you're proud to live. This is tied completely to how you view the health of the people in that community, and what are the efforts happening to preserve that health? To create long-term wellness in addition to the systems that are in place for people to rely upon in crisis or emergency.

The second thing we did after we started teaching gunshot-wound treatment, was asthma community care. For a couple of years, if you came to a gunshot-wound training, and we had enough time, we had a couple of hours, we would surprise you at the end, you're like, "Okay, that was gunshot wound. Now we're going to teach you how to help somebody having a breathing emergency." They were like, "Oh, well, I guess we're going to learn this." Chicago is one of the worst places, worst cities to live in, in the United States for people who have asthma. One in four Black children in Chicago have a diagnosed asthma, and so I remember this must have been 2016, perhaps December 2016, we started working on our asthma content, and we started adding that into the workshops, and we found out that there was a shooting somewhere on the South Side, where one of the witnesses was so distraught by what happened that she had an asthma attack.

Because somebody could say, "Well, gunshot wounds and asthma are two separate things." But if you understand what has happened to Black people in this country, and you understand how it affects our health, how it affects how stress relates to the wellness of the human body, and the long-term effects of stress and multigenerational effects of stress. You'll see that people being injured and traumatized by gun violence or any kind of traumatic violence, and what we deal with in terms of asthma are completely related, same causes. What we're trying to do in UMedics is about freedom, and the first aid and the health and wellness work that we do is a tool in that large project. The project and the goal is freedom. Our work is just a tool to get there.

COMMUNITY CARE DURING A HEALTH PANDEMIC

We did several online asthma workshops that year, and we integrated COVID-19 information as it was emerging, as it was changing into that workshop. We really ramped up the asthma work that we were doing there. The thing we had to make decisions about was our gunshot-wound workshop. We decided that that was not going to be a workshop we were going to do online. That was a workshop where we had to hold space in person, so we looked for opportunities to do that workshop when the weather permitted us to do it outside, so we did our gunshot-wound workshop exclusively outside.

We put together a cohort of about fourteen people from different organizations in Chicago, and we did the street-medic training. It was mostly online, and then some of it was in person outside. We did that between June and July of 2020, so we could have folks who were prepared to serve.

That's when I would say we developed the protest defense part of our work, which is now the whole training focus on developing Black street medics. We'll also open up to organizers, if they want to be trained for that, and then we do a protester public safety training, that is saying, "Hey, if you want to participate in an action, you should." These are some ways to help keep each other safer, and so we do that upon request.

For example, later that year, there was an organization who was having some trouble internally, like they had some disagreements about these vaccines. They were like, "We need somebody to help facilitate a conversation." We helped them out with that, came in and talked to them about that, so they could come to some decisions for themselves about how they wanted to deal with it. I think that also ended up being just a hard year emotionally for everybody. It was a hard year physically because a lot of folks were carrying a big burden of being out on the streets. They were either out on the street protesting or they were out on the street running street-medic trainings. When you go on medic duty [for protest mobilizations], you sign up for a shift, and it's hard to know when the action is going to be over, and sometimes you have to remind yourself of things like, "Do I also have to do jail support today?" You might be at that jail until four o'clock in the morning waiting for the last person to come out, so you can assess how they're doing.

Some of our members got brutalized by the police. One time, the police stole one of our members' bikes at an action. That was a tough year for a lot of us, and so I think we had to also think about, "Okay, what do we need to sustain us?" Because we were still all volunteers at the time. Almost everything we were doing was free or damn near free, and you had folks who were doing UMedics after work, before work or when they were underemployed or unemployed. It was definitely a leadership challenge to think about that. We had to be honest about the question, "What do we have to do to sustain people?"

People were able to get into some work and began thinking about new and different things we wanted to do as an organization, and so we experienced a lot of growth because of that. I would say that as far as COVID, we were impacted in the same way as everybody else was, but also I think because we had a group of people who were already thinking creatively about how Black people can practice self-determination in real time, how Black people can practice resilience, and how to respond to crises and how to respond to trauma? We were able to come out of that stronger.[15]

ON SUSTAINABILITY

That's a loaded question. I almost feel unequipped to answer this alone, but I'll do my best. What's needed to sustain? One thing that's needed is to be very clear about what your goals and values are. I'm not pulling that out of myself. This is something that we have to be very clear about what they are. It is something that a community elder told me before COVID, even like a few years ago when UMedics were struggling and like, "Oh my God, how do we keep doing this?" "We're all tired." She said, "Well, what are your goals? Have you reached your goals? If you have, and everybody's satisfied as you reach your goals, then you know you can rest. Put it down." If you haven't reached your goals, and you want to reach your goals, then find a way. Maybe finding a way relates to adjusting those goals so that they're actually reachable. Maybe it relates to adjusting your timeline. Maybe it relates to slowing down, but still keeping those goalposts ahead of you. Consider what your goals are. I would say that's been a big lifesaver for me in terms of how I think about working with UMedics. What are the goals, and then what are the values, right? Making sure that your values underpin everything that you're doing.

One of our values is this concept that comes from the Akan [people of Ghana]. There's an adinkra symbol associated with it, it's called *Denkyem*, and that relates to the idea of being fluid and dynamic and adjusting to changing circumstances. It doesn't mean you're wishy-washy flimflam. Instead, it means that you take a look at the conditions surrounding you and make your decisions based on that, so you're dynamic. This is one of the values that we use to help us to make decisions about what needs to happen. Then I think I have to think this way because we've transformed from being a volunteer-based collective to now being a collective where we have a mix of paid employees, people who are paid sometimes, and the volunteers. We have a mix.

MOVING FORWARD

I think it's important to recognize when our organization is having growing pains and that a lot of the life cycle of organizations isn't unusual or specific to one of them or another, but you do the best you can to look at, what point are we at in the cycle, and what do we need to navigate to the next point in the cycle? But the important thing is to maintain the relationships, and the bonds that will get you through.

I think that because there are strong relational bonds in the organization, that's one thing that has helped us, and I don't mean that the bonds are just based on "I like you," but the bonds are based on knowledge of each other's commitments to the mission and vision. Like, "Okay, at this moment in time, things are in a hard situation, but I know what your commitment is to this mission and vision, and I know what mine is, and therefore, we actually can figure this out." And we often do. I think that's important too.

At this moment in time, we do two kinds of gunshot workshops. We do a basic workshop, and then if you do the basic workshop, you're eligible for the advanced workshop, and then we do our asthma community-care workshop. We're also able to do CPR, AED, and first-aid certifications. On a limited basis, maybe once a year, we can do a street protest event for Black street medics, cohort trainings. We can do protest health and safety at request. We also have some of the community safety planning that started in 2020. That was a way to take some of the content about safety and awareness, and our approach to gunshot-wounds training, and put it online, so that's the online workshop.

We also have a collaboration going with the Chicago South Side Birth Center. It's called Birth Emergency Skills, and that's preparing people who have to respond to an unplanned out-of-hospital birth. That was developed as a response to the maternal-health crisis we are facing in our communities. The important thing in the work that we do is when we bring people together in the space of a workshop, or when we're doing skills work in street outreach. Sometimes we just talk to the people on the street, and we're doing the best we can to share what we can in two minutes, right? What we're trying to do is create or model a system of health care that is based on trust, where there is deep trust in the people, between the people who are providing care, and the people who need care. The line between those things is very fuzzy or barely exists.

I think that's why most of our focus is on bystanders, people who are in a position to be bystanders, whether they are people who are total civilians, non-professionals, or people who may be professionals, but not at work right now. This is a neighbor. And how are we thinking about it in that situation? How do we see young Black people especially, and where are we going to invest our time, and invest our material resources, while pressuring people who are holding material resources about how to distribute them?

One of our goals is to be intergenerational. We want to have a space across generations where we can be collaborative and co-create. It is a place where we can truly work together, and help and understand each other. I would love to see more of those kinds of spaces being created in our communities where it's not just what we're the organization that serves youth, but we're an organization where everybody is welcome. We're trying to figure out how to create the kinds of relations that we want amongst Black people in our communities. Like, what does that look like in general?

Equity and Transformation (EAT)

In reflecting on his organizing efforts in other parts of the city and country, Richard Wallace began to rethink the relationship of community-based organizations with the state. From his own experiences as someone who was formerly incarcerated, he understands the contradictions of those who are locked out of life-sustaining entities like education, living-wage employment, health care, and housing. Shifting his efforts to prioritize the marginalized (those returning home from incarceration, sex workers, people who run unauthorized home kitchens, etc.), he created Equity and Transformation (EAT).[16] As an organization "founded by and for post-incarcerated people," EAT offers important insight into what people often refer to as the "informal" economy. These are thought of as economic engagements that are outside of the mainstream, but I agree with Wallace that the only difference is that they are not recognized by the mainstream as "legitimate," or regulated by the state. If people use these services in a given community, they are legitimate to that community. In his thinking, Wallace pondered the question of whether people who participated in these "nontraditional" economies could be organized to protect their labor.

When he sent out an announcement that EAT was being introduced to the public, I attended one of their information sessions. There were conversations with Bucket Boys, sex workers, people who sold essential oils on the train, and people who operated candy stands outside of their houses.[*] The discussion centered around what they needed and what they could do for their communities if their needs were met. As EAT reimagines who a laborer is, they take into account "the history of exclusion of Black workers and the depth of creativity required to thrive within an alternative labor system in a capitalist country."[17] From this position they work to organize Informal Workers Associations (IWAs) as places where people can contemplate and implement their own versions of community safety.[18] Wallace contends that these spaces allow community members to provide tangible examples of collective care, which provide important building blocks in creating safe communities.

---

[*] "Bucket Boys" are groups of Black youth that play drums on buckets at frequently traveled street intersections for money. In the current moment, the Chicago Bulls basketball team employs a group of Bucket Boys to play at their home games.

ORIGIN STORY

For me, as I began to study the poor people's campaign, some of MLK's later work, and of course, Fred Hampton, I realized that I'm cut from that cloth. My mother raised us in movement. She raised us around Mama Akua, Fred Hampton Jr., and the Black Panther Party for Self-Defense. I studied their tactics to learn how do we organize the lumpen, how do we organize the proletariat, how do we create a class analysis within our movement? These were important questions to me at the time because far too often I would attend rallies, marches, and meetings, and the majority of the people in the space were non-Black or middle-class people. I felt like the experiences that I had as a formerly incarcerated person and the experiences that others [at the protests] had was different.

Mobilizing the most marginalized people means walking with the people at the people's pace, it means walking with those who have done harm and do harm because harm was done to them. It means being in service to the people, as opposed to the people being in service to the organization. It means that you have to use different tactics because of the vulnerabilities that are, I think, present within that base. I was like, "Somebody has to think about this at a scale, building a movement around it." I think the continuation of that is Equity and Transformation. That wasn't necessarily just thought of on my own. It was an assignment by my elder Denise Perry, movement allies like Barbara Ransby, Mary Hooks from Atlanta, Rukia Lumumba, folks that I went through the BOLD (Black Organizing for Leadership Development) workshop with, Aja Taylor from Philly, Brandon Sturtevant from Oakland. They were like, "You've been talking about this, it's time to build it."

I think oftentimes in movement, we critique without an actual commitment to do the work. My critique was that the national movement ecosystem needed FIP (formerly incarcerated people) voices in it. Opposed to offering a critique, I was like, "Let me offer a solution." Let's build the container that will hold our folks into movement and move them left . . . we're not losing them. We never attempted to get them. We left them. They're getting bought into neoliberal capitalism. They're getting bought away from cooperative work, even though cooperatives are what would benefit them the most.

We launched Equity and Transformation in 2018. I focused on informality because I felt like it humanized the lived experience of workers who had no other choice but to hustle. I wanted to provide a new way of thinking about people in street economies that decriminalized the people in it. A framework that went beyond unemployment, because I feel like unemployment doesn't mean you're not laboring; my people are always laboring. I think first year 2018, one thing . . . Where is the quote? I just used it. A quote by Cornel West says, "You can't lead the people if you don't love the people. You can't save the people if you don't serve the people." I think in the development of EAT, we grew, and I think through love and a commitment to the work, you grow. Sometimes it's a reverse growth at times, it's shrinking.

I think part of it is that when we started, we had this very robust analysis around informality, and it was really cute for academics and philanthropy. That didn't necessarily make it make sense to the communities that we were working with. I think at the time, the movement was extremely rigid as it related to accessibility. You had to know these authors, know these terms. You basically needed a freaking thesaurus, a glossary of terms, in order to enter and/or be associated with movement capital. I think in the beginning, because I was so connected to movement, that I led with a lot of that. It alienated me from the people who I knew the most and I needed to reach the most.

I think the first effort that we did is we began to carve our language out and made sure that it was accessible to the audience we were trying to reach. Even the name EAT. Of course, Equity and Transformation is the name of the organization, but we go by EAT because that's how simple it actually is . . . our people are just trying to eat. The name EAT came from a member who I saw. We had got him a job working in the temp-labor sector, and we knew it was not going to be the greatest job, but it was a job. I saw him back on the block hustling, I approached him and asked him what he was on lately and he was like, "Look, Rich, I'm just trying to eat."

Although I knew his decision could lead to jail, the penitentiary, or death, I really didn't have any other alternative for him. There was no co-op that I could point to that could provide a means to subsistence. I couldn't tell him to keep trying to find formal employment when I knew that nearly every option would end in either exploitation or discrimination. In fact, telling him to find a job felt like telling him to go find some more trauma. He told me, "The job let me go after ninety days," and that broke my heart because I knew that whether formally employed or unemployed, the demand for capital remains the same. Regardless of one's employment status, they still have to earn wages to pay for housing, groceries, water, and transportation.

In the absence of formal employment, Black workers don't sit idle, they hustle to make ends meet. Those hustles vary from childcare to drug trade. If you look back over the history of Black informality you see that occupations in the informal economy are not fixed, they often migrate from informal to formal. When a particular occupation or hustle is informal, you have a high rate of Black participation and innovation, ease of access, and Black folks hold ownership positions. The second the occupation becomes formalized, you see a reduction in Black ownership, participation, and innovation in the field.

In 2018 EAT began researching the medical cannabis industry in Illinois, to assess retention of Black informal workers in the formal cannabis market, and realized that out of the fifty-five licenses awarded to applicants, not one of the recipients was Black. That assessment led EAT to engage in the cannabis equity fight. We determined that any policy that created more barriers than bridges for Black informal workers was an anti-Black policy and should be interrupted at all costs. We released a series of reports titled "The Chronic Papers" to educate Black informal workers statewide. This included writing a series of op-eds[19] that changed the narrative in Illinois on informal workers. We also established and co-led the PURE cannabis coalition, which is the first Black-led cannabis equity coalition in the State. This included launching an organizing campaign to engage Black informal workers, identify their demands, and center their voice in Illinois's recreational-cannabis policy. Included in this process was organizing a dozen town halls across the state of Illinois titled "Chronic Conversations," engaging over ten thousand Illinois residents both in person and online.[20]

IF YOU MAKE IT REAL, PEOPLE WILL RESPOND

This is one funny story. We planned to organize these "cannabis equity forums" all throughout Illinois. The first one we literally titled "Cannabis Equity Forum." We're like, "Man, this is going to be busting." But nobody showed up. We're like, "What did we do wrong?" One of our members was like, "Cannabis Equity Forum? Ain't nobody coming to that shit." It was a humbling experience, so we made a collective decision to change the title of the forum to something that was culturally relatable to the people we wanted to attend the forum. We decided to rebrand the forums as "Chronic Conversations." One, *chronic* meaning "consistent," and two, *Chronic* being a Dr. Dre album that everybody from the nineties remembers. The first Chronic Conversation was max capacity; we literally had folks sitting on the floor because we ran out of seats. The lesson for us was that language is important. If you want the people to show up, if you want them to be confident that they are coming to a safe space, use language that is accessible to them and be intentional.

COVID CHALLENGES WHEN THE MARGINALIZED ARE EVEN MORE MARGINALIZED

The pandemic hits, had to be March of 2020. There were all of these "work from home," "quarantine" expressions coming from local news outlets in the city. We're like, "What does that mean for Black informal workers?" What does work from home mean for the unhoused? We met on Zoom, and we had a conversation with the members. They were like, "I don't know about COVID but I do know that I got to get out here and hustle. If I don't hustle, I don't eat." Additionally, many of the informal workers had to leave home to make ends meet, parents who shared their income with loved ones in exchange for childcare, food, and transportation, which in reality increased the demand to hustle during the pandemic.

Then we heard news about the CARES Act, and we were hopeful that the cash stipend from the government would provide some relief for Black informal workers. To the contrary, the CARES Act excluded many of our members due to their histories of being unemployed and/or owing child support.

Although the formal economy had to shut down, there was no incentive for the informal market to shut down in any way. Our team was in the streets from March 2020 until the pandemic concluded. We never left community. Through the grace of God, no one on our team caught COVID. In all, EAT provided direct financial assistance (DFA) to 849 households. The mediums for our direct financial assistance were cash, gift cards, and rent-support checks. The gift cards and cash DFA ranged from $25 to $100. The rent support ranged from $500 to $1,000. The goal of the DFA was to offset costs for general household expenses and reduce the risk of eviction.

Our initial intention was to target individuals that were not eligible for the federal stimulus, but the process to verify each participant was far too cumbersome. We decided to trust the process, and by focusing on communities that had per capita incomes nearly $20,000 below the average per capita income, we would have a higher rate of contact with our target population. By 2022 we had provided approximately $46,840 in direct financial support.

A GUARANTEED INCOME

The pandemic taught us a lot. One of the lessons was that direct financial assistance can save lives. When the CARES Act was announced, it excluded people who hadn't worked in the last five years or who owed child support. We thought that was a complete injustice because in our mind, people who haven't been able to find labor in the last five years, and those who don't have the resources to take care of their children, are probably in the most need right now. That was why we began providing direct financial support. That was our entry into the guaranteed-income space. It was through mutual aid.

I began to do some research on GI (guaranteed income) in 2021 and found a study on the SEED pilot in Stockton, California, launched by Mayor Michael D. Tubbs.[*] I was like, "Wow, look at the outcomes." You saw increases in psychological wellness, we saw income stabilization and increased economic mobility for folks. I was like, "Well, damn, ain't that what we want?"

I had a call during the pandemic. A bunch of allies had joined, and one of the allies, never forget, her name is Holly, she was a Korean sister. Her sister ended up coming on board with EAT as the research coordinator. Her name is Rachel Pyon. A brilliant young sister. Holly was like, "We want to do more than just donate money." I was like, "Well, shit. Yeah, we got a million things you can do. Come on." By our first call, Holly had organized five or six of her friends and family to join the call.

They're like, "What can we do?" I was like, "I got this idea. I want to create a guaranteed-income program solely for formerly incarcerated people." From 2020 to 2022, we designed that program, and in 2022 we launched. That was the Chicago Future Fund. It was the first guaranteed-income program in the nation that specifically provided cash payments to formerly

---

[*] The Stockton Economic Empowerment Demonstration (SEED) program is a guaranteed-income project that took place in Stockton, California, under the leadership of Mayor Michael Tubbs in 2019. Each of 125 families were given $500 dollars a month for twenty-four months. The program recorded increases in job attainment and financial security. See Stockton Economic Empowerment Demonstration, https://www.stocktondemonstration.org/.

incarcerated people. It was also a study, so it looked at income volatility, psychological wellness, physical functioning, and recidivism. I can remember a white progressive that is considered a thought leader in the guaranteed-income community told me not to study the impact GI has on recidivism. They said, "It will not change it." We did it anyway, and I'm glad we did. We proved in our study, which is detailed in our round two report, that GI does impact recidivism. Out of one hundred participants, only three people in our program had any engagement with the police after receiving GI support.

ON ABOLITION

I mean, for most formerly incarcerated people abolition is common sense. When you're incarcerated, all you dream about is life after prison, and life beyond prison. In fact, they also know what they need in order to heal. Which, at its core, is the foundation of abolition; seeing a world without prisons and transforming hurt to healing.

During the George Floyd uprising in 2020, millions flooded the streets declaring their vison of a world where police don't kill Black people. But many balked when asked what the alternative to police could actually be. Abolition is a twofold commitment, the way I interpret it: It is a commitment to dismantle and a commitment to rebuild. Those things happening simultaneously. Honestly, I feel like the vision around what we need to rebuild needs to precede the conversation of what we need to dismantle, because oftentimes, we lead with the "dismantle" argument.

Like TINA, "there is no alternative," becomes the omnipresent ideal. I think in the abolitionist world, we got to give our people some actual experience, tangible experience, in the alternatives to the systems we aim to dismantle, which is why we built the Chicago Future Fund. What can we give our folks as an example of what an alternative actually feels like? There was a number of conversations that were happening around guaranteed income at the state level, and there was very low, I think, comprehension within the Black community about the benefits of guaranteed income.

For me, I think at the time a lot of the advocates were like, "We need to go into Black communities and tell them what it does." I was like, "No. You need to create an example and let them sit in it." When I think about abolition, I feel like there's way more joy in the visioning and the experimenting of the alternatives, than there is in the work of dismantling the system. I think about our movement in Chicago and in the state, we have to build the muscle around building out these alternatives. I got lucky with the Chicago Future Fund because there was a group of allies down to throw down and help us build it out, and we had a community that was committed to supporting us in building it out.

BEYOND POLICY: BEING IN RIGHT RELATION WITH OUR COMMUNITIES

At the time, we were getting into this reparations framework because I was at my wit's end with criminal justice reform campaigns. During the uprising, we helped push a bill called HB 3653. It was an omnibus package that included pretrial fairness, it included prison gerrymandering, it included all of these criminal justice reform policies. I remember I was sitting up over that Christmas break, and I got a call from one of our members about the intercommunity violence that was taking place. I was like, "Man, the policies aren't moving fast enough to actually save the lives that we need to save."

Policy is an important part, but we have to do more. I took a trip to Aotearoa [New Zealand], and I got to sit at the feet of elders, Māori elders, the Indigenous people of that land . . . I got to sit at the feet of the elders, listen to them share their experience of strength and hope . . . They heard me, they listened to me talk. And then they asked me a few questions. They were like, "Well, what is your relationship with your first peoples?" I was like, "What do you mean?" I didn't even know that meant. I'm like, "You mean my folks back in Arkansas? What you talking about?" Then they started telling me the story of how about fifty years ago, they had turned from their fight against the state into a campaign that centered community healing and cultural decolonization.

They saw a lot of their Māori youth leaving Indigeneity, for the big city. They assumed that they too would acquire the material benefits produced in the neoliberal capitalist economy. They wanted the clothes, technology, and lifestyle. But in reality, when they got to the big city, they faced high rates of unemployment, drug addiction, intercommunity violence, domestic violence, and they ended up forming gangs to protect the little resources they were able to acquire. Their outcomes were spot on with Black outcomes in the city of Chicago. Essentially, they realized, "Oh, we're doing the wrong work right now. We actually got to work on healing our people."

They began building interventions. They began to intervene at the level of the courts and pull their people back from the grips of neoliberal capitalism and return them to Indigeneity and healing. When they said "healing," they weren't talking about massage therapy. They were like, "No. When we say 'healing,' we're talking about reorientating our people to their land, their language, and their lineage." Brothers who have been lost to the city who were now speaking in their Indigenous tongue, and they knew what mountain their ancestors came from, what river belonged to them, and what their relationship was to Aotearoa. Through that process, they healed a base of leaders that actually won reparations in New Zealand. There are monuments to remind them and others of what colonization did. Their cultural artifacts are in the spaces of local government.

I was like, "Bet." I came back home in 2023, and I'd already had a familiar connection to Benin in West Africa. I went there with new eyes this time though. I was thinking about, "What is my relationship to my first peoples? What is the Indigenous language there? What is their relationship to the land?" When I went there, I saw vast [swaths] of hustlers. Forget how US puts context on it, people that literally pick the coconut, sell the coconut, fish the water, and sell or trade the haul to acquire what they need to survive. I'm like, "Wouldn't it be awesome to actually bring the system impacting formerly incarcerated people through a process so that they have a deeper relation-ship with their first peoples?" Through that, we can provide a practical example of what restitution looks like for descendants of US slavery, which ultimately means restoring a survivor to the state they were in before the harm occurred. When we win reparations, I don't just mean the bag [compensation]. I want the relationship with land. I want to be reconnected with my relationship to land, language, and lineage.

This year, we're kicking off a fellowship program where we're bringing formerly incarcerated people through a six-month course, where they'll be learning Fongbe, which is an Indigenous language of Benin, so they'll be reconnected to the language. They will travel to Benin for two weeks and be reconnected to the land and their lineage, understanding that our story does not start with slavery. Our story started way beyond that, and we are connected to a vast Black diaspora. Just knowing that we are a part of the global majority is empowering.

In Benin, they don't preach prison abolition or police abolition. They just don't have many police. What exists there, what keeps the community safe, is history, conscience, and relationships. It is your lineage. It is your descendance of who you come from. That familial connection, that relational connection, which I feel like was dissolved through US colonization and transatlantic slave trade.

BUILDING OUR CHICAGO

The opposite of hate is love. And love is what is necessary in order to actually create those alternatives to police and prisons at scale. It's in our reconnection to who we are. Because we are love and trust. I think a lot of harm has occurred to us because of the amount of love and trust that we have for people. We've been violated, but we don't need to lose it. We don't need to lose it in this fight for abolition. We have to trust each other.

I think Chicago is a very unique city that has a ton of possibility. I think the work of organizing the proletariat is super necessary. We got to get out of solely focusing on the city politics and get into the rural. I think Fred Hampton was spot on with his commitment to organize white rural workers as well as Black. He was like, "We all got to get to this." I think that's necessary. What becomes possible for the city of Chicago is . . . true reparations.

We have established a commission, in the city of Chicago, that was included in the mayor's budget. We've elected a progressive Black mayor. For better or worse, I think it's a thing.

What becomes possible for me is that when movement and community are in rhythm and alignment, all of our freedom dreams are possible. But it requires a bit of a commitment from movement to move at pace with the people and a commitment from the people to move. Getting to that place is really the work of the organizer in this moment. It is the duality of, "We are sharp, but we can move from sharp to dull in order to be able to meet the people wherever they are on the arc of transformation."

Right now, I think what becomes possible for us over the next five years is a commitment for movement to be in lockstep with community. Once we get in lockstep with the community, it may be a few years of political education and building of these alternatives and dreaming together. I think that what comes after that is going to be real change. Substantive change is possible through organizing at pace with community, but it takes that commitment to just be like, "All right. I know what I believe in. But can I be in community with folks who may not believe in what I believe in, in this moment, because they've been socialized to believe in something else?" Walk with them. Sometimes you can crawl with them toward this destination of Black liberation.[21]

Conclusion—Fugitive Work Is Soul Work

Returning to the words of Ayana Contreras, I also "believe that Black Chicago has a unique culture, rooted in self-determination, creativity, optimism, and hustle."[22] The essence of the work of these three organizations should be considered part of our soul's work, as it challenges us to move beyond the contours of policy and pragmatism. As tangible examples of fugitive, abolitionist work, they challenge us to embrace possibility to do what we need, simply *because we need to*. Despite the evils of engineered conflict, it does not have to operate as a permanent fixture in the city. At the same time, contesting engineered conflict takes a specific will and determination. Marc Lamont Hill is correct in stating that, in the work of abolition, "there will not be perfection, but there has to be commitment."[23] In their own unique ways, these three organizations allow us to understand possibility despite deep precarity. Their embrace of a fugitive stance also brings us back to the necessity of engaging in principled, protracted struggle. Because this is long, slow work, it requires us to be in "right relationship" with each other, understanding that how we know and treat each other is the foundation of our commitment. All three organizations are clear that substantive change only happens when you center those who have been marginalized. Because more of the same will not work, we must turn to the radical imaginaries of fugitive thought that challenge us to look at reality while positioning ourselves to engage in our contradictions, while accepting the continual challenge of making abolition a reality.

EPILOGUE

On March 15, 2023, my partner and I attended the victory party for Mayor Brandon Johnson's election. As house music blasted through the speakers in the hotel ballroom, we encountered many of our comrades from struggles in education, immigration, housing, health care, employment, prison abolition, and support for LGBTQIA+ communities. Many people from these formations worked on his campaign. For many of us, we were genuinely pleased with the hard-won victory in a mayoral election against corporate neoliberal power. At the same time, we also knew that winning the election would be the smallest part of the victory condition. After an election, when you're trying to run a city, the *real work is around the corner.* Partisan elections rarely account for collective victories for the marginalized, but with Mayor Johnson's election there was at least the hope that some of our struggles would be given proper attention by the municipal government. This type of guarded optimism came about because Johnson comes from a teaching and a union-organizing background, rooted in a belief in collective victory against corporate power. As a teacher, he joined the grassroots, justice-centered faction of the Chicago Teachers Union (CTU) known as the Caucus of Rank and File Educators (CORE). Their takeover of the union in 2010 stood as a moment of interruption and possibility, as they shifted their efforts from solely employment and salary raises to understanding how neoliberalism, gentrification, food insecurity, lack of access to health care, and loss of living-wage employment directly impacted their teaching. When Johnson left the classroom, he stayed on with CORE and worked as a community organizer for CTU. When he entered electoral politics to run for Cook County commissioner, he was largely supported by his comrades in CORE and members of CTU.

Considered a longshot in comparison to candidates supported by corporate power, Johnson's initial victory in a deeply contested, hyper-segregated city like Chicago surprised many. For myself, Johnson's election was surreal because he was a person I remembered from his teaching days. I would run into him on the train and in the grocery store. He was a daily fixture in organizing efforts against school closings and gentrification. Unlike his opponents in the mayoral race, he knew the issues of marginalized Chicagoans, because he had experienced them himself. This brought ease to those of us who knew him from those days. The fact that this campaign for an openly progressive candidate was a collective effort by justice workers throughout the city was impressive. In his unexpected victory, there was a moment of hope and potential, considering the issues and concerns that had come with the previous administration, and many mayoral administrations before it. Although not without concerns (Johnson was raised in a nearby suburb and was not initially welcomed by older Black and Latinx voters), he was not a traditional "Chicago Machine" politician. Given the team of people who worked on his campaign, there was confidence that he would not succumb to the will of corporate neoliberal power.

But electoral victories are short lived. Before Johnson won the mayoral race, buses of migrants, primarily from Venezuela, were diverted to Chicago by way of Texas. This was the result of a combination of economic collapse by way of US foreign policy and a rift between outgoing mayor Lori Lightfoot and Republican Texas governor Greg Abbott. The rift was centered in the definition of *sanctuary city*, of which Chicago has the designation. Abbott's argument was that if southern border states were left to deal with a "porous" immigration system, then the sanctuary cities with Democratic mayors in the north should begin to take some of the burden. Since August of 2022, over thirty thousand migrants have come to Chicago. The process has brought out significant contradictions and tensions. Abbott's diversion of buses to Chicago has placed considerable strain on the city's shelter infrastructure. Venezuelan migrants (many of whom are Afro-Venezuelan) have been pitted against Black communities, as some of the first and largest shelters were located in historically under-resourced Black communities, which led long-term residents to feel that their long-standing issues had been ignored by the city while the concerns of recent migrants have been prioritized. Where this is the furthest thing from the truth (considerable numbers of migrants remain housing insecure and can only live in shelters for up to sixty days), the perception has deepened tensions in historically disinvested Black communities.

Mayor Johnson's victory party also occurred on Nakba Day, the day Palestinians commemorate the forced removal of seven hundred and fifty thousand people from their homeland. While we could not predict the loss of life that would take place in Gaza after October 7, 2023, Nakba Day stands as a grim reminder of the lasting consequences of seventy-five years of forced removal. Black Chicagoans understand similar remnants in relationship to engineered conflict. The declaration of disposability is an unfortunate reality that plays itself out locally and internationally. But in the same way that our Palestinian comrades continue to resist Zionist state power in Gaza, the West Bank, and the Golan Heights, Black Chicagoans will need to continue to resist state and corporate power positioned to remove them from the city's boundaries.

As the first progressive mayor in over forty years, Johnson must make the decision to work in solidarity with people on the ground who are willing to resist corporate, capitalist state power. It is uncommon for Chicago mayors to move in community with its residents, but the Johnson administration can pull lessons from the historical interruption of Mayor Harold Washington (1983–1987). His mayoral victory provides important instructions in what it means to center the needs of the marginalized and disenfranchised. Despite the perpetual racist opposition from members of city council, the Washington administration showed what is possible in turbulent times. Before Mayor Washington's untimely death in 1987, his administration fought for health care, education, and housing for communities on the margins, standing as tangible proof of possibility in a moment where justice work can appear to be more grueling by the second.

Returning to my neighborhood of Woodlawn, the migrant shelter at the old Wadsworth school building that housed over two hundred migrants was vacated on May 13, 2024. All of its residents have been relocated to other parts of the city. While it is important to secure housing for migrant families displaced by economic collapse in their home country, the concern now is whether or not they will be placed into deeper precarity if they are moved into spaces where people are unfamiliar with them. The intraracial tensions of engineered conflict have already ravaged the city in many of its Black neighborhoods. We must do the work to see that similar tensions do not rise again.

NOTES

Introduction: Engineering Conflict in the "New" Chicago

1. James Petty, "The London Spikes Controversy: Homelessness, Urban Securitisation, and the Question of 'Hostile Architecture,'" *International Journal for Crime, Justice, and Social Democracy* 5, no. 1 (2016): 67–81; Don Mitchell, *The Right to the City: Social Justice and the Fight for Public Space* (Guilford Press, 2003). Both contributions speak to the design of cities, particularly how cities function to contain the marginalized.
2. Saidiya Hartman, *Scenes of Subjection: Terror, Slavery, and Self-Making in Nineteenth-Century America* (New York: W. W. Norton & Company, 1997).
3. Kendrick Lamar, *To Pimp a Butterfly*, Top Dawg Entertainment, March 15, 2015.
4. Mike Davis, *City of Quartz: Excavating the Future in Los Angeles* (New York: Verso, 1990).
5. Stephen Haymes, *Race, Culture and the City: A Pedagogy of Black Urban Struggle* (Albany, NY: State University of New York Press, 1995).
6. Rashad Shabazz, *Spatializing Blackness: Architectures of Confinement and Black Masculinity in Chicago* (Urbana, IL: University of Illinois Press, 2015).
7. David A. Philoxène, "Navigating Everyday Precarity and (Un)Knowable Risks: Youth Sense-Making in Racialized Spaces of Safety and Risk," unpublished manuscript submitted for publication to *Children's Geographies*.
8. Frantz Fanon, *The Wretched of the Earth* (New York: Grove Press, 1963).
9. Katherine McKittrick, *Demonic Grounds: Black Women and the Cartographies of Struggle* (Minneapolis: University of Minnesota Press, 2006).
1. "Structural Violence," University of Washington Department of Global Health, https://depts.washington.edu/globalhealthjustice/category/structural-violence/.
2. Ruth Wilson Gimore quoted in Taylor Riley, Julia P. Schleimer, and Jaquelyn L. Jahn, "Organized Abandonment Under Racial Capitalism: Measuring

Accountable Actors of Structural Racism for Public Health Research and Action," *Social Science and Medicine* 343 (2024): 1–13.

3. Personal conversation with Dr. Katherine Cho on March 28, 2025.

4. Notes from phone call with former leader of a Chicago Police Department gang tactical unit on March 16, 2016 (identity withheld).

5. Eve Tuck, "Suspending Damage: A Letter to Communities," *Harvard Education Review* 79, no. 3 (2009): 409–27.

6. Amanda Wills, Sergio Hernandez, and Marlena Baldacci, "762 Murders. 12 Months. 1 American City," CNN, January 2, 2017, https://www.cnn.com/2017/01/02/us/chicago-murder-rate-2016-visual-guide/.

7. Robert Davis, "Bell Out to Disconnect Pay Phones," *Chicago Tribune,* June 7, 1990.

8. Rob Karwath, "Bell to Restrict Pay Phone Use in Drug War," *Chicago Tribune,* July 16, 1991.

9. William Scarborough, Ivan Arenas, and Amanda Lewis, *Between the Great Migration and Growing Exodus: The Future of Black Chicago?* (Chicago: Institute for Research on Race and Public Policy, 2020).

10. Michael J. Dumas, "Against the Dark: Antiblackness in Education Policy and Discourse," *Theory into Practice* 55, (2016): 11–19.

11. Carol Caref, Sarah Rothschild, Kurt Hilgendorf, Pavlyn Jankov, and Kevin Russell, *The Black and White of Education in Chicago Public Schools* (Chicago: Chicago Teachers Union, 2013), 1.

12. D. Bradford Hunt, *Blueprint for Disaster: The Unraveling of Chicago Public Housing* (Chicago: University of Chicago Press, 2009).

13. Scarborough, Arenas, and Lewis, *Between the Great Migration*, 20.

14. Christina Sharpe, *In the Wake: On Blackness and Being* (Durham, NC: Duke University Press, 2016), 116.

15. DeMarcus A. Jenkins, "Unspoken Grammar of Place: Anti-Blackness as a Spatial Imaginary in Education," *Journal of School Leadership* 31, nos. 1–2 (2021): 107.

16. Jenkins, "Unspoken Grammar of Place."

17. John P. Koval, "An Overview and Point of View" in *The New Chicago: A Social and Cultural Analysis,* ed. John P. Koval, Larry Bennett, Michael I. J. Bennett, Fassill Demissie, Roberta Garner, and Kiljoong Kim (Philadelphia: Temple University Press, 2006), 6.

18. Joel Rast, *The Origins of the Dual City: Housing, Race, and Redevelopment in Twentieth-Century Chicago* (Chicago: University of Chicago Press, 2019).

19. Tom Tresser, *Chicago Is Not Broke: Funding the City We Deserve* (Chicago: CivicLab, 2016).

20. Rachel Weber, *From Boom to Bubble: How Finance Built the New Chicago* (Chicago: University of Chicago Press, 2015).

21. Eve L. Ewing, *Ghosts in the Schoolyard: Racism and School Closings on Chicago's South Side* (Chicago: University of Chicago Press, 2018), 151.

22. David Philoxène, "Navigating Geographies of Urban Violence: Oakland Youth Sense-Making of Racialized Safety and Space," presentation delivered at the Institute for the Study of Societal Issues, University of California, Berkeley, April 10, 2022.

23. Brandi Thompson-Summers, *Black in Place: The Spatial Aesthetics of Race in a Post-Chocolate City* (Chapel Hill, NC: University of North Carolina Press, 2019).

24. David Harvey, *A Brief History of Neoliberalism* (London: Oxford University Press, 2005), 106.

25. Personal communication with Patrick Camangian via text message on August 8, 2019.

26. Personal conversation with Janet Smith on September 1, 2010.

27. Zoé Samudzi and William G. Anderson, *As Black as Resistance: Finding the Condition for Liberation* (Chico, CA: AK Press, 2018), 2.

28. Donald A. Norman, "Design Rules Based on Analysis of Human Error," *Communications of the ACM* 26, no. 4 (1983): 254–58.

29. Norman, "Design Rules Based on Analysis," 254.

30. Rob Nixon, *Slow Violence and the Environmentalism of the Poor* (Cambridge, MA: Harvard University Press, 2013), 445.

31. Ewing, *Ghosts in the Schoolyard*, 127.

32. Nixon, *Slow Violence*.

33. Brendan Bakala, "390,000 Drivers Set to Receive Refunds for Red Light and Speed Camera Tickets," *Illinois Policy*, January 30, 2018, https://www.illinoispolicy.org/390000-drivers-set-to-receive-refunds-for-red-light-and-speed-camera-tickets/.

34. CityXones, "The New Woodlawn: An Innovative Look at the Promise and Perils of Woodlawn's Transformation," *Hyde Park Herald*, 2019, https://www.cityxones.com/hyde-park-herald-special.

35. Rob Wilderboer, "In Cook County, the Costs of Catching a Case," WBEZ, March 13, 2012, https://www.wbez.org/shows/wbez-news/in-cook-county-the-costs-of-catching-a-case/1a705488-d4ba-42ea-aa47-cfacc4a30575.

36. bell hooks, *Yearning: Race, Gender, and Cultural Politics* (Boston: South End Press, 1990), 40.

37. Carlo Rotella, *The World Is Always Coming to an End: Pulling Together and Apart in a Chicago Neighborhood* (Chicago: University of Chicago Press, 2019), 3.

38. Frantz Fanon, *The Wretched of the Earth* (New York: Grove Press, 1963), 81.

39. Stuart Hall and Doreen Massey, "Interpreting the Crisis," *Soundings* 1, no. 1 (2010): 51–71.

40. Hall and Massey, "Interpreting the Crisis," 58.

41. David Harvey, *A Brief History of Neoliberalism* (London: Oxford University Press, 2005), 3.

42. American Medical Association, "What Is Racial Capitalism?" November 10, 2021, https://www.ama-assn.org/delivering-care/health-equity/what-racial-capitalism.

43. American Medical Association, "What Is Racial Capitalism?"

44. See Beryl M. Satter, *Family Properties: How the Struggle over Race and Real Estate Transformed Chicago and Urban America* (New York: Macmillian Publishing, 2009); Ta-Nehisi Coates, "The Case for Reparations," *Atlantic*, (June 2014), https://www.theatlantic.com/magazine/archive/2014/06/the-case-for-reparations/361631/; and Keeanga-Yamahtta Taylor, *Race for Profit: How Banks and the Real Estate Industry Undermined Black Homeownership* (Chapel Hill, NC: University of North Carolina Press, 2019).

45. Taylor, *Race for Profit.*

46. Harvey, *Brief History of Neoliberalism.*

47. Rasul Mowatt, *The Geographies of Threat and the Production of Violence: The State and the City Between Us* (New York: Routledge, 2022), 4.

48. Eric K. Yamamoto, *Interracial Justice: Conflict and Reconciliation in Post–Civil Rights America* (New York: New York University Press, 1999), 20.

49. Veronica Velez and Daniel Solorzano, "Critical Race Spatial Analysis: Using GIS as a Tool for Critical Race Research in Education" in *Critical Race Spatial Analysis: Mapping to Understand and Address Educational Inequity,* eds. Deb Morrison, Subini Ancy Annamma, and Darrell D. Jackson (Sterling, VA: Stylus Publishing, 2017), ix.

50. Velez and Solorzano, "Critical Race Spatial Analysis," 21.

51. Charles W. Mills, *The Racial Contract* (Ithaca, NY: Cornell University Press), 1997.

52. Michael J. Dumas, "Losing an Arm: Schooling as a Site of Black Suffering," *Race Ethnicity and Education* 17, no. 1 (2014): 1–29.

53. Andrew J. Baranauskas, "Exploring the Social Construction of Crime by Neighborhood: News Coverage of Crime in Boston," in *Sociological Focus* 53, no. 2 (2020): 159.

54. Ruth Wilson Gilmore, "What Is to Be Done?" in *American Quarterly* 63, no. 2 (2011): 245–65.

55. See Roderick Ferguson, *One-Dimensional Queer* (London: Wiley Publishing, 2018) and *Aberrations in Black: Toward a Queer of Color Critique* (Minneapolis: University of Minnesota Press, 2003).

Chapter 1: Schools as Sites
of Displacement and Dispossession

1. Excerpt taken from David Stovall, "Reflections on the Perpetual War: School Closings, Public Housing, Law Enforcement, and the Future of Black Life," in *Education at War: The Fight for Students of Color in America's Public Schools*, eds. Arshad Ali and Tracy Lachica Buenavista (New York: Fordham University Press, 2018).

2. See Ryan Lugalia-Hollon and Daniel Cooper, *The War on Neighborhoods: Policing, Prison and Punishment in a Divided City* (New York: Beacon Press, 2018).

3. See Beryl Satter, *Family Properties: How the Struggle Over Race and Real Estate Transformed Chicago and Urban America* (New York: Picador, 2010).

4. Lugalia-Hollon and Cooper, *War on Neighborhoods*, 21.

5. See Dionne Danns, "Chicago School Desegregation and the Role of the State of Illinois," *American Educational History Journal* 37, no. 1 (2010): 55–74.

6. Lugalia-Hollon and Cooper, *War on Neighborhoods*, 38.

7. Lugalia-Hollon and Cooper, *War on Neighborhoods*, 36.

8. Elizabeth Duffrin, "Slow Progress Amid Strife: While Students Who Were Shut Out by School Closings Show Some Signs of Academic Progress, Most Land in Schools That Are Not Much Better Than the Ones They Left," *Catalyst Chicago* 17, no. 6 (March 2006): 10.

9. Duffrin, "Slow Progress Amid Strife," 9.

10. "Principal Shocks Clemente with Resignation," *Chicago Tribune*, March 2, 2006, Section 2C, 6.

11. Pauline Lipman, "The Landscape of Education 'Reform' in Chicago: Neoliberalism Meets a Grassroots Movement," *Education Policy Analysis Archives* 25, no. 54 (2017), http://dx.doi.org/10.14507/epaa.25.2660.

12. David Stovall, "Mayoral Control: Reform, Whiteness, and Critical Race Analysis of Neoliberal Educational Policy," in *What's Race Got to Do with It?: Understanding Racism, Neoliberalism, and Education Reform*, eds. Bree Picower and Edwin Mayorga (New York: Peter Lang Publishers, 2015).

13. Samantha Smylie and Kalyn Belsha, "Chicago Will Have the Largest Elected School Board of Any Major U.S. City," *Chalk Beat*, July 30, 2021, https://chicago.chalkbeat.org/2021/7/30/22602068/illinois-governor-approves-elected-chicago-school-board.

14. Pauline Lipman and David Hursh, "Renaissance 2010: The Reassertion of Ruling Class Power Through Neoliberal Policies in Chicago," *Policy Futures in Urban Education* 5, no.2 (2007): 160–78.

15. Lipman and Hursh, "Renaissance 2010."

16. Lipman and Hursh, "Renaissance 2010."

17. David Stovall, *Born Out of Struggle: Critical Race Theory, School Creation, and the Politics of Interruption* (Albany, NY: SUNY Press, 2016).

18. Lipman and Hursh, "Renaissance 2010," 170.

19. Madeline Parrish and Chima Ikoro, "Chicago Public Schools and Segregation," *South Side Weekly*, February 24, 2022, https://southsideweekly.com/chicago-public-schools-and-segregation/.

20. Wendy Plotkin, "Deeds of Mistrust: Race, Housing, and Restrictive Covenants in Chicago, 1900–1953," (PhD diss., University of Illinois Chicago, 1999).

21. Plotkin, "Deeds of Mistrust."

22. Parrish and Ikoro, "Chicago Public Schools and Segregation."

23. Shawn L. Jackson, "An Historical Analysis of the Chicago Public Schools Desegregation Consent Decree (1980–2006): Establishing Its Relationship with the *Brown v. Board* Case of 1954 and the Implications of Its Implementation on Educational Leadership" (PhD diss., Loyola University, 2010), http://ecommons.luc.edu/luc_diss/129.

24. Parrish and Ikoro, "Chicago Public Schools and Segregation."

25. Mila Koumpilova, "Can Chicago Revitalize Its Tiny High Schools?" *Chalkbeat,* September 27, 2022, https://chicago.chalkbeat.org/2022/9/27/23375249/chicago-public-schools-pedro-martinez-small-neighborhood-high-schools.

26. Koumpilova, "Can Chicago Revitalize," 17.

27. Koumpilova, "Can Chicago Revitalize," 21.

28. Koumpilova, "Can Chicago Revitalize," 13.

29. Federico Waitoller and Joshua Radinsky, "Geo-spatial Perspectives on Neoliberal Education Reform: Examining Intersections of Ability, Race, and Social Class," in *Critical Race Spatial Analysis: Mapping to Understand and Address Educational Inequity,* eds. Deb Morrison, Subini Ancy Annamma, and Darrell D. Jackson (New York: Routledge, 2023): 147–64.

30. Rachel Weber, Stephanie Farmer, and Mary Donoghue, *Why These Schools: Explaining School Closures in Chicago 2000–2013* (Chicago: Great Cities Institute, University of Illinois at Chicago, 2017).

31. Catalyst Chicago, "Table: School Closings Over 10 Years" *Chicago Reporter,* December 7, 2011, https://www.chicagoreporter.com/table-school-closings-over-10-years/.

32. Marisa de la Torre and Julia Gwynne, *When Schools Close: Effects on Displaced Students in Chicago Public Schools* (Chicago: University of Chicago Consortium of School Research, 2009), 1–48.

33. Molly F. Gordon, Marisa de la Torre, Jennifer R. Cowhy, Paul T. Moore,

Lauren Sartain, and David Knight, *School Closings in Chicago Staff and Student Experiences and Academic Outcomes* (Chicago: University of Chicago Consortium on Chicago School Research, 2018).

34. Gordon et al., *School Closings in Chicago.*
35. Adeshina Emmanuel, "'War Zone' Described at Uptown School After Courtenay Stockton Merger," *DNA Info*, January 7, 2014, https://www.dnainfo.com/chicago/20140107/uptown/war-zone-described-at-uptown-school-following-courtenay-stockton-merger/.
36. Emmanuel, "'War Zone.'"
37. "Courtenay: School Overview," Chicago Public Schools, https://www.cps.edu/schools/schoolprofiles/courtenay.
38. Anthony S. Bryk, G. Alfred Hess Jr., Jeffrey Mirel, and Kenneth Wong, "Policy Lessons from Chicago's Experience with Decentralization," *Brookings Papers on Education Policy*, no. 2, (1999), 71.
39. Bryk et al., "Policy Lessons from Chicago's Experience," 106.
40. Michelle Mbekeani-Wiley, *Handcuffs in Hallways: The State of Policing in Chicago Public Schools* (Chicago: Sargent Shriver National Center on Poverty Law, 2017).
41. See Dan Weissman, "Austin High School Recovering After 'Reform from Hell,'" *Catalyst Chicago*, July 22, 2005, https://www.chicagoreporter.com/austin-high-school-recovering-after-reform-hell.
42. Richard Kahlenburg and Halley Potter, "Restoring Shanker's Vision for Charter Schools," *Journal of the American Federation of Teachers* (Winter 2014): 1–19.
43. Pauline Lipman, *The New Political Economy of Urban Education: Neoliberalism, Race, and the Right to the City* (New York: Routledge, 2011).
44. Gerald Bracey, *Charter Schools' Performance and Accountability: A Disconnect* (Education Policy Studies Laboratory: George Mason University, 2005).
45. Tammy Webber, "Chicago School Draws Scrutiny over Student Fines," *Herald Tribune*, February 21, 2012, https://www.heraldtribune.com/story/news/2012/02/21/chicago-school-draws-scrutiny-over-student-fines/29083100007/.
46. Carla Shedd, *Unequal City: Race, Schools and Perceptions of Injustice* (New York: Russell Sage Foundation, 2015), 11.
47. Weber et al., *Why These Schools?*
48. Elizabeth Todd-Breland, *A Political Education: Black Politics and Education Reform in Chicago Since the 1960s* (Chapel Hill, NC: University of North Carolina Press, 2018).
49. "History," Orr Academy High School, https://orracademy.org/apps/pages/index.jsp?uREC_ID=377292&type=d.

50. Chip Mitchell, "Chicago's 'Safe Passage' Curbs Street Violence Without Police, Studies Show," WBEZ, June 5, 2019, https://www.wbez.org/chicago/2019/06/05/chicagos-safe-passage-curbs-street-violence-without-police-studies-show.

51. Robert Gonzalez and Sarah Kosmisarow, "Community Monitoring and Crime: Evidence from Chicago's Safe Passage Program," *Journal of Public Economics* 191 (2020): 1–18.

52. Mitchell, "Chicago's 'Safe Passage.'"

53. Linda Lutton, "Closing Schools Diaspora," WBEZ, August 26, 2013, https://www.wbez.org/stories/closing-schools-diaspora/32d8158c-e379-4ebd-8c56-13609855b2aa.

Chapter 2: Plans That Did Not Transform

1. "Project," *The Oxford Pocket Dictionary of Current English*, July 19, 2025, https://www.encyclopedia.com/humanities/dictionaries-thesauruses-pictures-and-press-releases/project-0.

2. Catherine Fennell, *Last Project Standing: Civics and Sympathy in Post Welfare Chicago* (Minneapolis: University of Minnesota Press, 2015), 38.

3. Fennell, *Last Project Standing*, 32.

4. See D. Bradford Hunt, *Blueprint for Disaster: The Unraveling of Public Housing* (Chicago: University of Chicago Press, 2009); Arnold Hirsch, *Making the Second Ghetto: Race and Housing in Chicago, 1940–1960* (Chicago: University of Chicago Press).

5. See Devereux Bowly, *The Poorhouse: Subsidized Housing in Chicago, 1895–1976* (Carbondale, IL: Southern Illinois University Press, 1978).

6. J. S. Fuerst, *When Public Housing Was Paradise: Building Community in Chicago* (Chicago: University of Illinois Press, 2005), 3.

7. Bowly, *Poorhouse*, 18.

8. Bowly, *Poorhouse*, 26–27.

9. Bowly, *Poorhouse*, 20–21.

10. Bowly, *Poorhouse*, 27.

11. Bowly, *Poorhouse*, 56.

12. Bowly, *Poorhouse*, 37.

13. Fuerst, *When Public Housing Was Paradise*, 5.

14. Fuerst, *When Public Housing Was Paradise*, 11.

15. Fuerst, *When Public Housing Was Paradise*, 54.

16. Fuerst, *When Public Housing Was Paradise*, 56.

17. Michelle Boyd, *Jim Crow Nostalgia: Reconstructing Race in Bronzeville* (Minneapolis: University of Minnesota Press, 2008), xiii.

18. Bowly, *Poorhouse*, 80–83.

19. Bowly, *Poorhouse*, 78.

20. Bowly, *Poorhouse*, 18.

21. Edward G. Goetz, *New Deal Ruins: Race, Economic Justice, and Public Housing Policy* (London: Cornell University Press, 2013), 33.

22. Marah A. Curtis, Sarah Garlington, and Lisa Schottenfeld, "Alcohol, Drug and Criminal History Restrictions in Public Housing," *Cityscape* 15, no. 3 (2013): 37–52, 2013.

23. Goetz, *New Deal Ruins*, 13.

24. Bowly, *Poorhouse*, 77.

25. Bowly, *Poorhouse*, 83–84.

26. Hunt, *Blueprint for Disaster*, 159.

27. Hunt, *Blueprint for Disaster*, 180.

28. See Roberta Feldman and Susan Stall, *The Dignity of Resistance: Women Residents' Activism in Chicago Public Housing* (New York: Cambridge University Press, 2004).

29. Fuerst, *When Public Housing Was Paradise*, 11.

30. Bowly, *Poorhouse*, 112.

31. Rashad Shabazz, *Spatializing Blackness: Architectures of Confinement and Black Masculinity in Chicago* (Urbana, IL: University of Illinois Press, 2015), 56.

32. Shabazz, *Spatializing Blackness*, 58.

33. David E. B. Smith, "Clean Sweep or Witch Hunt: Constitutional Issues in Chicago's Public Housing Sweeps," *Chicago Kent Law Review* 69, no. 505 (1993): 508.

34. Goetz, *New Deal Ruins*, 79.

35. Goetz, *New Deal Ruins*.

36. Goetz, *New Deal Ruins*.

37. Smith, "Clean Sweep or Witch Hunt," 540.

38. Goetz, *New Deal Ruins*, 85.

39. Goetz, *New Deal Ruins*, 19.

40. See Audrey Petty, *High Rise Stories: Voices from Chicago Public Housing* (Chicago: Haymarket Press, 2021). Ben Austen, *High Risers: Cabrini-Green and the Fate of American Public Housing* (New York: Harper Publishers, 2018). There are also two documentary films on the struggle in Cabrini-Green, *Voices of Cabrini* and *77 Acres*, both produced by Ronit Films.

41. See Jeffrey Duncan-Andrade and Ernest Morell, *The Art of Critical Pedagogy: Moving from Theory to Practice in Urban Schools* (New York: Peter Lang, 2008).

42. Duncan-Andrade, *Art of Critical Pedagogy*, 87.

43. Smith, "Clean Sweep or Witch Hunt," 542.

44. See Feldman and Stall (2004) and Fennell (2015). Feldman and Stall discuss in detail the court victory won by residents of Wentworth Gardens, who effectively became tenant managers. Wentworth Gardens is the oldest tenant-managed public housing development in the county. Catherine Fennell documents the story of tenants in the Henry Horner Homes, who sued CHA to remain in their homes during the renovation.

45. Susan Popkin, Bruce Katz, Mary K. Cunningham, Karen Brown, Jeremy Gustafson, Margery A. Turner, *A Decade of Hope VI: Research Findings and Policy Challenges* (Washington, DC: The Urban Institute, 2004).

46. Goetz, *New Deal Ruins*, 84.

47. James E. Rosembaum, Linda K. Stroh, and Cathy Flynn, "Lake Parc Place: A Study of Mixed-Income Housing," *Housing Policy Debate* 9, no. 4 (1998): 703–40.

48. Chicago Housing Authority, "Chicago Housing Authority: Plan for Transformation. Improving Public Housing in Chicago and the Quality of Life," January 6, 2000.

49. Janet Smith, "The Chicago Housing Authority's Plan for Transformation," in *Where Are Poor People to Live?: Transforming Public Housing Communities*, eds. Larry Bennett, Janet L. Smith, and Patricia A. Wright (London: M.E. Sharpe, 2006), 93.

50. Popkin et. al., *Decade of Hope VI*, 14.

51. Jacqueline Thompson, "Harold Ickes Homes News," *Residents Journal*, December 9, 2008, https://wethepeoplemedia.org/harold-l-ickes-homes-news/.

52. Mary C. Piemonte, "Tenants Protest CHA's Plan for Lathrop," *Residents Journal*, December 15, 2012, https://wethepeoplemedia.org/tenants-protest-chas-plans-for-lathrop/.

53. Smith, "Chicago Housing Authority's Plan," 104.

54. Chicago Housing Authority, *Plan for Transformation*, 13.

55. Smith, "Chicago Housing Authority's Plan," 115.

56. Natalie Moore, "Why the Chicago Housing Authority Failed to Meet Its Mixed-Income Ambitions," WBEZ, March 23, 2019, www.interactive.wbez.org/cha.

57. Russell W. Rumberger, "The Causes and Consequences of Student Mobility," *Journal of Negro Education* 72, no.1 (2003): 6–21.

58. "Beethoven: School Overview," Chicago Public Schools, www.cps.edu/schools/schoolprofiles/beethoven.

59. Moore, "Why the Chicago Housing Authority Failed."

60. Mick Dumke, "Chicago Claims Its 22-Year 'Transformation' Plan Revitalized 25,000 Homes. The Math Doesn't Add Up," *ProPublica*, December 16, 2022,

https://www.propublica.org/article/chicago-housing-authority-hud-transformation-plan.

61. Barbara, Kenya. "The Plan for Transformation: How a Plan with Lofty Goals Has Underperformed and Forever Changed Public Housing in Chicago," *Public Interest Law Reporter* 24, no. 1 (2018): 7.

62. Barbara, "Plan for Transformation."

Chapter 3: This Is Not a Gang Problem

1. John Hagedorn, Roberto Aspholm, Teresa Cordova, Andrew Papachristos, and Lance Williams, *The Fracturing of Gangs and Violence in Chicago: A Research-Based Reorientation of Violence Prevention and Intervention Policy* (Chicago: Great Cities Institute, 2018), 2.

2. Hagedorn, *Fracturing of Gangs and Violence*, 135.

3. Roberto Aspholm, *Views from the Streets: The Transformation of Gangs and Violence on Chicago's South Side* (New York: Columbia University Press, 2019), 3.

4. Aspholm, *Views from the Streets*.

5. Ruth Wilson Gilmore, *Golden Gulag: Prisons, Surplus, Crisis, and Opposition in Globalizing California.* (Berkeley, CA: University of California Press, 2007), 28.

6. See David Harvey, "The New Imperialism: Accumulation by Dispossession," *Socialist Register* 40 (2004): 63–87.

7. Natalie Moore and Lance Williams, *The Almighty Black P Stone Nation: The Rise Fall and Resurgence of an American Gang* (Chicago, IL: Lawrence Hill Books, 2011), 19–20.

8. See Moore and Williams, *Almighty Black P Stone Nation*, 31–48.

9. See Moore, Natalie and Lance Williams, *Almighty Black P Stone Nation*, 49–69; Lance Williams, *King David and Boss Daley: The Black Disciples, Mayor Daley and Chicago on the Edge* (Essex, CT: Prometheus Books, 2023), 217–26.

10. Moore and Williams, *Almighty Black P Stone Nation*, 7–30.

11. Williams, *King David and Boss Daley*, 215–16.

12. See Elizabeth Hinton, *From the War on Poverty to the War on Crime: The Making of Mass Incarceration in America* (Cambridge, MA: Harvard University Press, 2017).

13. See Timuel Black, *Bridges of Memory: Chicago's First Wave of Black Migration Volume 1* (Chicago: Northwestern University Press, 2005); and *Bridges of Memory Volume 2: Chicago's Second Generation of Black Migration* (Chicago: Northwestern University Press, 2008).

14. Asphlom, *Views from the Streets*, 33, 41.

15. Simon Balto, *Occupied Territory: Policing Black Chicago from Red Summer to Black Power* (Chapel Hill, NC: University of North Carolina Press, 2019), 4.

16. "Erase the Gang Database," Erase the Database Coalition, erasethedatabase.com.

17. Chicago Crime Commission, *The Gang Book*, chicagocrimecommission.org.

18. Spencer Ackerman, "Homan Square Revealed: How Chicago Police Disappeared 7,000 People," *Guardian*, October 19, 2015, https://www. theguardian.com/us-news/2015/oct/19/homan-square-chicago-police-dis-appeared-thousands.

19. Flint Taylor, *The Torture Machine: Racism and Police Violence in Chicago* (Chicago: Haymarket Books, 2019).

20. Balto, *Occupied Territory*, 11.

21. United States Department of Justice, *Federal Report on Police Killings: Ferguson, Cleveland, Baltimore, and Chicago* (London: Melville House Publishing, 2017), 412.

22. *State of Illinois v. City of Chicago,* United States District Court for the Northern District of Illinois, Eastern Division. CN 17cv-6260.

23. Alex Vitale, *The End of Policing* (London: Verso, 2017).

24. Jeffrey Duncan-Andrade and Ernest Morrell, *The Art of Critical Pedagogy: Possibilities for Moving from Theory to Practice in Urban Schools* (New York: Peter Lang, 2008).

25. Alex Nitkin, "Police Conduct Lawsuits Cost Taxpayers $40 Million in 2020 Report Shows—And Costs Are Growing," *Block Club Chicago,* March 10, 2022, https://blockclubchicago.org/2022/03/10/police-misconduct-law-suits-cost-chicago-taxpayers-40-million-in-2020-report-shows-and-costs-are-growing%EF%BF%BC/.

26. Brian Mullgardt, "'Further Harassment and Neutralization': The FBI's Counterintelligence in Illinois," *Journal of the Illinois State Historical Society* 113, no. 3–4 (2020): 94.

27. Frank Donner, *Protectors of Privilege: Red Squads and Police Repression in Urban America* (Los Angeles: University of California Press, 1990), 91–92.

28. Balto, *Occupied Territory,* 202.

29. Balto, *Occupied Territory,* 203.

30. Balto, *Occupied Territory,* 206.

31. Gerald E. Lynch, "A Conceptual, Practical, and Political Guide to RICO Reform," *Vanderbilt Law Review* 769, no. 43 (1990), 770.

32. Lynch, "A Conceptual, Practical, and Political Guide," 776–77.

33. Lynch, "A Conceptual, Practical, and Political Guide."

34. Over the years, prosecutors have been critical of RICO cases in government corruption cases because prosecutors often do not have the resources to investigate powerful politicians at the local level. Another critique is offered against white-collar crime cases, where local and federal penalties are thought

to often be inadequate to the magnitude of wrongdoing. Lynch, "A Conceptual, Practical, and Political Guide," 778–81.

35. U.S. v. Larry Hoover et. al. (95 CR 508)

36. In addition to U.S. v. Hoover, the two other cases in Operation Headache were U.S. v. Keith McCain (95 CR 509) and U.S. v. Jeffrey C. Hatcher (95 CR 510).

37. Neyfakh, Leon. "How Did Chicago Get So Violent?: Did the Effort to Eradicate the City's Gangs in the 1990s Inadvertently Lead to Its Bloody Present?" *Slate*, September 23, 2016, https://slate.com/news-and-politics/2016/09/is-chicagos-ghastly-murder-rate-the-result-of-its-1990s-anti-gang-policies.html.

38. Neyfakh, "How Did Chicago Get So Violent?"

39. Neal Pollack, "The Gang That Could Go Straight," *Chicago Reader* 4, no, 26 (January 26, 1995), https://chicagoreader.com/news-politics/the-gang-that-could-go-straight/.

40. U.S. v. Larry Hoover et. al., 3.

41. U.S. v. Larry Hoover et. al., 4.

42. U.S. v. Larry Hoover et. al., 5–7.

43. Pollack, "Gang That Could Go Straight."

44. Finnin McCown, "Making Peace, Making Revolution: Black Gangs in Chicago Politics, 1992–1993," *Chicago Studies* (2017), 112.

45. Larry Hoover, "Larry Hoover Political Prisoner, Growth and Development, 21st Century VOTE, Control Your Community and Politicians," *New Afrika History*, November 30, 2016, https://newafrikan77.wordpress.com/2016/11/30/larry-hoover-political-prisonergrowth-and-development-21st-century-vote-control-your-community-and-politicians/.

46. Hoover, "Larry Hoover Political Prisoner."

47. Pollack, "Gang That Could Go Straight."

48. Ann Scott Tyson, "The Many Faces of a Reputed Gangster," *Christian Science Monitor*, May 6, 1997, https://www.csmonitor.com/1997/0506/050697.us.us.3.html?cmpid=shared-email.

49. Quote is from CPD captain Donald Hilbring in reference to the hopes of limiting the scope of the GDs' operations. See Ann Scott Tyson, "True Colors: Trial of Chicago's 'Disciples,'" *Christian Science Monitor*, February 27, 1996, https://www.csmonitor.com/1996/0227/27011.html.

50. Ron Levi, "Making Counterlaw: On Having No Apparent Purpose in Chicago," *British Journal of Criminology* 49, (2009), 132.

51. Supreme Court of the United States of America, Chicago v. Morales, 527 U.S. 41 (1999).

52. Supreme Court of the United States of America, Chicago v. Morales, 527 U.S. 41 (1999).

53. Dennis P. Rosenbaum and Cody Stephens, *Reducing Public Violence and Homicide in Chicago: Strategies and Tactics of the Chicago Police Department* (Center for Law and Justice, University of Illinois at Chicago), 24.

54. Rosenbaum and Stephens, *Reducing Public Violence*, 24–25.

55. Timothy Bella, "Will Illinois RICO Law 'with Teeth' Help Chicago?," *Al Jazeera*, August 22, 2012.

Chapter 4: When It All Comes Together

1. *Judgment Night*, directed by Stephen Hopkins (MCA Universal, 1993).

2. Conversation with Ada and Ronald Stovall on July 9, 2024. The Pershing Hotel is the recording site of the famous album *Live at the Pershing* by pianist Ahmad Jamal.

3. Veronica Velez and Daniel Solorzano, "Critical Race Spatial Analysis: Conceptualizing GPS as a Tool for Critical Race Research in Education," in *Critical Race Spatial Analysis: Mapping to Understand and Address Educational Inequity*, eds. Deb Morrison, Subini A. Annamma, and Darrell D. Jackson (Sterling, VA: Stylus Publishing, 2017), 16.

4. "The History of Woodlawn," Chicago Studies, https://chicagostudies.uchi-cago.edu/woodlawn/woodlawn-history-woodlawn.

5. Michelle Boyd, *Jim Crow Nostalgia: Reconstructing Race in Bronzeville* (Minneapolis: University of Minnesota Press, 2008).

6. Arnold Hirsch, *Making the Second Ghetto: Race and Housing in Chicago 1940–1960* (Chicago: University of Chicago Press, 1998), 148.

7. Hirsch, *Making the Second Ghetto*, 148.

8. Quoted in Hirsch, *Making the Second Ghetto*, 154.

9. Community Benefits Agreement for the Area Around the Obama Center, Obama Community Benefits Agreement Coalition, http://www.obamacba.org/.

10. Community Benefits Agreement.

11. Robert McCoppin, "Big Plans Near Obama Center Stuck in Bunker," *Chicago Tribune,* October 2, 2023, https://digitaledition.chicagotribune.com/tribune/article_popover.aspx?guid=18473455-4db3-41af-a18d-903e3e36c3f8.

12. Lauren Fitzpatrick, "Ahead of Opening Nearby Obama Center, Hyde Park Academy HS Gets $40 Million Boost," *Chicago Sun Times,* September 11, 2018, https://chicago.suntimes.com/2018/9/11/18374583/ahead-of-opening-of-nearby-obama-center-hyde-park-academy-hs-gets-40m-boost.

13. Dennis Rodkin, "This Is the Most Expensive Home Sale Ever in Woodlawn," *Crain's Chicago Business Report*, March 16, 2023, https://www.chicagobusiness.com/residential-real-estate/

most-expensive-home-sale-ever-woodlawn-chicagos-south-side.

14. "6519 S Ingleside Ave, Chicago, IL 60637," Redfin, https://www.redfin.com/ IL/Chicago/6519-S-Ingleside-Ave-60637/home/13928513.

15. *Woodlawn Area Community Analysis: Final Draft* (AECOM, 2019), 40.

16. J. W. Mason, "Losing Track," *Chicago Reader,* November 6, 1997, https://chicagoreader.com/news-politics/losing-track/.

17. "Woodlawn, Chicago, Cook County, IL Demographics," Point2Homes, 2023, https://www.point2homes.com/US/Neighborhood/IL/Cook-County/Chicago/Woodlawn-Demographics.html.

18. "Woodlawn, Chicago."

19. "6522-26 S Ingleside Ave, Chicago, IL 60637," Redfin, https://www.redfin.com/IL/Chicago/6522-S-Ingleside-Ave-60637/home/17557912.

20. "6522 S Ingleside Ave Unit 3S, Chicago, IL 60637" Realtor.com, https://www.realtor.com/realestateandhomes-detail/6522-S-Ingleside-Ave_Chicago_IL_60637_M81622-62417.

21. Velez and Solorzano, "Critical Race Spatial Analysis," 16.

22. Elizabeth Todd-Breland, *A Political Education: Black Politics and Education Reform in Chicago Since the 1960s* (Chapel Hill, NC: University of North Carolina Press, 2018), 61.

23. Todd-Breland, *Political Education.*

24. Todd-Breland, *Political Education,* 52.

25. Todd-Breland, *Political Education.*

26. Todd-Breland, *Political Education,* 63.

27. Todd-Breland, *Political Education,* 211.

28. Maureen Kelleher, "Woodlawn: Activists Make Housing School Connection," *Catalyst Chicago,* March 20, 2006, https://www.chicagoreporter.com/woodlawn-activists-make-housing-schools-connection/.

29. Maureen Kelleher, "Charter Provides New School Option: Faced with Community Pressure, University Will Serve Local Kids First," *Catalyst Chicago* 17, no. 6, (March 2006): 16–17.

30. Todd-Breland, *Political Education,* 214.

31. Grant Pick, "A Tour of Duties," *Catalyst Chicago,* September 14, 2005, https://www.chicagoreporter.com/tour-duties/.

32. Pick, "A Tour of Duties."

33. "Till School Overview," Chicago Public Schools, https://www.cps.edu/schools/schoolprofiles/till.

34. Eve L. Ewing, *Ghosts in the Schoolyard: Racism and School Closings on Chicago's South Side* (Chicago: University of Chicago Press, 2018), 127.

35. Lauren Fitzpatrick, Andy Boyle, and Caroline Hurley, "Who Are Chicago

Schools Named For?," *Chicago Sun Times,* December 30, 2020, https://graph-ics.suntimes.com/education/school-names/.

36. "Designate Alexandre Dumas Elementary School as a Technology Cluster Magnet School, Change the School's Educational Focus to a Technology Program and Change the School's Name to Dumas Technology Academy," Chicago Public Schools, April 23, 2008, https://www.cpsboe.org/content/actions/2008_04/08-0423-EX2.pdf.

37. Clifford Meacham, "The Matter of the Proposal to Close Dumas Technology Academy and Relocation of James Wadsworth Elementary School, Chicago, IL., Hearing Report and Recommendations," April 25, 2013. Possible to add publication info or a url? Or should this be citing a court decision?

38. Meacham, "Matter of the Proposal."

39. Sam Cholke, "Woodlawn Faced with Big Empty School After U of C Charter Moves," *Block Club Chicago,* January 12, 2017, https://www.dnainfo.com/chicago/20170112/woodlawn/university-of-chicago-woodlawn-charter-school-moves-wadsworth-building/.

40. Lee Harris, "UChicago Charter Schools Opens New Woodlawn Campus, First Development South of 61st Since '60s Agreement," *Chicago Maroon,* February 1, 2018, https://chicagomaroon.com/25412/news/uchicago-charter-schools-opens-new-woodlawn-campus/.

41. Maxwell Evans, "New Patio Planned for Migrants at Wadsworth Shelter in Woodlawn," *Block Club Chicago,* July 7, 2023, https://blockclubchicago.org/2023/07/07/new-patio-planned-for-migrants-at-wadsworth-shelter-in-woodlawn/.

42. Susan Zupan, "Vallas Connection to Wadsworth: Why Didn't the Powers-That-Be Fold Dumas into Wadsworth's School Building in 2013?" *Substance News,* February 9, 2023, https://www.substancenews.net/articles.php?page=7984.

43. Zupan, "Vallas Connection to Wadsworth."

44. Paddy McNamara, "Proceedings Before the Board of Education of the Chicago Public Schools Independent Hearing Officer's Report: The Proposed Closure of Austin O. Sexton Elementary School and the Relocation of John Fiske Elementary School," April 29, 2013, 4–5, https://schoolinfo.cps.edu/SchoolActions/Download.aspx?fid=2703.

45. McNamara, "Proceedings Before the Board," 3.

46. Shaka Rawls, "Watching the Asphalt Grow: How One Community Experienced and Was Impacted by Educational Reform Policies" (PhD diss., University of Illinois at Chicago, 2024), 87–89.

47. Eve L. Ewing, "Commentary" in *Research Report: School Closings in Chicago—Staff and Student Experiences and Academic Outcomes,* eds. Molly

F. Gordon, Marisa de la Torre, Jennifer R. Cowhy, Paul T. Moore, Lauren Sartain, and David Knight (University of Chicago Consortium on Chicago School Research, May 2018).

48. John Hall Fish, *Black Power/White Control: The Struggle of the Woodlawn Organization in Chicago* (Princeton, NJ: Princeton University Press, 1973; Princeton Legacy Library, 2016), 71.

49. Hall Fish, *Black Power/White Control*, 93.

50. Hall Fish, *Black Power/White Control*, 92.

51. Mason, "Losing Track."

52. Mason, "Losing Track."

53. Lilydale Gibson, "Due South: After Decades of Mistrust and Misunderstanding, the University Is Getting Reacquainted with Woodlawn," *University of Chicago Magazine* 98, no. 3 (February 2006), https://magazine.uchicago.edu/0602/features/south.shtml.

54. Woodlawn East Community and Neighbors (WECAN), *The Woodlawn Housing Data Project Summary Report*, September 2019, 11, https://d35xwg-5b6z69e9.cloudfront.net/store/5ccca34e4d20d7648120722b0ddbcc36.pdf.

55. WECAN, *Woodlawn Housing Data*.

56. WECAN, *Woodlawn Housing Data*, 6.

57. Hall Fish, *Black Power/White Control*, 292.

58. See Moore and Williams, *Almighty Black P Stone Nation*, specifically chapter 4.

59. Hall Fish, *Black Power/White Control*, 71–72.

60. Hall Fish, *Black Power/White Control*.

61. Hall Fish, *Black Power/White Control*, 77.

62. Hall Fish, *Black Power/White Control*, 76.

63. Max Budovitch, "The Fight to Remain," *South Side Weekly*, January 23, 2019, https://southsideweekly.com/the-fight-to-remain-woodlawn-organization-grove-parc-poah/.

64. Budovitch, "The Fight to Remain."

65. Budovitch, "The Fight to Remain."

66. Budovitch, "The Fight to Remain."

67. *Chicago Sun-Times* Editorial Board, "Rise of 63rd Street Continues with Plan for $48 Million 'Woodlawn Social,'" *Chicago Sun-Times*, May 17, 2023, https://chicago.suntimes.com/2023/5/17/23727173/63rd-street-woodlawn-development-obama-center-green-line-editorial.

68. "About Us," One Woodlawn, https://onewoodlawn.org/#about-us.

69. "Chicago Police Return to Community Policing," *Chicago Tribune*, May 20, 2013, https://www.officer.com/home/news/10945759/chicago-police-department-signals-return-to-community-policing.

70. See Moore and Williams, *Almighty Black P Stone Nation*. Chapter 4 explains the relationship between the Stones, TWO, and the federal government by way of programming for the "War on Poverty."

71. "Black Disciples," Chicago Gang History, https://www.chicagoganghistory. com/gang/black-disciples/.

72. Roberto Asphlom, *Views from the Streets: The Transformation of Gangs and Violence on Chicago's South Side* (New York: Columbia University Press, 2019), 31.

73. Matthew D. Wilson, "Youth Employment Data: Employment to Population Ratios for 16 to 19 and 20 to 24 Year Olds by Chicago Community Area, 2005–2009 to 2010–2014," Great Cities Institute, University of Illinois at Chicago, February 16, 2016, 5, https://greatcities.uic. edu/2016/09/02/youth-employment-data-employment-to-population-ratios-for-16-to-19-and-20-to-24-year-olds-by-chicago-community-area-2009-2014/.

74. Maxwell Evans, "City Council Approves Woodlawn Affordable Housing Ordinance Near Obama Center: 'A Step in the Right Direction,'" *Block Club Chicago,* September 10, 2020, https://blockclubchicago.org/2020/09/09/ city-council-approves-woodlawn-affordable-housing-ordinance-a-step-in-the-right-direction/.

75. Kelly Bauer, "Woodlawn Residents Push for Anti-Displacement Ordinance amid Fears over Obama Library," *Block Club Chicago,* October 23, 2018, https://blockclubchicago.org/2018/10/23/woodlawn-residents-push-for-anti-displacement-ordinance-amid-fears-over-obama-library/.

76. "Woodlawn Housing Preservation Ordinance Overview," City of Chicago, https://www.chicago.gov/city/en/depts/doh/supp_info/woodlawn-housing-ordinance.html.

77. "Woodlawn Housing Preservation."

Chapter 5: Black Fugitive Futures

1. Andrea Ritchie, "Ending the War on Black Women," in *Abolition for the People: The Movement for a Future Without Policing and Prisons,* ed. Colin Kaepernick (Chicago: Haymarket Books, 2023), 198.

2. Ayana Contreras, *Energy Never Dies: Afro-Optimism and Creativity in Chicago* (Chicago: University of Illinois Press, 2021), xiv.

3. Kelly Hayes and Mariame Kaba, *Let This Radicalize You: Organizing and the Revolution of Reciprocal Care* (Chicago: Haymarket Books, 2023), xii.

4. 725 ILCS 5/Article 100, The Safety, Accountability, Fairness and Equity

– Today Act (SAFE-T Act). Passed on September 18, 2023.

5. Quote from Michael Dumas during an April 17, 2018, presentation at the American Educational Research Association, as part of a panel on abolition.

6. Zoe Samudzi and William G. Anderson, *As Black as Resistance: Finding the Condition for Liberation* (Chico, CA: AK Press, 2018), xviii.

7. Stefano Harney and Fred Moten, *The Undercommons: Fugitive Planning and Black Study* (New York: Minor Compositions, 2013), 20.

8. Samudzi and Anderson, *As Black as Resistance,* 13.

9. Hayes and Kaba, *Let This Radicalize You,* 224.

10. "Mission," Let Us Breathe Collective, https://www.letusbreathecollective.com/about.

11. "Mission," Let Us Breathe Collective.

12. "Mission," Let Us Breathe Collective.

13. Damon Williams, interview by the author, July 29, 2024.

14. Williams, July 29, 2024.

15. Martine Caverl, interview by the author, March 27, 2024.

16. "About EAT," Equity and Transformation, 2025, https://www.eatchicago.org/about.

17. "About EAT."

18. "About EAT."

19. Richard Wallace, "Chicago's Black Community Needs an Equity-First Legalized Cannabis Policy," *Crain's Chicago Business,* December 19, 2018, https://www.chicagobusiness.com/opinion/chicagos-black-community-needs-equity-first-legalized-cannabis-policy.

20. "Equity and Transformation Presents 'Chronic Conversation,'" posted March 29, 2019, by Equity and Transformation (EAT), YouTube, https://www.youtube.com/watch?v=sK7F7Jo2Xow.

21. Richard Wallace, interview by the author, September 27, 2024.

22. Contreras, *Energy Never Dies,* ix.

23. Quote from Marc Lamont Hill during panel discussion with Dr. Angela Y. Davis sponsored by Haymarket Books in Chicago on October 2, 2024.

BIBLIOGRAPHY

Adelman, Robert M. and Christopher Mele, eds. *Race, Space, and Exclusion: Segregation and Beyond in Metropolitan America*. New York: Routledge, 2014.

Ali, Arshad and Tracy Lachia Buenavista, eds. *Education at War: The Fight for Students of Color in America's Public Schools*. New York: Fordham University Press, 2018.

Amin, Reema. "Chicago Board of Education Votes to Remove Police Officers from Schools." *Chalkbeat*, February 22, 2024. https://www.chalkbeat.org/chicago/2024/02/23/chicago-board-of-education-votes-out-police-officers/.

Anderson, William C. *The Nation on No Map: Black Anarchism and Abolition*. Chico, California: AK Press, 2021.

Andrews, Kehinde. *Back to Black: Retelling Black Radicalism for the Twenty-First Century*. London: Zed Books, 2018.

Ansell, David. *The Death Gap: How Inequality Kills*. Chicago: University of Chicago Press, 2017.

Architecture, Engineering, Construction, and Management (AECOM). *Woodlawn Area Community Analysis: Final Draft*. April 22, 2019.

Aspholm, Roberto. *Views from the Streets: The Transformation of Gangs and Violence on Chicago's South Side*. New York: Columbia University Press, 2020.

Babwin, Don. "Ex-Chicago Officer Convicted of Murdering Laquan McDonald Released Early." *PBS News*, February 3, 2022. https://www.pbs.org/newshour/nation/ex-chicago-officer-convicted-of-murdering-laquan-mcdonald-released-early.

Bakala, Brendan. "390,000 Drivers Set to Receive Refunds for Red Light and Speed Camera Tickets." *Illinois Policy*, January 30, 2018. https://www.illinoispolicy.org/390000-drivers-set-to-receive-refunds-for-red-light-and-speed-camera-tickets/.

Balto, Simon. *Occupied Territory: Policing Black Chicago from Red Summer to Black Power*. Chapel Hill: University of North Carolina Press, 2019.

Baranauskas, Andrew J. "Exploring the Social Construction of Crime by Neighborhood: News Coverage of Crime in Boston." *Sociological Focus* 53, no. 2 (2020): 156–76.

Barbara, Kenya. "The Plan for Transformation: How a Plan with Lofty Goals Has Underperformed and Forever Changed Public Housing in Chicago." *Public Interest Law Reporter* 24, no. 1 (2018): 1–8.

Basaldua, Fructoso M., Maximillian Cuddy, Amanda Lewis, and Ivan Rodriguez. *Chicago's Racial Wealth Gap: Legacies of the Past, Challenges in the Present, Uncertain Future*. Chicago: Institute for Research on Race and Public Policy, 2022.

Bauer, Kelly. "Woodlawn Residents Push for Anti-Displacement Ordinance Amid Fears over Obama Library." *Block Club Chicago*, October 23, 2018. https://blockclubchicago.org/2018/10/23/woodlawn-residents-push-for-anti-displacement-ordinance-amid-fears-over-obama-library/.

Bell, Michael. *My Peace: A Prison Insider's Guide to Gang Violence*. Chicago: Create Space Publishers, 2014.

Bella, Timothy. "Will Illinois RICO Law 'with Teeth' Help Chicago?" *Al Jazeera*, August 22, 2012.

Bennett, Larry. *The Third City: Chicago and American Urbanism*. Chicago: University of Chicago Press, 2010.

Bennett, Larry, Janet Smith, and Patricia A. Wright, eds. *Where Are Poor People to Live?: Transforming Public Housing Communities*. London: M.E. Sharpe, 2006.

Bennett, Larry, Roberta Garner, and Euan Hague, eds. *Neoliberal Chicago*. Urbana, IL: University of Illinois Press, 2017.

Betancur, John, and Janet Smith. *Claiming Neighborhood: New Ways of Understanding Urban Change*. Urbana, IL: University of Illinois Press, 2016.

Biehl, João. *Vita: Life in a Zone of Social Abandonment*. Los Angeles: University of California Press, 2013.

Black, Timuel. *Bridges of Memory: Chicago's First Wave of Black Migration*. Chicago: Northwestern University Press, 2005.

———. *Bridges of Memory Volume 2: Chicago's Second Generation of Black Migration*. Chicago: Northwestern University Press, 2008.

Bowly, Devereux. *The Poorhouse: Subsidized Housing in Chicago, 1895–1976*. Carbondale, IL: Southern Illinois University Press, 1978.

Boyd, Michelle. *Jim Crow Nostalgia: Reconstructing Race in Bronzeville*. Minneapolis: University of Minnesota Press, 2008.

Bracey, Gerald. *Charter Schools' Performance and Accountability: A Disconnect*. Education Policy Studies Laboratory: George Mason University, 2005.

Bryk, Anthony S., G. Alfred Hess Jr., Jeffrey Mirel, and Kenneth Wong. "Policy Lessons from Chicago's Experience with Decentralization." *Brookings Papers on Education Policy*, no. 2 (1999): 67–127.

Budovitch, Max. "The Fight to Remain." *South Side Weekly*, January 23, 2019. https://southsideweekly.com/the-fight-to-remain-woodlawn-organization-grove-parc-poah/.

Burden-Stelly, Charisse. "Modern U.S. Racial Capitalism: Some Theoretical Insights." *Monthly Review* 72, no. 3 (2020). https://monthlyreview.org/2020/07/01/modern-u-s-racial-capitalism/.

Byrd, Dustin J., and Seyed Javad Miri, eds. *Frantz Fanon and Emancipatory Social Theory: A View from the Wretched.* Chicago: Haymarket Press, 2020.

Camp, Jordan, and Christina Heatherton, eds. *Policing the Planet: Why the Policing Crisis Led to Black Lives Matter.* London: Verso, 2016.

Caref, Carol, Sarah Rothschild, Kurt Hilgendorf, Pavlyn Jankov, and Kevin Russell. *The Black and White of Education in Chicago Public Schools.* Chicago: Chicago Teachers Union, 2013.

Catalyst Chicago. "Table: School Closings over 10 Years." *Chicago Reporter*, December 7, 2011. https://www.chicagoreporter.com/table-school-closings-over-10-years/.

Carbado, Devon. *Unreasonable: Black Lives, Police Power, and the Fourth Amendment.* New York: The New Press, 2022.

Chicago Housing Authority. "Chicago Housing Authority: Plan for Transformation. Improving Public Housing in Chicago and the Quality of Life." January 6, 2000.

Chicago Public Schools. "Chief Executive Officer Recommendation: Designate Alexandre Dumas Elementary School as a Technology Cluster Magnet School, Change the School's Educational Focus to a Technology Program, and Change the School's Name to Dumas Technology Academy." April 23, 2008.

Chicago Tribune. "Chicago Police Return to Community Policing." May 20, 2013. https://www.officer.com/home/news/10945759/chicago-police-department-signals-return-to-community-policing.

——. "Principal Shocks Clemente with Resignation." March 2, 2006.

Cholke, Sam. "Woodlawn Faced with Big Empty School After U of C Charter Moves." *Block Club Chicago*, January 12, 2017. https://www.dnainfo.com/chicago/20170112/woodlawn/university-of-chicago-woodlawn-charter-school-moves-wadsworth-building/.

CityXones. "The New Woodlawn: An Innovative Look at the Promise and Perils of Woodlawn's Transformation." *Hyde Park Herald*, 2019. https://www.cityxones.com/hyde-park-herald-special.

Clements, Mark, Marvin Reeves, Ronald Kitchen, and Stanley Howard. *Tortured by Blue: The Chicago Police Torture Story.* Bloomington, IN: Balboa Press, 2019.

Coates, Ta-Nehisi. "The Case for Reparations." *The Atlantic*, June 2014. https://www. theatlantic.com/magazine/archive/2014/06/the-case-for-reparations/361631/.

Contreras, Ayana. *Energy Never Dies: Afro-Optimism and Creativity in Chicago.* Urbana, IL: University of Illinois Press, 2021.

Correia, David and Tyler Wall. *Police: A Field Guide.* London: Verso, 2018.

Curtis, Marah A., Sarah Garlington, and Lisa Schottenfeld. "Alcohol, Drug, and Criminal History Restrictions in Public Housing." *Cityscape* 15, no. 3 (2013): 37–52.

Danns, Dionne. "Chicago School Desegregation and the Role of the State of Illinois." *American Educational History Journal* 37, no. 1 (201): 55–74.

Davis, Robert. "Bell Out to Disconnect Pay Phones." *Chicago Tribune*, June 7, 1990.

Dawley, David. *A Nation of Lords: The Autobiography of the Vice Lords.* Long Grove, IL: Waveland Press, 1992.

Dazey, Margot. "Rethinking Respectability Politics." *The British Journal of Sociology* 72, no. 3 (2021): 580–93.

De la Torre, Marisa, and Julia Gwynne. *When Schools Close: Effects on Displaced Students in Chicago Public Schools.* Chicago: University of Chicago Consortium of School Research, 2009.

Diamond, Andrew. *Chicago on the Make: Power and Inequality in a Modern City.* Los Angeles: University of California Press, 2017.

Doering, Jan. *Us Versus Them: Race, Crime, and Gentrification in Chicago Neighborhoods.* New York: Oxford University Press.

Donner, Frank. *Protectors of Privilege: Red Squads and Police Repression in Urban America.* Los Angeles: University of California Press, 1990.

Duffrin, Elizabeth. "Slow Progress Amid Strife: While Students Who Were Shut Out by School Closings Show Some Signs of Academic Progress, Most Land in Schools That Are Not Much Better Than the Ones They Left." *Catalyst Chicago* 17, no. 6 (March 2006): 6–10.

Dumas, Michael J. "Against the Dark: Antiblackness in Education Policy and Discourse." *Theory into Practice* 55 (2016): 11–19.

———. "Losing an Arm: Schooling as a Site of Black Suffering." *Race Ethnicity and Education* 17, no. 1 (2014): 1–29.

Dumas, Michael J., and kihanna miraya ross. "Be Real Black for Me: Imagining BlackCrit in Education." *Urban Education* 51, no. 4 (2016): 415–42.

Dumke, Mick. "Chicago Claims Its 22-Year 'Transformation' Plan Revitalized 25,000 Homes. The Math Doesn't Add Up." *ProPublica*, December 16, 2022. https://www.propublica.org/article/chicago-housing-authority-hud-transformation-plan.

Duneier, Mitchell. *Ghetto: The Invention of a Place, the History of an Idea.* New York: Farrar, Straus and Giroux, 2016.

Emmanuel, Adeshina. "'War Zone' Described at Uptown School After Courtenay Stockton Merger." *DNAInfo*, January 7, 2014. https://www.dnainfo.com/chicago/20140107/uptown/war-zone-described-at-uptown-school-following-courtenay-stockton-merger/.

Evans, Maxwell. "New Patio Planned for Migrants at Wadsworth Shelter in Woodlawn." *Block Club Chicago*, July 7, 2023. https://blockclubchicago.org/2023/07/07/new-patio-planned-for-migrants-at-wadsworth-shelter-in-woodlawn/.

———. "City Council Approves Woodlawn Affordable Housing Ordinance Near Obama Center: 'A Step in the Right Direction.'" *Block Club Chicago*, September 10, 2020. https://blockclubchicago.org/2020/09/09/city-council-approves-woodlawn-affordable-housing-ordinance-a-step-in-the-right-direction/.

Ewing, Eve L. *Ghosts in the Schoolyard: Racism and School Closings on Chicago's South Side*. Chicago: University of Chicago Press, 2018.

———. "Commentary," in Gordon, Molly F., Marisa de la Torre, Jennifer R. Cowhy, Paul T. Moore, Lauren Sartain, and David Knight. *Research Report: School Closings in Chicago—Staff and Student Experiences and Academic Outcomes*. University of Chicago Consortium on Chicago School Research, May 2018.

Fanon, Frantz. *Voices of Liberation*. Edited by Leo Zeilig. Chicago: Haymarket Books, 2016.

———. *The Wretched of the Earth*. New York: Grove Press, 1963.

Feldman, Roberta, and Susan Stall. *The Dignity of Resistance: Women Residents' Activism in Chicago Public Housing*. New York: Cambridge University Press, 2004.

Fennell, Catherine. *Last Project Standing: Civics and Sympathy in Post-Welfare Chicago*. Minneapolis: University of Minnesota Press, 2015.

Ferguson, Roderick. *One-Dimensional Queer*. London: Wiley Publishing, 2018.

———. *Aberrations in Black: Toward a Queer of Color Critique*. Minneapolis: University of Minnesota Press, 2003.

Finkel, Ed. "Suder's Old Students Shut Out: District Touts New Magnet but Activists Say Poorest Preschoolers Are Not Reaping the Benefit." *Catalyst Chicago* 17, no. 6 (March 2006): 12–13.

Finnin McCown, Michael. "Making Peace, Making Revolution: Black Gangs in Chicago Politics, 1992–1993." *Chicago Studies* (2014–15): 111–43.

Fitzpatrick, Lauren. "Ahead of Opening Nearby Obama Center, Hyde Park Academy HS Gets $40 Million Boost. *Chicago Sun Times*, September 11, 2018. https://chicago.suntimes.com/2018/9/11/18374583/ahead-of-opening-of-nearby-obama-center-hyde-park-academy-hs-gets-40m-boost.

Fitzpatrick, Lauren, Andy Boyle, and Caroline Hurley. "Who Are Chicago

Schools Named For?" *Chicago Sun Times,* December 30, 2020. https://graphics.suntimes.com/education/school-names/.

Forman Jr., James. *Locking Up Our Own: Crime and Punishment in Black America.* New York: Farrar, Straus and Giroux, 2017.

Fuerst, J. S. *When Public Housing Was Paradise: Building Community in Chicago.* Urbana, IL: University of Illinois Press, 2005.

Gibran Muhammad, Khalil. *The Condemnation of Blackness: Race, Crime, and the Making of Modern Urban America.* Cambridge, MA: Harvard University Press, 2010.

Gibson, D. W. *The Edge Becomes the Center: An Oral History of Gentrification in the Twenty-First Century.* New York: The Overlook Press, 2015.

Gilmore, Ruth Wilson. *Golden Gulag: Prisons, Surplus, Crisis, and Opposition in Globalizing California.* Los Angeles: University of California Press, 2007.

———. "What Is to Be Done?" *American Quarterly* 63, no. 2 (2011): 245–65.

Goetz, Edward G. *Clearing the Way: Deconcentrating the Poor in Urban America.* Washington, DC: The Urban Institute, 2003.

———. *New Deal Ruins: Race, Economic Justice, and Public Housing Policy.* London: Cornell University Press, 2013.

Gonzalez, Robert and Sarah Kosmisarow. "Community Monitoring and Crime: Evidence from Chicago's Safe Passage Program." *Journal of Public Economics* 191 (2020): 1–18

Gonzalez Van Cleve, Nicole. *Crook County: Racism and Injustice in America's Largest Criminal Court.* Stanford, CA: Stanford Law Books, 2016.

Gordon, Molly F., Marisa de la Torre, Jennifer R. Cowhy, Paul T. Moore, Lauren Sartain, and David Knight. *School Closings in Chicago Staff and Student Experiences and Academic Outcomes.* Chicago: University of Chicago Consortium on Chicago School Research, 2018.

Grant, Carl A., Ashley Woodson, and Michael J. Dumas, eds. *The Future Is Black: Afropessimism, Fugitivity, and Radical Hope in Education.* New York: Routledge, 2021.

Great Cities Institute. *Youth Employment Data: Employment to Population Ratios for 16 to 19 and 20 to 24 Year Olds by Chicago Community Area, 2005–2009 to 2010–2014.* University of Illinois at Chicago, February 16, 2016.

Hagedorn, John, Roberto Aspholm, Teresa Córdova, Andrew Papachristos, and Lance Williams. *The Fracturing of Gangs and Violence in Chicago: A Research-Based Reorientation of Violence Prevention and Intervention Policy.* Chicago: University of Illinois at Chicago Great Cities Institute, 2018.

Hale, Charles R., ed. *Engaging Contradictions: Theory, Politics and Methods of Activist Scholarship.* Los Angeles: University of California Press, 2008.

Hall Fish, John. *Black Power/White Control: The Struggle of the Woodlawn Organization in Chicago.* Princeton, NJ: Princeton Legacy Library, 1973.

Hall, Stuart, and Doreen Massey. "Interpreting the Crisis." *Soundings* 1, no. 1 (2010): 51–71.

Harris, Lee. "UChicago Charter Schools Opens New Woodlawn Campus, First Development South of 61st Since '60s Agreement: The New Woodlawn Campus of University of Chicago Charter Schools Has Opened to Students." *The Chicago Maroon*, February 1, 2018. https://chicagomaroon.com/25412/news/uchicago-charter-schools-opens-new-woodlawn-campus/.

Harney, Stefano, and Fred Moten. *The Undercommons: Fugitive Planning and Black Study.* Brooklyn: Minor Compositions, 2013.

———. *All Incomplete.* Brooklyn: Minor Compositions, 2021.

Harvey, David. *A Brief History of Neoliberalism.* London: Oxford University Press, 2005.

———. "The New Imperialism: Accumulation by Dispossession." *Socialist Register* 40 (2004): 63–87.

Hayes, Kelly, and Mariame Kaba. *Let This Radicalize You: Organizing and the Revolution of Reciprocal Care.* Chicago: Haymarket, 2023.

Haymes, Stephen Nathan. *Race, Culture, and the City: A Pedagogy for Black Urban Struggle.* Albany, NY: SUNY Press, 1995.

Helfenbein, Robert J. *Critical Geographies of Education: Space, Place, and Curriculum Inquiry.* New York: Routledge, 2021.

Henricks, Kasey, Amanda E. Lewis, Ivan Arenas, and Deana G. Lewis. *A Tale of Three Cities: The State of Racial Justice in Chicago Report.* Chicago: Institute for Research on Race and Public Policy, 2017.

Hill, Marc Lamont. *Nobody: Casualties of America's War on the Vulnerable, from Ferguson to Flint and Beyond.* New York: Atria, 2016.

Hinton, Elizabeth. *From the War on Poverty to the War on Crime: The Making of Mass Incarceration in America.* Cambridge, MA: Harvard University Press, 2017.

———. *America on Fire: The Untold History of Police Violence and Black Rebellion Since the 1960s.* New York: Liveright Publishing Company, 2021.

Hirsch, Arnold. *Making the Second Ghetto: Race and Housing in Chicago 1940–1960.* Chicago: University of Chicago Press, 1998.

hooks, bell. *Yearning: Race, Gender, and Cultural Politics.* Boston: South End Press, 1990.

Hoover, Larry. "Larry Hoover Political Prisoner, Growth and Development, 21st Century VOTE, Control Your Community and Politicians!" https://newafrikan77.wordpress.com/2016/11/30/larry-hoover-political-prisonergrowth-and-development-21st-century-vote-control-your-community-and-politicians/.

Hugh, Caroline. "Constructing a 'Compatible Community': A Drama of University-Led Urban Renewal, in Five Acts." *Expositions Magazine,* Winter 2024. https://cegu.uchicago.edu/2023/11/30/university-led-renewal/.

Hunt, D. Bradford. *Blueprint for Disaster: The Unraveling of Chicago Public Housing.* Chicago: University of Chicago Press, 2009.

Hutchison, Ray, and Bruce D. Haynes. *The Ghetto: Contemporary Global Issues and Controversies.* Boulder, CO: Westview Press, 2012.

Jackson, Shawn L. "An Historical Analysis of the Chicago Public Schools Desegregation Consent Decree (1980–2006): Establishing Its Relationship with the *Brown v. Board* Case of 1954 and the Implications of Its Implementation on Educational Leadership" (2010). PhD. diss., Loyola University Chicago, 2010. http://ecommons.luc.edu/luc_diss/129.

James, Joy. *Resisting State Violence: Radicalism, Gender and Race in U.S. Culture.* Minneapolis: University of Minnesota Press, 1996.

Jenkins, DeMarcus A. "Unspoken Grammar of Place: Anti-Blackness as a Spatial Imaginary in Education." *Journal of School Leadership* 31, nos. 1–2 (2021): 107–26.

Johnson, Gaye Therese, and Alex Lubin, eds. *Futures of Black Radicalism.* London: Verso, 2017.

Jurkanin, Thomas, and Terry Hillard. *Chicago Police: An Inside View—The Story of Superintendent Terry G. Hillard.* Springfield, IL: Charles C. Thomas Publishing, 2006.

Kahlenburg, Richard, and Halley Potter. "Restoring Shanker's Vision for Charter Schools." *Journal of the American Federation of Teachers* (Winter 2014): 1–19.

Karwath, Rob. "Bell to Restrict Pay Phone Use in Drug War." *Chicago Tribune,* July 16, 1991.

Kelleher, Maureen. "A Battle, A Truce, and New Alliance: Grassroots Activism Still Alive and Well in Gentrifying Community." *Catalyst Chicago* 17, no. 6 (March 2006): 14–15.

———. "Charter Provides New School Option: Faced with Community Pressure, University Will Serve Local Kids First." *Catalyst Chicago* 17, no. 6 (March 2006): 16–17.

———. "Woodlawn: Activists Make Housing School Connection." *Chicago Reporter,* March 20, 2006. https://www.chicagoreporter.com/woodlawn-activists-make-housing-schools-connection/.

Koval, John P., Larry Bennett, Michael I. J. Bennett, Fassill Demissie, Roberta Garner, and Kiljoong Kim, eds. *The New Chicago: A Social and Cultural Analysis.* Philadelphia: Temple University Press, 2006.

Koumpilova, Mila. "Can Chicago Revitalize Its Tiny High Schools?" *Chalkbeat,*

September 27, 2022. https://chicago.chalkbeat.org/2022/9/27/23375249/
    chicago-public-schools-pedro-martinez-small-neighborhood-high-schools.

Levi, Ron. "Making Counterlaw: On Having No Apparent Purpose in Chicago."
    British Journal of Criminology 49 (2009): 132–50.

Lipman, Pauline. *The New Political Economy of Urban Education: Neoliberalism,
    Race and the Right to the City.* New York: Routledge, 2011.

———. "TheLandscape of Education 'Reform' in Chicago: Neoliberalism Meets a
    Grassroots Movement." *Education Policy Analysis Archives* 25, no. 54 (2017).
    http://dx.doi.org/10.14507/epaa.25.2660.

Lipman, Pauline, and David Hursh. "Renaissance 2010: The Reassertion of Ruling
    Class Power Through Neoliberal Policies in Chicago." *Policy Futures in Urban
    Education* 5, no. 2 (2007): 160–78.

Lipsitz, George. *How Racism Takes Place.* Philadelphia: Temple University Press,
    2011.

Lugalia-Hollon, Ryan and Daniel Cooper. *The War on Neighborhoods: Policing,
    Prison, and Punishment in a Divided City.* New York: Beacon Press, 2018.

Lutton, Linda. "Closing Schools Diaspora." WBEZ Chicago, August 26, 2013.
    https://www.wbez.org/stories/closing-schools-diaspora/32d8158c-e379-
    4ebd-8c56-13609855b2aa.

Lynch, Gerald E. "A Conceptual, Practical, and Political Guide to RICO Reform."
    Vanderbilt Law Review 769, no. 43 (1990): 769–802.

Main, Frank. "'O Block': The Most Dangerous Block in Chicago, Once Home to
    Michelle Obama." *Chicago Sun-Times,* November 2, 2014. https://chicago.
    suntimes.com/2014/11/2/18458059/o-block-most-dangerous-block-in-chi-
    cago-michelle-obama-chief-keef-parkway-gardens-south-king-drive.

Mason, J. W. "Losing Track: Many People Think Tearing Down a Neglected Stretch of
    the El Is Good for Woodlawn. Many People with Cars, That Is." *Chicago Reader,*
    November 6, 1997. https://chicagoreader.com/news-politics/losing-track/.

Masterson, Matt. "Ex-Chicago Detective Acquitted in Rekia Boyd Killing Wants
    Court Records Expunged." WTTW News, November 14, 2019. https://news.
    wttw.com/2019/11/14/ex-chicago-detective-acquitted-rekia-boyd-kill-
    ing-wants-court-records-expunged.

Mbekeani-Wiley, Michelle. *Handcuffs in Hallways: The State of Policing in Chicago
    Public Schools.* Chicago: Sargent Shriver National Center on Poverty Law, 2017.

McCoppin, Robert. "Big Plans Near Obama Center Stuck in Bunker: Emanuel-Backed
    Tiger Woods Golf Project Stalled, but Hopes Remain for Restoration of Existing
    Courses." *Chicago Tribune,* October 2, 2023. https://www.proquest.com/newspa-
    pers/big-plans-near-obama-center-stuck-bunker/docview/2870869918/.

McKittrick, Katherine. *Demonic Grounds: Black Women and the Cartographies of*

Struggle. Minneapolis: University of Minnesota Press, 2016.

McKittrick, Katherine, and Clyde Adrian Woods, eds. *Black Geographies and the Politics of Place*. Boston: South End Press, 2007.

McNamara, Paddy. "Proceedings Before the Board of Education of the Chicago Public Schools Independent Hearing Officer's Report: The Proposed Closure of Austin O. Sexton Elementary School and the Relocation of John Fiske Elementary School." April 29, 2013. https://schoolinfo.cps.edu/SchoolActions/Download.aspx?fid=2703.

Meacham, Clifford. "The Matter of the Proposal to Close Dumas Technology Academy and Relocation of James Wadsworth Elementary School, Chicago, IL., Hearing Report and Recommendations." April 25, 2013.

Melamed, Jodi. *Represent and Destroy: Rationalizing Violence in the New Racial Capitalism*. Minneapolis: University of Minnesota Press, 2011.

Mills, Charles W. *The Racial Contract*. Ithaca, NY: Cornell University Press, 1997.

Mitchell, Chip. "Chicago's Safe Passage Curbs Street Violence Without Police." WBEZ Chicago, June 5, 2019. https://www.wbez.org/chicago/2019/06/05/chicagos-safe-passage-curbs-street-violence-without-police-studies-show.

Moore, Natalie Y. "Chicago awards grants to spur development near transit in disinvested neighborhoods." WBEZ Chicago, November 23, 2021. https://www.wbez.org/race-class-communities/2021/11/24/chicago-funds-11-transit-oriented-development-projects.

———. *The South Side: A Portrait of Chicago and American Segregation*. New York: St. Martin's Press, 2016.

Moore, Natalie Y., and Lance Williams. *The Almighty Black P Stone Nation: The Rise, Fall, and Resurgence of an American Gang*. Chicago: Lawrence Hill Books, 2011.

Morrison, Deb, Subini Ancy Annamma, and Darrell D. Jackson, eds. *Critical Race Spatial Analysis: Mapping to Understand and Address Educational Inequity*. Sterling, VA: Stylus Publishing, 2017.

Mowatt, Rasul A. *The Geographies of Threat and the Production of Violence: The State and the City Between Us*. New York: Routledge, 2022.

Mullgardt, Brian. "Further Harassment and Neutralization: The FBI's Counterintelligence in Illinois." *Journal of the Illinois State Historical Society* 113, no. 3–4 (2020): 94–120.

Neyfakh, Leon. "How Did Chicago Get So Violent?: Did the Effort to Eradicate the City's Gangs in the 1990s Inadvertently Lead to Its Bloody Present?" *Slate*, September 23, 2016. https://slate.com/news-and-politics/2016/09/is-chicagos-ghastly-murder-rate-the-result-of-its-1990s-anti-gang-policies.html.

Nitkin, Alex. "Police Conduct Lawsuits Cost Taxpayers $40 Million in 2020, Report Shows—and Costs Are Growing." *Block Club Chicago*, March 10, 2022. https://

blockclubchicago.org/2022/03/10/police-misconduct-lawsuits-cost-chicago-taxpayers-40-million-in-2020-report-shows-and-costs-are-growing.

Nixon, Rob. *Slow Violence and the Environmentalism of the Poor*. Cambridge, MA: Harvard University Press, 2013.

Norman, Donald A. "Design Rules Based on Analysis of Human Error." *Communications of the ACM* 26, no. 4 (1983): 254–8.

Parrish, Madeline, and Chima Ikoro. "Chicago Public Schools and Segregation: A Historical View of How Education Decisions Have Perpetuated Segretation." WTTW. https://interactive.wttw.com/firsthand/segregation/chicago-public-schools-and-segregation.

Pick, Grant. "A Tour of Duties." *Catalyst Chicago,* September 14, 2005. https://www.chicagoreporter.com/tour-duties/.

Peterson, Ruth D., and Lauren J. Krivo. *Divergent Social Worlds: Neighborhood Crime and the Racial-Spatial Divide*. New York: Russell Sage Foundation, 2010.

Petty, Audrey, ed. *High Rise Stories: Voices from Chicago Public Housing*. Chicago: Haymarket Books, 2021.

Philoxène, David. "Navigating Geographies of Urban Violence: Oakland Youth Sense-Making of Racialized Safety and Space." Presentation delivered at the Institute for the Study of Societal Issues, University of California, Berkeley, April 10, 2022.

Piemonte, Mary C. "Tenants Protest CHA's Plan for Lathrop." *Residents Journal,* December 15, 2012. https://wethepeoplemedia.org/tenants-protest-chas-plans-for-lathrop/.

Plotkin, Wendy. "Deeds of Mistrust: Race, Housing, and Restrictive Covenants in Chicago, 1900–1953." PhD diss., University of Illinois Chicago, 1999.

Pollack, Neal. "The Gang That Could Go Straight." *Chicago Reader,* January 26, 1995. https://chicagoreader.com/news-politics/the-gang-that-could-go-straight/.

Popkin, Susan J. *No Simple Solutions: Transforming Public Housing in Chicago*. New York: Rowman and Littlefield, 2016.

Popkin, Susan, Bruce Katz, Mary K. Cunningham, Karen Brown, Jeremy Gustafson, and Margery A. Turner. *A Decade of Hope VI: Research Findings and Policy Challenges*. Washington DC: The Urban Institute, 2004.

Ralph, Laurence. *Renegade Dreams: Living Through Injury in Gangland Chicago*. Chicago: University of Chicago Press, 2014.

Rast, Joel. *The Origins of the Dual City: Housing, Race, and Redevelopment in Twentieth-Century Chicago*. Chicago: University of Chicago Press, 2019.

Rawls, Shaka. "Watching the Asphalt Grow: How One Community Experienced and Was Impacted by Educational Reform Policies." PhD diss., University of Illinois at Chicago, 2024.

Riley, Taylor, Julia P. Schleimer, and Jaquelyn L. Jahn. "Organized Abandonment Under Racial Capitalism: Measuring Accountable Actors of Structural Racism for Public Health Research and Action." *Social Science and Medicine* 343 (2024): 1–13.

Ritchie, Andrea. "Ending the War on Black Women." In *Abolition for the People: The Movement for a Future Without Policing and Prisons*, edited by Colin Kaepernick. Chicago: Haymarket Books, 2023.

———. *Practicing New Worlds: Abolition and Emergent Strategies*. Chico, CA: AK Press, 2023.

Rodkin, Dennis. "This Is the Most Expensive Home Sale Ever in Woodlawn." *Crain's Chicago Business Report*, March 16, 2023. https://www.chicagobusiness.com/residential-real-estate/most-expensive-home-sale-ever-woodlawn-chicagos-south-side.

Rodriguez, M. "The Story of King Von: The War in Chiraq." Medium, October 20, 2021. https://medium.com/@mrodriguez0/the-story-of-king-von-57b7ff2c78fd.

Rosembaum, Dennis P., and Cody Stephens. "Reducing Public Violence and Homicide in Chicago: Strategies and Tactics of the Chicago Police Department." Center for Law and Justice, University of Illinois at Chicago, 2005.

Rosembaum, James E., Linda K. Stroh, and Cathy Flynn. "Lake Parc Place: A Study of Mixed-Income Housing." *Housing Policy Debate* 9, no. 4 (1998): 703–40.

Rotella, Carlo. *The World Is Always Coming to an End: Pulling Together and Apart in a Chicago Neighborhood*. Chicago: University of Chicago Press, 2019.

Rumberger, Russell W. "The Causes and Consequences of Student Mobility." *Journal of Negro Education* 72, no.1 (2003): 6–21.

Sampson, Robert. *Great American City: Chicago and the Enduring Neighborhood Effect*. Chicago: University of Chicago Press, 2012.

Samudzi, Zoé, and William G. Anderson. *As Black as Resistance: Finding the Condition for Liberation*. Chico, CA: AK Press, 2018.

Satter, Beryl M. *Family Properties: How the Struggle over Race and Real Estate Transformed Chicago and Urban America*. New York: Macmillian Publishing, 2009.

Scarborough, William, Ivan Arenas, and Amanda Lewis. *Between the Great Migration and Growing Exodus: The Future of Black Chicago?* Chicago: Institute for Research on Race and Public Policy, 2020.

Scott Tyson, Ann. "True Colors: Trial of Chicago's Disciples." *Christian Science Monitor*, February 26, 1997. https://www.csmonitor.com/1996/0227/27011.html.

———. "The Many Faces of a Reputed Gangster: Larry Hoover, Drug Baron or Community Activist? A Jury Will Now Make the Call." *Christian Science Monitor*, May 6, 1997. https://www.csmonitor.com/1997/0506/050697.us.us.3.html.

Schuba, Tom. "$100K Bounty Was Placed on Killing Chicago Rapper FBG Duck,

Informant Told Chicago Police." *Chicago Sun Times,* January 27, 2023. https://chicago.suntimes.com/2023/1/27/23569891/fbg-duck-king-von-drill-rap-carlton-weekly-oblock-chicago-gangs-gang-violence-parkway-gardens.

Shabazz, Rashad. *Spatializing Blackness: Architectures of Confinement and Black Masculinity in Chicago.* Urbana, IL: University of Illinois Press, 2015.

Sharpe, Christina. *In the Wake: On Blackness and Being.* Durham, NC: Duke University Press, 2016.

Shedd, Carla. *Unequal City: Race, Schools, and Perceptions of Injustice.* New York: Russell Sage Foundation, 2015.

Shiller, Helen. *Daring to Struggle, Daring to Win: Five Decades of Resistance in Chicago's Uptown Community.* Chicago: Haymarket Press, 2022.

Smith, David E. B. "Clean Sweep or Witch Hunt: Constitutional Issues in Chicago's Public Housing Sweeps." *Chicago Kent Law Review* 69, no. 505 (1993).

Soja, Edward W. *Seeking Spatial Justice.* Minneapolis: University of Minnesota Press, 2010.

Soss, Joe, Richard C. Fording, and Sanford F. Schram. *Disciplining the Poor: Neoliberal Paternalism and the Persistent Power of Race.* Chicago: University of Chicago Press, 2011.

Stein, Samuel. *Capital City: Gentrification and the Real Estate State.* London: Verso Books, 2019.

Stewart, Forrest. *Ballad of the Bullet: Gangs, Drill Music, and the Power of Online Infamy.* Princeton, NJ: Princeton University Press, 2020.

Stovall, David. *Born Out of Struggle: Critical Race Theory, School Creation, and the Politics of Interruption.* Albany, NY: SUNY Press 2016.

———. "Mayoral Control: Reform, Whiteness, and Critical Race Analysis of Neoliberal Educational Policy." In *What's Race Got To Do With It?: Understanding Racism, Neoliberalism and Education Reform,* edited by Bree Picower and Edwin Mayorga. New York: Peter Lang Publishers, 2015.

———. "Reflections on the Perpetual War: School Closings, Public Housing, Law Enforcement and the Future of Black Life." In *Education at War: The Fight for Students of Color in America's Public Schools,* edited by Arshad Imtiaz Ali and Tracy Lachica Buenavista. New York: Fordham University Press, 2018.

Taylor, Flint. *The Torture Machine: Racism and Police Violence in Chicago.* Chicago: Haymarket Books, 2019.

Taylor, Keeanga-Yamahtta. *Race for Profit: How Banks and the Real Estate Industry Undermined Black Homeownership.* Chapel Hill, NC: University of North Carolina Press, 2019.

Thompson, Jacqueline. "Harold Ickes Homes News." *Residents Journal,* December 9, 2008. https://wethepeoplemedia.org/harold-l-ickes-homes-news/.

Thompson-Summers, Brandi. *Black in Place: The Spatial Aesthetics of Race in a Post-Chocolate City.* Chapel Hill: University of North Carolina Press, 2019.

Todd-Breland, Elizabeth. *A Political Education: Black Politics and Education Reform in Chicago Since the 1960s.* Chapel Hill: University of North Carolina Press, 2018.

Tresser, Tom. *Chicago Is Not Broke: Funding the City We Deserve.* Chicago: CivicLab, 2016.

Trouillot, Michel-Rolph. *Silencing the Past: Power and the Production of History.* New York: Beacon Press, 1995.

Tuck, Eve. "Suspending Damage: A Letter to Communities." *Harvard Education Review* 79, no. 3 (2009): 409–27.

Turner, David C. "#ResistCapitalism to #FundBlackFutures: Black Youth, Political Economy and the Twenty-First-Century Black Radical Imagination." *Abolition: A Journal of Insurgent Politics* 1, no. 1 (2018).

United States Department of Justice. *Federal Reports on Police Killings: Ferguson, Chicago, Cleveland, and Baltimore.* Brooklyn, NY: Melville House, 2017.

Vitale, Alex S. *The End of Policing.* London: Verso, 2017.

Wacquant, Loïc. *Punishing the Poor: The Neoliberal Government of Social Insecurity.* Durham, NC: Duke University Press, 2004.

Waitoller, Federico, and Joshua Radinsky. "Geo-spatial Perspectives on Neoliberal Education Reform: Examining Intersections of Ability, Race, and Social Class." In *Critical Race Spatial Analysis: Mapping to Understand and Address Educational Inequity,* edited by Deb Morrison, Subini Ancy Annamma, and Darrell D. Jackson. New York: Routledge, 2023.

Walcott, Rinaldo. *On Property: Policing, Prisons, and the Call for Abolition.* Windsor, Ontario: Biblioasis, 2021.

Wang, Jackie. *Carceral Capitalism.* South Pasadena, CA: Semiotext(e), 2018.

Webber, Tammy. "Chicago School Draws Scrutiny over Student Fines." *Herald Tribune,* February 21, 2012. https://www.heraldtribune.com/story/news/2012/02/21/chicago-school-draws-scrutiny-over-student-fines/29083100007/.

Weber, Rachel, Stephanie Farmer, and Mary Donoghue. *Why These Schools: Explaining School Closures in Chicago 2000–2013.* Chicago: Great Cities Institute, University of Illinois at Chicago, 2017.

Weber, Rachel. *From Boom to Bubble: How Finance Built the New Chicago.* Chicago: University of Chicago Press, 2015.

Weissman, Dan. "Austin High School Recovering After 'Reform from Hell.'" *Catalyst Chicago,* July 22, 2005. https://www.chicagoreporter.com/austin-high-school-recovering-after-reform-hell/.

Wiegmann, Douglas A., and Scott A. Shappell. *A Human Error Approach to Aviation Accident Analysis: The Human Factors Analysis and Classification System.* New York: Routledge, 2003.

Wilderboer, Rob. "In Cook County, the Costs of Catching a Case." WBEZ, March 13, 2012. https://www.wbez.org/shows/wbez-news/in-cook-county-the-costs-of-catching-a-case/1a705488-d4ba-42ea-aa47-cfacc4a30575.

Williams, Lance. *King David and Boss Daley: The Black Disciples, Mayor Daley and Chicago on the Edge.* Essex, CT: Prometheus Books, 2023.

Wills, Amanda, Sergio Hernandez, and Marlena Baldacci. "762 Murders. 12 Months. 1 American City." CNN, January 2, 2017, https://www.cnn.com/2017/01/02/us/chicago-murder-rate-2016-visual-guide/.

Wilson, David. *Inventing Black-on-Black Violence: Discourse, Space and Representation.* Syracuse, NY: Syracuse University Press.

Wilson, Matthew D. "Youth Employment Data: Employment to Population Ratios for 16 to 19 and 20 to 24 Year Olds by Chicago Community Area, 2005–2009 to 2010–2014." Great Cities Institute, University of Illinois at Chicago, February 16, 2016. https://greatcities.uic.edu/2016/09/02/youth-employment-data-employment-to-population-ratios-for-16-to-19-and-20-to-24-year-olds-by-chicago-community-area-2009-2014/.

Woodlawn East Community and Neighbors (WECAN). "The Woodlawn Housing Data Project Summary Report." September 2019.

Yamamoto, Eric K. *Interracial Justice: Conflict and Reconciliation in Post–Civil Rights America.* New York: New York University Press, 1999.

Zupan, Susan. "Vallas Connection to Wadsworth: Why Didn't the Powers-That-Be Fold Dumas into Wadsworth's School Building in 2013?" *Substance News*, February 9, 2023. https://www.substancenews.net/articles.php?page=7984.

INDEX

Bold indicates photos, charts, and maps.

ABOUT THE AUTHOR

David Omotoso Stovall is a professor in the Black Studies and Criminology, Law, and Justice Departments at the University of Illinois at Chicago and the author of *Born Out of Struggle: Critical Race Theory, School Creation, and the Politics of Interruption.*

ABOUT HAYMARKET BOOKS

Haymarket Books is a radical, independent, nonprofit book publisher based in Chicago. Our mission is to publish books that contribute to struggles for social and economic justice. We strive to make our books a vibrant and organic part of social movements and the education and development of a critical, engaged, and internationalist left.

We take inspiration and courage from our namesakes, the Haymarket Martyrs, who gave their lives fighting for a better world. Their 1886 struggle for the eight-hour day—which gave us May Day, the international workers' holiday—reminds workers around the world that ordinary people can organize and struggle for their own liberation. These struggles—against oppression, exploitation, environmental devastation, and war—continue today across the globe.

Since our founding in 2001, Haymarket has published more than nine hundred titles. Radically independent, we seek to drive a wedge into the risk-averse world of corporate book publishing. Our authors include Angela Y. Davis, Arundhati Roy, Keeanga-Yamahtta Taylor, Eve Ewing, Aja Monet, Mariame Kaba, Naomi Klein, Rebecca Solnit, Mohammed El-Kurd, José Olivarez, Noam Chomsky, Winona LaDuke, Robyn Maynard, Leanne Betasamosake Simpson, Howard Zinn, Mike Davis, Marc Lamont Hill, Dave Zirin, Astra Taylor, and Amy Goodman, among many other leading writers of our time. We are also the trade publishers of the acclaimed Historical Materialism Book Series.

Haymarket also manages a vibrant community organizing and event space in Chicago, Haymarket House, the popular Haymarket Books Live event series and podcast, and the annual Socialism Conference.

ALSO AVAILABLE
FROM HAYMARKET BOOKS

1919 and *Electric Arches*
Eve L. Ewing

Abolish Rent: How Tenants Can End the Housing Crisis
Tracy Rosenthal and Leonardo Vilchis

Abolition. Feminism. Now.
Angela Y. Davis, Gina Dent, Erica R. Meiners, and Beth E. Richie

Black History Is for Everyone
Brian Jones

I Didn't Come Here to Lie: My Life and Education
Karen G. J. Lewis and Elizabeth Todd-Breland
Foreword by Angela Y. Davis, afterword by Stacy Davis Gates

No Cop City, No Cop World: Lessons from the Movement
Edited by Kamau Franklin, Micah Herskind, and Mariah Parker

Teach Truth: The Struggle for Antiracist Education
Jesse Hagopian

Their End Is Our Beginning: Cops, Capitalism, and Abolition
brian bean, illustrated by Charlie Aleck

To Washington Park, with Love
Documentary Photographs from Summer 1987
Rose Blouin, foreword by Adrienne Brown and Eve L. Ewing